The Shadow Workforce

The Shadow Workforce

Perspectives on Contingent Work in the United States, Japan, and Europe

Sandra E. Gleason
Editor

2006

W.E. Upjohn Institute for Employment Research
Kalamazoo, Michigan

Library of Congress Cataloging-in-Publication Data

The shadow workforce : perspectives on contingent work in the United States, Japan, and Europe / Sandra E. Gleason, editor.
  p. cm.
  Includes bibliographical references and index.
  ISBN-13: 978-0-88099-288-6 (pbk. : alk. paper)
  ISBN-10: 0-88099-288-3 (pbk. : alk. paper)
  ISBN-13: 978-0-88099-289-3 (hardcover : alk. paper)
  ISBN-10: 0-88099-289-1 (hardcover : alk. paper)
1. Temporary employment—United States. 2. Temporary employment—Japan.
3. Temporary employment—Europe. 4. Part-time employment—United States.
5. Part-time employment—Japan. 6. Part-time employment—Europe. 7. Contracting
out—United States. 8. Contracting out—Japan. 9. Contracting out—Europe.
I. Gleason, Sandra E.
  HD5854.2.U6S53 2006
  331.25'729—dc22

© 2006
W.E. Upjohn Institute for Employment Research
300 S. Westnedge Avenue
Kalamazoo, Michigan 49007-4686

Cover design by Alcorn Publication Design.
Index prepared by Diane Worden.
Printed in the United States of America.
Printed on recycled paper.

Dedicated to

Daniel H. Kruger
(1923–2003)

Distinguished Professor
School of Labor and Industrial Relations
Michigan State University

A true friend and colleague who inspired students and faculty
throughout his 43 years of service to Michigan State University.

Contents

Acknowledgments

Most of the work on this book was completed after I joined the Office of the Dean of the former Commonwealth College of Pennsylvania State University. I want to thank the three deans for whom I worked for their support: Joseph Strasser, John Leathers, and Diane M. Disney.

The authors in this volume wrote interesting chapters that introduce the reader to nonstandard employment. I am very appreciative of their hard work.

Several other individuals also helped with the development of this book. Richard N. Block, Lonnie Golden, and two anonymous reviewers provided helpful comments. My assistant, LeAnn Anderson, prepared some of the tables and figures. Allison Colosky, for the W.E. Upjohn Institute for Employment Research, provided helpful editorial guidance.

1
Introduction

Sandra E. Gleason
Pennsylvania State University

As early as the mid-1970s, observers of private sector employment practices in the United States commented on an emerging new phenomenon: the increasing use of nonstandard workers—that is, employees who are hired under a variety of nonstandard arrangements without a permanent connection to an employer. These include part-time employment; hiring through temporary help employment agencies, such as "Kelly Girl" clerical services; self-employed consultants; employees leased, contracted, or subcontracted from business service firms such as advertising or janitorial firms; multiple-job holders; and day laborers.[1]

Although companies historically have used nonstandard workers, the relatively rapid growth rate of these workers in a wide range of industries and occupations has become pervasive (see Nye [1998] for examples). At the time the change was identified, the available data made it difficult to measure exactly what was occurring, although the trend appeared to be similar in both the private and public sectors (see Light [1999] for examples in the federal government). Today we have better data but they provide disparate estimates of the extent of nonstandard employment.

Nonstandard employment arrangements have received increased attention due to several factors. First, ongoing changes suggest that the trend toward greater use of nonstandard employment is likely to continue. The restructuring of the economy in the post–World War II era in an increasingly global economy has continued. The pace of this change has been heavily driven by technological advances and the "information age," and encouraged by the increase in the share of total compensation (i.e., wages and fringe benefits) represented by legally required benefits such as Social Security and nonwage benefits such as health care. These economic forces have encouraged employers to seek more options to control or reduce labor costs. Illustrative examples include the use of temporary workers during a short period of peak demand and long-term strategies to improve productivity by subcontracting the peripheral activities of the firm to companies specializing in services such as accounting. Several terms are used interchangeably to identify these employment arrangements, including nonstandard work or nonstandard employment, atypical employment, contingent work, alternative staffing strategies, flexible work arrangements, as well as the phantom workforce and the shadow workforce (Belous 1989; Carré et al. 2000; Delson 1995; Light 1999; Nollen and Exel 1996; Nye 1988; Polivka, Cohany, and Hipple 2000; Reilly 2001).[2]

Second, while nonstandard employment provides for many employers a buffer for market changes, it often provides relatively unstable employment for workers due to their dependence on the varying needs of the employer. Also, wages can be lower, and many workers do not receive benefits such as health care and pensions. Consequently, the perceived movement away from the twentieth-century model of "good jobs," defined as full-time employment with a continuous attachment to one employer, has raised questions about how "good jobs" will be defined in the future.[3]

Finally, it has become apparent as we have learned more about the nonstandard workforce that it is disproportionately staffed by women, younger workers, and minorities (see Fagan and O'Reilly [1998] and Zeytinoğlu and Muteshi [1999] for further discussion). Indeed, early research in the United States particularly stressed the negative impact on women.[4] Furthermore, not all of these workers are voluntarily in contingent employment. Some would prefer full-time employment in a standard work arrangement.

Our understanding of the growth of nonstandard employment and its impact on employers, employees, the labor force, and public policy has evolved over the past two decades. In the 1980s much attention was focused on the identification of the dimensions of the change and trying to explain why it was occurring. During the 1990s, more sophisticated explanatory models were developed and tested. These models explained the advantages and disadvantages of nonstandard work from the perspectives of both the employer (the demand side of the labor market) and employee (the supply side of the labor market). This was a departure from previous research, which tended to focus primarily on either the demand or the supply side of the market, and treated this workforce as a relatively homogeneous group without appropriate attention to the multiple forms of nonstandard employment arrangements. Not surprisingly, different authors with varying foci reached different conclusions about the positive, negative, or neutral impact of these arrangements. For example, those studying the implications for unions typically saw the impact on the labor force as highly negative, while those analyzing the benefits for employers generally concluded that there were many positive benefits.

Researchers today present a more balanced outlook, which has synthesized the divergent perspectives of employers and employees. It recognizes the heterogeneity of this group of workers and both the advantages and disadvantages of nonstandard employment to the parties involved. This in turn is encouraging more attention to the public policy measures designed to provide more protections and improve working conditions for nonstandard employees.

This book provides an overview of the facts and issues of nonstandard employment in the countries where this labor market phenomenon has been most studied: the United States, Japan, and the European Union.[5] Although the authors have used nontechnical language for general readers who are not specialists in labor market analysis, scholars and human resource professionals also will find these essays of interest. The book presents a balanced perspective on the advantages and disadvantages of nonstandard employment arrangements from the viewpoint of employers and employees; it does not advocate a particular philosophical perspective. Chapters 2 through 6 focus on the United States, while Chapters 7 through 9 focus on Japan and Europe. The final chapter summarizes the future directions for research identified by the authors.

KEY CONCEPTS

A number of concepts are used repeatedly throughout the book that are key to understanding the discussions. These concepts include the measurement of the shadow workforce, the heterogeneity of these workers, labor market flexibility as seen from both the employer and employee perspectives, the use of core and noncore workers in strategic hiring decisions, and the tension between regulation and deregulation in the public policy debates.

Measuring the Nonstandard Workforce

Those interested in studying the nonstandard workforce initially were hindered by the lack of labor market employment data designed to focus in detail on this segment of the workforce. Also, the variety of forms of nonstandard employment made it difficult to determine how many people were in each employment category. In response to the need for data, in 1995 the U.S. Bureau of Labor Statistics (BLS) added more questions to the Current Population Survey (CPS) in a supplemental survey conducted every two years called the "Contingent and Alternative Work Survey" (CWS). The CWS measures the size of the labor force in nonstandard work arrangements by the type of employment arrangement and for workers employed for less than one year in jobs that are contingent on the needs of the employers. We now have time-series data indicating that, since 1995, the characteristics of contingent workers have changed little.

As discussed in more detail in Chapter 2, the data show that, by 2005, workers hired in nonstandard employment arrangements represented about 4.1 percent of the labor force based on the broadest measure of contingent work developed by the BLS, but this is about a 1.1 percent decrease from 1995.[6] These facts sharply contrast with the popular perception that nonstandard work is rapidly replacing standard work arrangements. However, the estimate is based on the responses provided by workers, but not all workers were able to answer the question of whether their employment was contingent. If the respondents who were uncertain about the contingency of their employment arrangements were included, contingent employment would be about 10 percent (Belman and Golden 2000).

The BLS definition of alternative employment arrangements indicates that about 10.7 percent of the workforce fell into this group in 2005, but there is some overlap between this measure and the contingent work measure.[7] Several studies have analyzed this overlap. Even when using the broadest measure of contingency, one-third of the employees of temporary help agencies were not contingent workers in 1995, and in 1997 about 19 percent of total employment was in regular self-employment or regular part-time employment (Cohany 1996; Polivka 1996). However, if the regular self-employed and regular part-time workers also are included, 29.9 percent of the labor force in 1999 was in a non-standard employment arrangement (Hipple 2001; Polivka, Cohany, and Hipple 2000). Because this group of employees has been relatively invisible to employers, as well as within the total labor force, it has been labeled as a "phantom" of the larger full-time labor force employed in standard employment arrangements; its true size is unknown.[8]

The Heterogeneity of the Nonstandard Workforce

Analysis increasingly has taken into account the substantial differences between the various subgroups of nonstandard employees, whether the choice to be in nonstandard employment is voluntary or involuntary, and the resulting economic impact of the employment arrangement on the employee. For example, a male computer programmer who is a college graduate and voluntarily chooses to work as a well-paid, full-time consultant to a software firm is in a very different arrangement than a female with a high school education who works part time in a retail store earning the minimum wage when she prefers a full-time position. She usually has no fringe benefits such as health insurance or an employer-provided pension, and she experiences inferior working conditions and has little or no job security.

Although both workers are in nonstandard employment arrangements, it is clear that the consultant is not harmed by this arrangement; he may in fact be employed for several years on a project with the same employer. In contrast, the female retail clerk is disadvantaged in the labor market by her contingent status. Consequently, relatively few policy concerns have been articulated about workers such as the computer consultant. Most of the public policy discussion has focused on workers who, like the retail clerk, are relatively disadvantaged by involuntary contingent employment, particularly those who are working-class, minority or immigrant, and less educated (Bernasek and Kinnear 1999; Carré et al. 2000; Zeytinoğlu 1999). Without careful attention to this heterogeneity, research may either over- or understate the labor market problems faced by these workers. This, in turn, can result in inappropriate and ineffective policy recommendations (Lester 1998).

Consequently, care must be taken to avoid generalizations about the impact these highly varied employment arrangements have on workers. Such generalizations do not provide useful insights and can be misleading. The impact of being in a contingent job varies greatly with the type of employment arrangement, industry sector, occupation, education, and employee demographic characteristics such as age, gender, and race (Belman and Golden 2000). As Ferber and Waldfogel (2000, p. 214) note: ". . . the answer to the question of whether part-time jobs are bad jobs is 'it depends.'"

Core and Noncore Workers

Discussions about the use of nonstandard employment arrangements frequently draw a distinction between two groups of employees. The first is the "core" workers who perform the work most closely tied to the primary economic activities of the employer. Core employees are in standard employment arrangements, which means they have full-time jobs with a permanent connection to a single employer, usually receive a range of social insurance benefits, and have some protection from arbitrary dismissal (Vosko 1998). The second is the noncore, or "peripheral," workers whose work is not the core work of the organization (see Reilly [2001, pp. 47–49] for a typical discussion of core and peripheral workers). An example for a manufacturing company would be the use of a core employee trained to perform a specialized task on an assembly line, while a peripheral employee would be hired to perform janitorial work through a subcontract with a firm that specializes in janitorial services.

The use of noncore workers in various types of nonstandard employment arrangements offers the firm more flexible opportunities to do its work while protecting the employment security and avoiding layoffs of its trained and experienced core workers. The use of contingent employees can be an ad hoc tactical approach to address short-term needs, such as covering the maternity leave of a core employee, or a strategic response developed to deal over time with an increasingly global and dynamic economic environment. Nonstandard employees allow an employer to use "just-in-time" management of labor to increase, decrease, or reassign its workforce (Lewis and Molloy 1991). Nonstandard employment arrangements can be used, for example, to adjust to fluctuations in the demand for its products, reduce labor costs, reduce the in-house time spent on a variety of human resource administrative and monitoring functions for peripheral workers, subcontract for special projects for which a set of skills is needed for only a limited time period, manage unexpected or temporary staffing needs such as an illness or vacations, and to temporarily add a position as a way to determine whether a new core position is needed. To achieve the flexibility desired for both tactical and strategic adjustments one employer may use one or more of these different employment arrangements simultaneously. For a detailed discussion of how to determine whether to hire a core or non-core employee for a particular job, see Roberts and Gleason (2000).

Flexibility

As discussed earlier, flexibility gives employers more options for rapid and nimble adjustments to changes in the economic environment through internal adjustments to their strategic hiring and staffing plans. Similarly, some employees want greater flexibility so they can more easily combine work with their lifestyle preferences.

Much of the discussion of employer flexibility has focused primarily on numerical flexibility at the enterprise level, i.e., adjusting the number of workers or hours of work in response to product demand. However, two other types of flexibility also are important to employers. Functional flexibility, the design and organization of jobs so that employees can be used in a wide range of tasks, permits rapid reassignment to different jobs. Financial flexibility includes hiring decisions designed to control or reduce short- and long-term labor costs and the use of different systems of compensation such as subcontracting.[9] However, when this results in contingent employment with lower-wage jobs and fewer benefits for workers, the welfare of workers is reduced, and some workers are unable to exercise their preferences for full-time employment.

Some employees voluntarily choose nonstandard employment because of lifestyle preferences or because it provides the flexibility to combine employment with other daily demands. For example, women with small children may be conceptualized as making a labor market choice among three options: not working, working part time, or working full time. Some women will voluntarily choose part-time work so they have time to care for their children (Tam 1997). As a result, greater workforce diversity had placed new demands on employers to develop employment options that are more family-friendly and recognize the different needs of employees.

The concept of the "flexibilisation of labor" was coined by Delson (1995) to denote an inclusive framework of factors that result in great-er labor market flexibility. This includes employer actions, employee choices, and the legal and institutional framework that structures labor market relationships. Reilly (2001) discusses the concept of "mutual flexibility" which ". . . lies in balancing the understandable needs of employers to be efficient and competitive with the equally understand-able needs of employees to protect their incomes and lead the lifestyle that suits them" (p. xi). These are both multidimensional views of flex-ibility, broadly defined.

Regulation or Deregulation

Fundamental transformations are under way in the global economy. New forms of technology are developing, and the structure of the indus-trialized nations is continuing to shift away from traditional manufactur-ing toward services and information technology industries. In response to these changes, nations are evaluating the laws and labor market in-stitutions created in the past to identify the changes required for the dynamic global economy of the twenty-first century. A frequent tension encountered is whether, or to what degree, good public policy should regulate or deregulate the institutions that structure labor market activi-ties. This is a debate about the role of government policy in supporting or limiting labor market flexibility. Tensions arise between regulation advocates, who seek to develop new laws to address problems faced by nonstandard employees, and deregulation advocates, who want to remove the legal and institutional barriers to flexibility created by exist-ing laws. Thus, what employers and workers can and cannot do is con-strained by public policy as embodied in law and other regulations. This public regulation is complemented by the private regulation negotiated by employers and unions through collective bargaining.

Each type of nonstandard employment exists in its current form because there is either a relative absence of a regulatory environment or a regulatory environment that frames its use. For example, in the

United States employers have been able to expand the use of part-time employees with few legal obstacles and little effort to change the institutional framework. Also, the temporary help industry has worked since the 1960s to establish the legal concept of a temporary help firm as the employer, instead of the client firm that actually uses the workers being defined as the employer.[10] This makes the client firm the customer firm, which may—but not always—relieve it of a number of costly legal responsibilities, as discussed in Chapters 5 and 6. This result has been achieved through lobbying and seeking influence over state administrative agencies, and has succeeded in achieving "conditional legitimacy" for the employer status of temporary help firms (Gonos 1997, p. 105). The business community in this case played a dominant role in the development of the law and public policy applied to temporary help firms. As a result the temporary help supply industry grew rapidly from 1972 to 1997 at an annual rate of more than 11 percent (Estevao and Lach 2000, p. 123).

The regulatory framework has, in turn, affected economic decision making. For example, in the United States the use of workers provided by temporary help firms is generally expected to reduce labor costs due to the relatively weak regulatory structure. In contrast, the European Union has created a regulatory environment designed to provide greater protections to these workers, which limits the degree to which client firms can expect to reduce labor costs (Vosko 1998, pp. 24–26).

Labor unions also are important labor market institutions that influence the legal and administrative framework. Many labor unions tend to oppose legal changes that will expand opportunities for part-time and temporary work at the expense of full-time employment. Recent evidence in the United States suggests that this opposition is not based on the lower hours of employment per se, but instead reflects the concern that part-time workers are paid a lower wage per hour than full-time workers. Various strategies are used to address unions' concerns. Unions in the United States have used collective bargaining to limit or control the growth of nonstandard employment. In Japan and Europe unions have supported regulation by the government to control temporary employment agencies (Delson 1995, p. 108).

OVERVIEW OF THE BOOK

This book is organized into three sections. The primary focus is the nonstandard workforce in the United States. Chapter 2 provides an overview of the nonstandard workforce in the United States, its demographic characteristics, and why it has grown. Chapters 3–6 build on this foundation, with discussions about the employer's decision to hire contingent workers, labor union responses to the threats and challenges created by contingent work for unionized employees, the legal framework in which the decision to hire nonstandard workers of various types is made, and the impact of current public programs such as unemployment insurance on these workers. Chapters 7–9 focus on Japan and Europe and explore how these mature industrialized nations are coping with, and adapting to, contingent work within different socioeconomic and legal systems. Finally, Chapter 10 presents a summary and ideas for future research.

Perspectives from the United States

In Chapter 2, von Hippel et al. provide an overview of the facts, theories, and issues related to the nonstandard workforce in the United States. As the authors note, even the seemingly simple question "How large is this segment of the workforce?" does not have an easy answer due to the variety of definitions used to measure this heterogeneous group of workers and the associated methodological challenges encountered by the Bureau of Labor Statistics (BLS). The BLS uses three estimates ranging from narrow to broad to measure "contingent employment," which is work that is expected to last less than one year, and a fourth measure of "alternative employment arrangement," which groups workers into four categories: 1) independent contractors, 2) on-call workers, 3) temporary help agency workers, and 4) workers provided by contract. The characteristics of the nonstandard workforce are identified by type of alternative employment arrangement, age, gender, race, level of educational attainment, occupational category, and industrial sector.

The chapter then provides an overview of the demand and supply sides of the labor markets employing contingent workers. Data are provided on workers' preferences for nonstandard work arrangements, as well as the impact of these arrangements on their earnings and selected fringe benefits. Workers' preferences for contingent or permanent work reflect their interests in flexibility for lifestyle or life cycle reasons. Employers use these workers to address the challenges they face, including the need to control or reduce labor costs, to be more flexible in adjusting to dynamic market conditions, and to avoid legal and other restrictions.

The authors argue that the changing nature of the employment relationship within the current global economic context suggests that the size of the nonstandard workforce is likely to increase in the future. As employers and employees understand more clearly the changing nature of employment relationships, both see the benefits from more flexible employment arrangements. This in turn means that we need to overcome some of the negative stereotypes previously associated with part-time and other forms of nonstandard work; we also need to address inequities in the operation of our social support systems, which were designed to serve primarily full-time employees in standard employment arrangements.

Miller and Barney discuss in detail in Chapter 3 how employers are responding to the rapidly changing competitive environment that has encouraged their increased use of contingent workers. They recognize that the use of contingent workers is only one option for managing the monetary expenses of wages and benefits and nonmonetary labor costs. Nonmonetary costs include a variety of transactions costs such as time spent interviewing job candidates, teaching firm-specific skills, and handling the administrative costs associated with contingent employees. The empirical research on the impact on labor costs of various transactions costs is summarized.

The authors argue, however, that the creation of a flexible workforce through appropriate investments in permanent employees, such as training in a broad range of skills, is an alternative to the use of contingent workers. The relative productivity of contingent and permanent workers depends on the employment situation. Consequently, when monetary and nonmonetary costs are considered, hiring contingent workers is not always the most cost-effective strategy.

Miller and Barney's analysis extends the basic benefit/cost analysis used by employers to evaluate strategic hiring decisions by combining two perspectives: the real-options approach and the resource-based approach. The real-options approach borrows from financial analysis the concept of "real options," that is, investing in a real asset under conditions of uncertainty about demand, technology, and the actual productivity of employees. The owner of the option uses it for financial benefit when there are favorable conditions. For example, hiring temporary employees can be considered a real option during periods of high uncertainty, but companies may desire a larger and more flexible permanent workforce under low uncertainty. Thus, the employer can adjust the mix of contingent work arrangements and flexible permanent employees to address demand, technological, and measurement uncertainties. Similarly, the resource-based approach focuses on how organizations gain competitive advantages by managing resources that are rare, valuable, hard to imitate, and uniquely used due to the culture, history, and structure of an organization. Consequently, the use of a hard-to-imitate flexible permanent workforce can be a least-cost strategy for a firm seeking flexibility. Depending on the circumstances, a flexible permanent workforce and contingent workers are substitute methods to create value under conditions of uncertainty. Bringing the two frameworks together generates some additional insights into how managers can gain competitive advantage through adjustments in their labor forces.

Chapter 4, by Lundy, Roberts, and Becker, discusses U.S. labor unions' responses to the use of contingent work. In an era when union membership has been declining, the potential loss of additional full-time union members due to nonstandard employment arrangements threatens the strength of unions and the job security and economic welfare of their members.[11] Labor unions in the United States, like those in Japan and Europe, generally oppose nonstandard employment. Most unions continue to focus solely on their traditional membership of full-time permanent employees. They have done little to organize contingent workers, or to seek to provide protections in wages, hours, and conditions of work similar to those provided traditionally to organized workers.

Lundy, Roberts, and Becker reviewed the collective bargaining contracts from a variety of private and public sector employers to determine how unions are addressing contingent work as reflected in the contract language. Their analysis indicates that the economic sector in which the union operates is an important although imperfect predictor of union tactics. Unions in industrial or goods-producing sectors are more likely to use strategies of exclusion to prohibit or limit contingent employment arrangements, such as subcontracting or outsourcing. In contrast, unions in the service sector are more likely to use strategies of inclusion so that these workers are covered by their collective bargaining agreement, such as including part-time employees in the bargaining unit and negotiating prorated benefits for them.

The authors discuss the guidelines provided by the National Labor Relations Board (NLRB), which governs the inclusion in a bargaining unit of temporary, part-time, and leased employees, as well as some less common employee categories, such as students. Also, employers' use of outsourcing, privatization, and independent contractors limits union membership and is resisted by unions. However, when unions are able to organize contingent workers, unions may face tensions over what is negotiated for contingent workers relative to the full-time members who want more family-friendly policies and greater scheduling flexibility, as well as improved economic welfare through better wages, benefits, and conditions of work. In this context unions face challenges when bargaining for seniority, wages, and prorated benefits for contingent workers.[12]

Chapters 5 and 6 review in more detail the public policies that affect contingent workers in the United States. Chapter 5 reviews the legal framework that structures the contingent work arrangements between employers and employees. Chapter 6 reviews public policies affecting workers' economic welfare and the conditions of work that affect individual workers directly, such as unemployment insurance and job safety. Although some of these topics are briefly discussed in earlier chapters, the focus here is a more detailed analysis of the effects of these policies on contingent workers.

In Chapter 5, Coens and Storrs note that much of the literature about employers' advantages in nonstandard employment arrangements creates the impression that these arrangements are options for escaping a variety of legal obligations and liabilities related to employment. The authors discuss in detail why this impression is incorrect and why there is "no safe harbor" from these obligations; employers are responsible for complying with the laws. However, understanding compliance is complicated for employers because there is no single definition of employee that is used consistently throughout U.S. labor law. In addition, the terminology used to describe the various contingent employment arrangements, such as independent contractor, also varies. Consequently, the same nonstandard employment arrangement can be treated differently under different laws.

The authors focus on the definitions and legal interpretations used by federal agencies to differentiate "employees" from independent contractors, temporary employees, and leased employees. For example, the Internal Revenue Service (IRS) uses the multifactor "common law test" to determine whether a worker is considered an employee or an independent contractor for tax purposes. This test focuses on how much direct control the employer has over the work done by the employee. However, the Wage-Hour Division of the Department of Labor uses the broader multifactor "economic realities" test to determine which workers should be covered as employees by the federal minimum wage law. This test incorporates the control issues of the narrower common law test but focuses on the degree to which the individual depends on the employer for his or her economic livelihood. As a result of the differences in these approaches, the same worker might be classified as an employee for the purposes of minimum wage coverage and as an independent contractor for tax purposes. The chapter discusses the need to change the present fragmented approach to defining employees to provide greater consistency and uniformity, as well as to provide more guidance to help employers understand what they must do to comply with the current complex and often confusing laws.

Wenger in Chapter 6 discusses the relative lack of public policy responses to date in both federal and state public policy to the growth of nonstandard employment. This lack of responses reflects the history of existing labor market policies which were developed to protect full-time employees in standard employment arrangements. Furthermore, there is no true national labor market policy in the United States, but rather a fragmented system in which the states implement federal legislation while the courts interpret it. When workers in nonstandard employment arrangements are covered by public policies, it is unintended since the definitions of eligibility for coverage were designed for full-time employees. Understanding the eligibility rules for coverage thus is critical, since these rules determine who is covered and who is not. The broader the definition of "employee," the more workers are covered.

The major programs and policies that directly affect contingent workers are reviewed by Wenger: health care and pensions, unemployment insurance, Family and Medical Leave Act (FMLA), minimum wage law, and occupational safety and health. The eligibility requirements for each policy are reviewed. Also, the impact on contingent workers is evaluated based on four standard criteria used for public policy evaluations: economic efficiency, equity, security, and liberty. His analysis and these four criteria guide the identification of appropriate policy reforms. Wenger argues that the ongoing changes on both the supply and demand sides of the labor force require public policy responses to provide benefits, social insurance, and work site protections to nonstandard workers equivalent to those provided to full-time workers. He provides six recommendations for reforms that will help adapt U.S. social welfare protections to provide better protection for nonstandard employees.

Perspectives from Japan and Europe

The same basic forces for change generated by the increasing impact of global economic competition on national economies have affected all of the mature industrialized nations, including those of Japan and Europe. Not surprisingly, the phenomenon of the increase in the use of nonstandard employment also has been experienced in these countries, and has given rise to concerns similar to those discussed for the United States. Like the United States, other nations have struggled with measurement issues and finding the most appropriate way to measure the growth of these varied employment arrangements. However, due to different institutions and cultures, the focus on nonstandard employment has taken some unique twists when compared with the experience in the United States. For example, in Japan the adjustments to expanding nonstandard employment reflect a movement away from a national labor market policy commitment to employment stability embodied in the concept of "lifetime employment" that has dominated the Japanese labor market since World War II.[13] In Europe, the growth of temporary employment agencies reflects a movement away from a historical public policy commitment to institutions that support full employment rather than labor market flexibility. Consequently, both Japan and Europe are working to devise an appropriate infrastructure through deregulation to encourage a previously prohibited or limited labor market institution—private sector temporary employment agencies.

The discussion of the growth of nonstandard employment in Japan is set in the context of the "bursting of the bubble" of economic prosperity in 1989.[14] As a consequence of the economic changes that resulted, Japanese employers have been moving away from "lifetime employees" or "regular employees" to use alternative employment arrangements.

A by-product of the bursting of the bubble was the Japanese government's recognition that its labor markets had to become more flexible as the economy was opened to both more domestic and global competition (Porter and Sakakibara 2004). National policy initiatives to support flexibility included the expansion of public employment offices and services as well as training. Temporary employment agencies also were given greater freedom to operate. Prior to 1985 such employment arrangements were prohibited by law in Japan in part as a way to encourage hiring for lifelong employment. However, as the need for greater labor market flexibility was recognized, temporary employment agencies were legalized and the types of jobs they could fill were expanded.

Ozeki and Wakisaka in Chapter 7 provide an overview of the different types of nonregular employment in Japan and the demographic and industrial characteristics of these workers. As a group, nonregular workers represented 33 percent of the labor force in 2005, an increase of more than 5 percent since 1999, and tended to be more heavily concentrated in the service-oriented industries. Like U.S. employers, Japanese firms attribute the use of contingent workers to factors such as labor cost savings and more flexible adjustments to changes in demand. Furthermore, Japanese workers' explanations for why they are nonregular employees are similar to those of American workers.

The chapter pays particular attention to two groups of nonregular workers: part-time workers, who are the largest group of nonregular workers, and "dispatched workers" sent by temporary employment agencies to client companies. Dispatched workers are the component of the nonregular workforce that is expected to grow the most quickly in the foreseeable future.

There are two categories of part-time workers in Japan: those who work shorter hours (similar to the definition used in the United States) and those who are not on the lifetime employment career path but may work 35–40 hours a week (fewer hours than "lifetime" employees). The large number of women in part-time employment reflects not only the cultural norms of employment for men and women, but also financial inducements provided by the Japanese government and many companies to encourage women to work less than full time. The chapter also discusses the effects of contingent employment on pay, unemployment insurance, bonus programs, and retirement benefits. Although wages and benefits generally are lower for nonregular employees in Japan, the national health insurance system ensures that everyone has health care.

In Chapter 8 Honda builds on the discussion by Ozeki and Wakisaka by providing more detail about the Japanese government's employment policies and the labor unions' responses to the growth of part-time and dispatched workers. He discusses the three major employment policies used for these two groups of workers: the Part-Time Work Law (PWL) and job placement assistance focused on part-time workers, and the Worker Dispatching Law (WDL) developed to protect workers dispatched by temporary employment agencies.[15] The PWL was developed to provide protections for part-time workers by improving job security, providing better management practices where they are employed, and improving the social security system. Unfortunately, since the PWL is not legally binding, it appears to have had little impact; indeed, many employers are only vaguely aware of its existence. As discussed earlier, temporary employment agencies are relatively new in Japan. The WDL was created to permit a legal private sector mechanism to match employers and employees that would supplement the public employment services while regulating these temporary agencies to protect employee welfare.

The chapter also discusses unions' responses to the growth of nonregular employees. The Japanese union structure is dominated by enterprise unions in relatively large companies—the same companies that have built their human resource management structures around lifetime employment for regular employees. Japanese labor unions have been heavily involved in the development of Japanese government labor policies for part-time and dispatched workers. However, like U.S. unions, they have shown little interest in organizing these workers.

Chapter 9 by Michon provides an overview of nonstandard work in Europe and discusses one institutional response—the growth of temporary help firms (also called temporary work agencies [TWAs]). As the need for more flexible labor markets has become evident, temporary work agencies have emerged as institutions that facilitate flexibility. However, like Japan, a number of European countries previously have prohibited or severely limited temporary employment agencies as part of their national policies to support full employment; the notable exception is France. Consequently, these relatively new labor market institutions still are evolving within each country as well as in the context of the European Union (EU). The EU is working toward common approaches to regulating employment policies and labor markets and institutions such as temporary work agencies to facilitate greater labor market integration.[16]

Michon provides an overview of temporary agency work (TAW) in the member nations of the EU. He discusses the difficulties of comparative analysis across countries because there is no common definition of TAW or common method of regulating TAW through laws and collective bargaining.[17] The heterogeneity of national differences in the regulation of TAW has resulted in differing workforce characteristics. For example, in Germany TAW is primarily used in the industrial sector and employs male manual laborers, while in Denmark it is found primarily in the service sector employing white-collar females.

The chapter provides an overview of the complexities of the various national approaches to regulating TAW and the activities of the "social partners" (employers and unions). While employers have created national TWA employer organizations, unions typically have not created comparable associations due to their hostility to TAW. Michon discusses the ways in which the differences in perspectives on public policy of the employer organizations and unions are being negotiated in some countries, and he reviews the attention being given in varying degrees to protections of TAW workers in the member nations. The chapter concludes with a brief discussion of the challenges of developing within the EU a more standardized approach to regulating temporary agency work.

Where Do We Go from Here?

Chapter 10 discusses the directions for future research. The research challenges created by the available data and theoretical models are reviewed, and attention is focused on options to develop public policies that are more customized to address the needs of those workers who are involuntarily contingent employees (Bendapudi, Mangum, and Tansky 2001). In addition, the chapter discusses recommendations for future research provided by the contributors to this volume. These include further analysis of employer decision-making processes, analysis of factors affecting the extension of coverage of employment protections and benefits, comparative research to provide insights into the impact of different models of regulation, and evaluations of the impact of the activities of unions and nonprofit organizations.

CONCLUSION

One of the most challenging labor market developments in the past three decades has been the increased use in the United States, Japan, and Europe of nonstandard employment arrangements. These employment arrangements are not new; however, their use has raised questions about what workers in these countries can expect for their future career paths. Also, there is increasing recognition that social systems have not changed appropriately to support nonstandard workers who are disadvantaged in the labor market, whether by the provision of training to support lifelong learning, the accommodation of variations in life cycle preferences for work for men and women, or the provision of health care and pensions.

The countries discussed in this volume are struggling to find answers to many questions that will help define the future of work and what a "good job" should provide for workers. Each country is trying to determine how to create a new approach to the social and psychological contracts previously provided by the standard employment relationship.[18] As our understanding of the forces creating the nonstandard workforce has improved, more discussion has focused on the implications of this change as part of a larger conversation about the future of work.

Notes

1. For a more detailed discussion of the definitions of these various employment arrangements see Polivka, Cohany, and Hipple (2000).
2. Although in 1996 there were about 1.9 million civil servants, Light (1999) estimates that the "shadow of government" was 12.7 million full-time-equivalent jobs due to job creation by federal contracts, and through grants and funds allocated to state and local governments. If the military and postal workers are counted, a total of nearly 17 million people were employed through federal expenditures for this shadow workforce (p. 1).
3. However, it should be noted that this twentieth-century model differs from the historical model of employment in which contingent employment was the norm for most workers (Kelloway, Gallagher, and Barling 2004).
4. For example, 9to5, National Association of Working Women published a report in 1986 noting that almost two-thirds of the part-time workforce in 1985 was female, and over 62 percent of the temporary help industry jobs in 1984 were filled by women. Furthermore, the report documented the poor wages and conditions of employment of these workers (DuRivage 1996).
5. Counting contingent workers is not an easy task, even in mature countries with well-established procedures for collecting accurate labor market data, as discussed in Chapter 2. Unfortunately, the evolving data collection systems in rapidly developing countries such as China generate unreliable or incomplete labor market measures. This makes it impossible to evaluate nonstandard employment in a meaningful way. See Banister (2005) for a discussion of the problems.
6. To determine the employment status of workers, BLS survey respondents are asked a series of questions to determine the absence of either an implicit or explicit commitment by an employer for long-term employment. The key factor used to make this determination is whether the job is temporary or not expected to continue (Hipple 2001).
7. Polivka (1996, p. 56) states ". . . not all workers in alternative work arrangements are contingent, and conversely, not all contingent workers are in alternative arrangements. Therefore, by and large, contingent workers and workers in alternative arrangements are analyzed separately."
8. Belous (1989) illustrates the challenge this creates for employers, as well as data collection, by quoting senior executives in two companies. The ". . . senior human resource executive admitted, 'I don't call it a contingent workforce; I call it a phantom workforce. In many cases, we just don't know what we are doing. We don't know the size of this phantom workforce, but we think it is very large. We don't know our liability in terms of benefits to this phantom workforce. We don't know how to control it or who in the company should control it' " (p. 58). A second executive states: "We call it the hidden workforce, and our hidden workforce is out of control . . . We are trying to get a handle on it" (p. 60).
9. In addition, some authors discuss wage flexibility, that is, changing wages to reflect the external labor market supply and demand conditions as well as pay flex-

ibility internally. For a more detailed discussion of flexibility see Reilly (2001) and Ozaki (1999).

10. The standard two-party employment relationship provides a direct relationship between the employer (the firm hiring and paying the employee) and the employee (the worker performing the services for the employer). This contrasts with the temporary employment agency, which creates a triangular employment relationship: the agency with the client (customer) company, the agency with the worker, and the client company with the worker. The temporary employment agency has a contract with the client company to which temporary workers are sent. The agency handles the activities that would otherwise be undertaken by the human resource department of the client firm, such as recruiting workers, conducting reference checks, evaluating qualifications, and perhaps providing training, and places the workers with employers. In addition, the agency generally is held responsible for paying various taxes such as payroll and Social Security taxes, protecting the safety and health of their workers, and ensuring equal employment opportunity laws are followed. Thus, the agency generally is considered the legal employer (see Chapter 5 for legal uncertainties arising from these "coemployment" situations), and is paid an hourly fee by the client which covers the wage of the employee plus the firm's markup for its services. The temporary agency also has an employment contract with the temporary employee and pays the employee. Some agencies provide benefits in addition to pay. Finally, the temporary employee provides services to and receives direction from the client company (Gonos 1997).

    Temporary employment agencies are distinguished from leasing companies which take over from a client company the payroll of an existing workforce and handle hiring and firing. Leasing companies also are more likely to provide benefits. Typically work assignments are for longer term than those of temporary workers. The leasing company is the legal employer in these situations. The number of leasing companies also has grown rapidly (Carey and Hazelbaker 1986; Lewis and Molloy 1991; Segal and Sullivan 1997).

11. However, some full-time workers also would be willing to accept a lower wage under certain conditions. A survey by Friedman and Casner-Lotto (2003) found that about one-quarter of unionized workers would reduce their scheduled work time if they could cut back without experiencing severe reductions in income, benefits, and job security. For example, they would find it acceptable to work 90 percent of a full-time work schedule and get paid 90 percent of their current wages and benefits.

12. In 2003, 14.2 percent of employed full-time workers in the United States were members of unions, while 6.8 percent of employed part-time workers were members (Bureau of Labor Statistics 2004).

13. Gao (2001) states that Japan privatized social protections by basing its strategy for total employment on

> . . . three pillars. First, big corporations institutionalized a permanent employment system, providing job security to their employees; second, medium-size and small companies, with support from

the state, organized numerous cartels to avoid bankruptcy and keep everyone in business; and third, family-owned mini shops were protected by heavy government regulations. All these measures served to reduce pressure on public spending for unemployment assistance. (p. 114)

This system created stability and protected inefficient companies. When unemployment grew, the Japanese government used public works projects to create a safety net.

For those employees hired by the big corporations that could provide lifetime employment, the benefits were significant. Employees knew that although their salaries started low they would rise steeply with the accumulation of training and experience, and they would be rewarded with seniority-based promotions within the company. These expectations typically tied employees to one employer for their entire careers. However, lifetime employment has been primarily enjoyed by male workers. The buffer in the Japanese employment system has been female employment heavily concentrated in part-time work. The female labor force participation remains low in Japan relative to the United States and most industrialized nations, but is expected to increase as more women achieve higher levels of education and delay marriage. For further discussion of this employment system see Durand and Durand-Sebag (1996) and Hart and Kawasaki (1999).

14. From 1985 to 1990 Japan recorded rapid economic growth averaging an increase in the real gross domestic product of 4.6 percent a year, as well as a tripling of the value of the Nikkei Stock index and rapidly increasing land prices. By 1991 it had become apparent that this "bubble economy" had grown due to gains from speculation on inflated stock and land prices. When this bubble burst, economic growth flattened and asset values fell; Japan went into the worst recession it had experienced since the 1940s. The Japanese government began in 1992 to develop macroeconomics policies to support a recovery. At this time it also began to address the major mismatches between Japanese institutions, which had been designed for a different set of economic forces, and the current global economy (Grimes 2001). Alexander (2002) argues that the relative stagnation and decline of the Japanese economy since the early 1990s is the result of the inability of both the Japanese government and businesses to replace the previously successful ways of doing things that generated the economic miracle of post World War II, and to emphasize employment stability with new approaches appropriate for the flexibility needed for the current economic environment.

15. Organizations that provide job placement assistance are referred to as "labor market intermediaries" because they facilitate matching workers seeking jobs (recruitment) with employers (placement). The national system of public employment services offices created in Japan provides free services, whereas private organizations may charge fees. Firms that provide placement are different from temporary employment agencies because their job is completed once a worker is placed in a job; these firms do not act as the employer and do not assume related responsibilities such as providing some fringe benefits.

16. See Vosko (1998) for the historical background to these multiple national approaches from the founding of the International Labor Organization in 1919 through the present.
17. Andresen (1992) identifies five particularly salient additional factors that result in differences between European nations that are substantially larger than regional differences in the United States and further complicate cross-national comparisons. These include language, social bonds to a local region which reduce labor mobility, educational systems, different experiences with migration, and distinct social security systems with different standards for benefits.
18. For an example of this type of discussion see Jouen and Caremier (2000). For a discussion of the "new" psychological contract for employment, see Stone (2004).

References

Alexander, A.J. 2002. *In the Shadow of the Miracle: The Japanese Economy since the End of High-Speed Growth*. Lanham, MD: Lexington Books.

Andresen, B. 1992. "A European Business View of European Labor Markets." In *European and American Labor Markets: Different Models and Different Results*, R.S. Belous, R.S. Hartley, and K.L. McClenahan, eds. Washington, DC: National Planning Association, pp. 96–108.

Banister, J. 2005. "Manufacturing Employment in China." *Monthly Labor Review* 128(7): 11–29.

Belman, D., and L. Golden. 2000. "Nonstandard and Contingent Employment: Contrasts by Job Type, Industry, and Occupation." In *Nonstandard Work: The Nature and Challenges of Changing Employment Arrangements*, F. Carré, M. A. Ferber, L. Golden, and S.A. Herzenberg, eds. Champaign, IL: Industrial Relations Research Association, pp. 167–212.

Belous, R.S. 1989. *The Contingent Economy: The Growth of the Temporary, Part-Time and Subcontracted Workforce*. Washington, DC: National Planning Association.

Bendapudi, V., S.L. Mangum, and J.W. Tansky. 2001. "Customizing Public Policy: A Typology of Contingent Employment." *Perspectives on Work* 5(2): 33–36.

Bernasek, A., and D. Kinnear. 1999. "Workers' Willingness to Accept Contingent Employment." *Journal of Economic Issues* 32(2): 461–469.

Bureau of Labor Statistics. 2004. "Household Data Annual Averages. Table 40. Union Affiliation of Employed Wage and Salary Workers by Selected Characteristics." http://stats.bls.gov/cps/cpsaat40.pdf (accessed April 14, 2006).

Carey, M.L., and K.L. Hazelbaker. 1986. "Employment Growth in the Temporary Help Industry." *Monthly Labor Review* 109(4): 37–44.

Carré, F., M.A. Ferber, L. Golden, and S. A. Herzenberg, eds. 2000. *Nonstandard Work: The Nature and Challenges of Changing Employment Arrangements*. Champaign, IL: Industrial Relations Research Association.

Cohany, S. R. 1996. "Workers in Alternative Employment Arrangements." *Monthly Labor Review* 119(10): 31–45.

Delson, L. 1995. *Atypical Employment: An International Perspective—Causes, Consequences and Policy*. Groningen, The Netherlands: Woltersgroep-Groningen bv.

Durand, J.P., and J. Durand-Sebag. 1996. *The Hidden Face of the Japanese Model*. Clayton, Australia: Monash Asia Institute.

DuRivage, V. 1996. *Working at the Margins: Part-Time & Temporary Workers in the United States*. Cleveland, OH: 9to5, National Association of Working Women.

Estevao, M., and S. Lach. 2000. "The Evolution of the Demand for Temporary Help Supply Employment in the United States." In *Nonstandard Work: The Nature and Challenges of Changing Employment Arrangements*, F. Carré, M.A. Ferber, L. Golden, and S.A. Herzenberg, eds. Champaign, IL: Industrial Relations Research Association, pp. 123–143.

Fagan, C., and J. O'Reilly. 1998. "Conceptualizing Part-Time Work: The Value of an Integrated Comparative Perspective." In *Part-Time Prospects: An International Comparison of Part-Time Work in Europe, North America and the Pacific Rim*, J. O'Reilly and C. Fagan, eds. London: Routledge, pp. 1–31.

Ferber, M.A., and J. Waldfogel. 2000. "The Effects of Part-Time and Self-Employment on Wages and Benefits: Differences by Race/Ethnicity and Gender." In *Nonstandard Work: The Nature and Challenges of Changing Employment Arrangements*, F. Carré, M.A. Ferber, L. Golden, and S.A. Herzenberg, eds. Champaign, IL: Industrial Relations Research Association, pp. 213–234.

Friedman, W., and J. Casner-Lotto. 2003. *Time Is of the Essence: New Scheduling Options for Unionized Employees*. Report from the Work in American Institute. Berkeley, CA: Work in American Institute and Labor Project for Working Families.

Gao, B. 2001. *Japan's Economic Dilemma: The Institutional Origins of Prosperity and Stagnation*. New York: Cambridge University Press.

Gonos, G. 1997. "The Contest over 'Employer' Status in the Postwar United States: The Case of Temporary Help Firms." *Law and Society Review* 31(1): 81–110.

Grimes, W.W. 2001. *Unmaking the Japanese Miracle: Macroeconomics Politics 1985–2000*. Ithaca, NY: Cornell University Press.

Hart, R.A., and S. Kawasaki. 1999. *Work and Pay in Japan*. New York: Cambridge University Press.

Hipple, S. 2001. Contingent Work in the Late 1990s. *Monthly Labor Review* 124(3): 3–27.

Jouen, M., and B. Caremier. 2000. *The Future of Work*. Luxembourg: European Commission.

Kelloway, E.K., D.G. Gallagher, and J. Barling. 2004. "Work, Employment, and the Individual." In *Theoretical Perspectives on Work and the Employment Relationship*, B.E. Kaufman, ed. Champaign, IL: Industrial Relations Research Association, pp. 105–131.

Lester, G. 1998. "Careers and Contingency." *Stanford Law Review* 51(1): 73–145.

Lewis, W.M., and N.H. Molloy. 1991. *How to Choose and Use Temporary Services*. New York: American Management Association.

Light, P.C. 1999. *The True Size of Government*. Washington, DC: Brookings Institution.

Nollen, S., and H. Exel. 1996. *Managing Contingent Workers: How to Reap the Benefits and Reduce the Risks*. New York: American Management Association.

Nye, D. 1988. *Alternative Staffing Strategies*. Washington, DC: The Bureau of National Affairs.

Ozaki, M., ed. 1999. *Negotiating Flexibility: The Role of the Social Partners and the State*. Geneva: International Labour Office.

Polivka, A.E. 1996. "Into Contingent and Alternative Employment: By Choice?" *Monthly Labor Review* 119(10): 55–74.

Polivka, A.E., S.R. Cohany, and S. Hipple. 2000. "Definition, Composition, and Economics Consequences of the Nonstandard Workforce." In *Nonstandard Work: The Nature and Challenges of Changing Employment Arrangements*, F. Carré, M.A. Ferber, L. Golden, and S.A. Herzenberg, eds. Champaign, IL: Industrial Relations Research Association, pp. 41–94.

Porter, M.E., and M. Sakakibara. 2004. "Competition in Japan." *Journal of Economic Perspectives* 18(1): 27–50.

Reilly, P. 2001. *Flexibility at Work: Balancing the Interests of Employer and Employee*. Burlington, VT: Gower Publishing Co.

Roberts, K., and S.E. Gleason. 2000. "Workforce Planning for Flexibility: Staffing with Temporary Employees." In *Managing Human Resources in the 21st Century*, E.E. Kossek and R.N. Block, eds. Cincinnati: South-Western College Publishing, Module 12.

Segal, L.M., and D.G. Sullivan. 1997. "The Growth of Temporary Services Work." *Journal of Economic Perspectives* 11(2): 117–136.

Stone, K.V.W. 2004. *From Widgets to Digits: Employment Regulations for the Changing Workplace*. New York: Cambridge University Press.

Tam, M. 1997. *Part-Time Employment: A Bridge or a Trap?* Brookfield, VT: Ashgate Publishing Company.

Vosko, L.F. 1998. "Regulating Precariousness? The Temporary Employment Relationship under the NAFTA and the EC Treaty." *Industrial Relations* 53(1): 2–34.

Zeytinoğlu, I.U., ed. 1999. *Changing Work Relationships in Industrialized Economies.* Philadelphia: John Benjamins Publishing Company.

Zeytinoğlu, I.U., and J.K. Muteshi. 1999. "Changing Work Relationships: Enacting Gender, Race/Ethnicity and Economic Class." In *Changing Work Relationships in Industrialized Nations*, I.U. Zeytinoğlu, ed. Philadelphia: John Benjamins Publishing Company, pp. 1–17.

Part 1

The Shadow Workforce
in the United States

2

Operationalizing the Shadow Workforce

Toward an Understanding of the Participants in Nonstandard Employment Relationships

Courtney von Hippel
University of New South Wales

Venkat Bendapudi
Ohio State University

Judith Tansky
Ohio State University

David B. Greenberger
Ohio State University

Stephen L. Mangum
Ohio State University

Robert L. Heneman
Ohio State University

Most individuals regard full-time, long-term employment as the preferred employment relationship. As such, those in alternative forms of employment may be cast as working in the "shadow" of the mainstream. The term *shadow workforce* thus refers to individuals engaged in forms of employment that differ from full-time, long-term employment. That is, they are engaged in *nonstandard work* (Carré and Joshi 2001). The shadow workforce garners public attention in headlines, titles, and statements proclaiming "The End of the Job," *The Downsizing of America,* and "Jobs in an Age of Insecurity," and in judicial decisions developing case law concerning this group (Bridges 1994; Cahill 1996; Church 1993).

Opinions on the shadow workforce are polarized. Some point to anxiety among workers about the disappearance of job security, career ladders, and benefits in the shadow workforce (Nollen 1996). Others argue that such sentiments are exaggerations of the extent of shadow work, its consequences, or both (Cohany 1998; Dennard 1996; Ettore 1994; Lenz 1996). The latter view suggests that nonstandard employment offers greater flexibility to employees and employers and benefits society as a result of a more efficient and cost-effective use of labor. Both extremes are stereotypical attitudes to nonstandard work. The reality is that the shadow workforce is not a homogeneous entity. Significant differences exist among shadow workers in demographics, skills, income and education levels, and motivation. Researchers should not view contingent workers as a monolith, for such amalgamation prompts overly simplistic diagnoses. Differences between types of contingent workers are so pronounced that, for some workers, the shadow workforce is preferred to the mainstream. For those strongly preferring the mainstream, some parts of the shadow are clearly darker than others.

We begin with data on the extent and composition of the shadow workforce to provide an overview of trends in contingent and nonstandard employment arrangements. We also examine differences in perspectives on the job consequences of such employment. We then adopt a psychological approach to understand growth in the shadow workforce from both the demand or employer perspective and the supply or labor perspective. We reflect upon attempts to incorporate contingent employment into standard models of the employment system, concluding with some questions still seeking answers, living true to the motto that good research should recommend further research.

DEFINING AND ESTIMATING THE SHADOW WORKFORCE

Computing the size of the shadow workforce is complicated by its heterogeneity. What unites its inhabitants is that they are not currently party to full-time, long-term employment and instead are engaged in nonstandard work (Carré and Joshi 2001). Early attempts to quantify the shadow workforce referred to "contingent employees" and operationally involved aggregating some or all of the following groups: part-time workers, individuals employed in the temporary help–supply industry, and contract workers with a single client (Callaghan and Hartmann 1991). This helped to narrow the group, but its imprecision led to unreliable estimates. Fortunately, significant progress has occurred over time in the sophistication of available estimates of the shadow workforce. The U.S. Bureau of Labor Statistics (BLS), beginning in 1995, has collected data on the phenomena through a supplement to the Current Population Survey (CPS), administered monthly to approximately 50,000 American households. The supplement employs two conceptualizations: "contingent employment" and "alternative employment arrangement."

The BLS defines *contingent* employment as work that does not involve explicit or implicit contracts for long-term employment. Contingent work was initially conceptualized as "conditional and transitory employment arrangements as initiated by a need for labor," or in other words, individuals in employment relationships where the conditions are likely to be immediately and directly contingent on changes in production processes and fluctuations in product and service demand (Freedman 1985). Such direct contingency might be illustrated by software programmers in the dotcom bust, when decreases in demand for software skills produced decreased demand and greater idle time for software programmers employed on a per-project basis. Thus, in the BLS data set, contingent work is employment expected to last less than a year; contingent workers are individuals who do not perceive themselves as having an explicit or implicit contract for ongoing employment (Hipple 1998).

Three alternative measures of contingent work are used by the BLS (Polivka and Nardone 1989). Estimate 1, the narrowest, measures contingent workers as wage and salary workers who both expect to work in their current jobs and have worked for their current employers for one year or less. Self-employed workers and independent contractors, as well as individuals working for temporary help employment agencies or contract companies who expect to be employed under these arrangements for more than one year, are excluded under this estimate.

Estimate 2 includes the self-employed and independent contractors who expect to be and have been in employment relationships for one year or less. This category also includes temporary help and contract company workers who expect to be working for the customers to whom they have been assigned for one year or less. For example, based on the above definitions, a temporary worker who has worked for the same temporary employment agency for five years but who moves from one client to another on a regular basis (e.g., weekly or monthly) would be considered contingent under Estimate 1 but not under Estimate 2.

Contingent employment is expanded in Estimate 3 to include all wage and salary workers who do not expect their employment to last for a year, except for those who, for personal reasons, expect to leave jobs that they would otherwise keep. For example, under Estimate 3, a worker who has been employed by a company for 15 years but expects to retire in four months would be contingent.

Using Estimate 3, there were 5.7 million contingent workers in 2005, representing 4.1 percent of the total U.S. workforce (Table 2.1). This is only a very slight increase from 2001 levels of 5.4 million contingent workers, representing 4.0 percent of total employment. Also of note is that 1995, the first year of the series, yielded the largest estimates of contingent workers in both raw number and percentage terms. As a percentage of total employment, contingent employment in these survey data decreased in the 1997, 1999, and 2001 surveys, leveling with very similar percentages of employment figures in 2001 and 2005. To the best of our knowledge these facts cannot be attributed to changes in definition or survey methodology. Whether this 10-year swath of data portrays a longer-term trend, a portion of a cyclical trend, or perhaps is linked to other phenomena, such as trends in international outsourcing, is grounds for healthy speculation.

A second conceptualization used in the supplement to the Current Population Survey (CPS) concerns "alternative employment arrangements." Specific alternative employment arrangements included are independent contractors, on-call workers, temporary help agency workers, and workers provided by contract firms (Cohany 1998).

Independent contractors work for themselves and thus are not employees in a traditional sense. They may work with several clients on different projects at the same time (e.g., a computer consultant). On-call workers are people who do not have a regular schedule for reporting to

Table 2.1 Contingent Worker Employment in the United States

	Number of contingent workers (in millions)					% of U.S. employment				
	1995	1997	1999	2001	2005	1995	1997	1999	2001	2005
Estimate 1	2,739	2,385	2,444	2,295	2,504	2.3	2.0	1.9	1.7	1.8
Estimate 2	3,422	3,096	3,038	2,963	3,177	2.9	2.6	2.3	2.2	2.3
Estimate 3	6,034	5,574	5,641	5,369	5,705	5.2	4.6	4.3	4.0	4.1

SOURCE: Bureau of Labor Statistics, Current Population Survey Supplements: Contingent and Alternative Employment Arrangements, Employed Contingent and Noncontingent Workers by Selected Characteristics, February 1995, 1997, 1999, 2001, 2005.

work. They fill in for regular, full-time positions due to staffing short-ages or temporary absences (e.g., substitute teachers). Temporary help agency workers and workers provided by contract firms are employees of one company who carry out work assignments for another organiza-tion. Temporary help services specialize in placing otherwise uncon-nected individuals temporarily with clients for specific projects, while contract firms typically lease out their employees for significantly lon-ger periods of time to client company sites (e.g., janitors, security staff, engineers, and information technology workers).

The 2005 survey identified 10.3 million independent contractors (7.4 percent of the U.S. workforce), 2.5 million on-call workers (1.8 percent), 1.2 million temporary help workers (0.9 percent), and 813,000 contract workers (0.6 percent). The proportion of people employed in alternative arrangements increased from 9.3 percent (12.5 million people) in 2001 to 10.7 percent (14.8 million) in 2005. As shown in Table 2.2, the largest alternative employment arrangement category in all five surveys (1995–2005) was independent contractors, four times

Table 2.2 U.S. Employment by Type of Work Arrangement

	Independent contractors	On-call workers	Temporary help agency	Contract workers	Traditional workers
Number of workers (000)					
1995	8,309	2,078	1,181	652	111,052
1997	8,456	1,996	1,300	809	114,199
1999	8,247	2,032	1,188	769	119,109
2001	8,585	2,089	1,169	633	121,917
2005	10,342	2,454	1,217	813	123,843
% of U.S. employment					
1995	6.7	1.7	1.0	0.5	90.1
1997	6.7	1.6	1.0	0.6	90.1
1999	6.3	1.5	0.9	0.6	90.7
2001	6.4	1.6	0.9	0.5	90.6
2005	7.4	1.8	0.9	0.6	89.1

SOURCE: Bureau of Labor Statistics, Current Population Survey Supplements: Con-tingent and Alternative Employment Arrangements, Employed Workers with Alterna-tive and Traditional Work Arrangements by Selected Characteristics, February 1995, 1997, 1999, 2001, 2005.

as large as "on-call workers," the next largest category. Interestingly, 2005 marked the highest absolute number and employment percentage for three of the four alternative employment arrangements: independent contractors, on-call workers, and contract workers. The only segment that was not at a historical high in absolute numbers was temporary help agency work, which was below the record 1997 levels in absolute numbers and in percentage representation. Viewing the shadow workforce through the lens of alternative work arrangements portrays a sense of greater stability in the phenomena than when viewed through the lens of contingent work. "Traditional" work arrangements characterized 90.1 to 90.7 percent of employment in the period 1995–2001, dropping to 89.1 percent only in the latest survey year of 2005.

In sum, whether viewed through the lens of alternative employment arrangements or that of contingent workers, the shadow workforce is a nontrivial proportion of the U.S. workforce, as measured from 1995 to 2005.

WHO IS IN THE SHADOW WORKFORCE?

The heterogeneity of the shadow workforce is evident in its demographic composition, briefly described here using CPS data on contingent workers and alternative employment arrangements.

Age

The age distribution of workers in contingent and alternative work arrangements in 2005, contrasted with noncontingent and traditional employment, is shown in Tables 2.3 and 2.4. The largest group of contingent workers was between 16 and 24 years of age (27.2 percent). This is in contrast to noncontingent workers, where the largest group was the category of 35–44-year-olds (25.1 percent). Contingent workers are twice as likely as noncontingent workers to be under 25 years of age. Table 2.4 provides an age breakdown across alternative work arrangements. Workers in temporary and on-call work arrangements were more heavily clustered in the younger age groups than was the case for other work arrangements: nearly 20 percent of both on-call and tem-

Table 2.3 Age Distribution of Contingent and Noncontingent Workers, 2005 (%)

Age	Contingent workers	Noncontingent workers
Over 55	13.8	16.5
45–55	15.3	24.1
35–44	18.3	25.1
25–34	25.4	21.5
16–24	27.2	12.8

SOURCE: Bureau of Labor Statistics, Current Population Survey Supplements: Contingent and Alternative Employment Arrangements, Employed Contingent and Noncontingent Workers by Selected Characteristics, February 2005.

Table 2.4 Age Distribution of Employment within Alternative Work Arrangements, 2005 (%)

Age	Independent contractors	On-call	Temporary	Contract	Traditional
Over 55	27.3	18.0	13.8	16.3	15.5
45–54	27.1	17.0	16.4	22.8	23.7
35–44	26.6	23.3	20.8	24.1	24.7
25–34	14.7	21.8	29.8	25.2	22.2
16–24	4.3	19.9	19.3	11.6	13.9

SOURCE: Bureau of Labor Statistics, Current Population Survey Supplements: Contingent and Alternative Employment Arrangements, Employed Workers with Alternative and Traditional Work Arrangements by Selected Characteristics, February 2005.

porary workers were between 16 and 24. The distribution of independent contractors was more skewed to the older-age categories compared with any other work arrangement, including traditional arrangements. For example, workers ages 55 and older represented 27.3 percent of independent contractors, as opposed to 13.8 percent of temporary workers. The age distribution of contract workers was most consistent with that of traditional work arrangements.

Gender and Ethnicity

The distribution of workers across contingent and alternative employment by gender and ethnicity is shown in Tables 2.5 and 2.6. In

Table 2.5 Selected Demographics of Contingent and Noncontingent Workers, 2005 (%)

Demographic group	Contingent workers	Noncontingent workers
Women	48.9	46.7
Black	11.6	10.5
Hispanic	20.8	12.7

SOURCE: Bureau of Labor Statistics, Current Population Survey Supplements: Contingent and Alternative Employment Arrangements, Employed Contingent and Noncontingent Workers by Selected Characteristics, February 2005.

Table 2.6 Selected Demographics of Workers in Alternative Work Arrangements, 2005 (%)

Demographic group	Independent contractors	On-call	Temporary	Contract	Traditional
Women	35.3	49.4	52.8	31.0	47.8
Black	5.6	8.6	22.7	14.9	10.9
Hispanic	9.2	15.7	21.0	16.4	13.1

SOURCE: Bureau of Labor Statistics, Current Population Survey Supplements: Contingent and Alternative Employment Arrangements, Employed Workers with Alternative and Traditional Work Arrangements by Selected Characteristics, February 2005.

2005, women and minorities comprised a greater percentage of contingent workers than noncontingent workers. Among alternative work arrangements, the percentage of employment in temporary help agencies for women, African Americans, and Hispanics was higher than their employment percentages in traditional work arrangements. The percentage of independent contractors who were female, African American, or Hispanic was lower than the percentage of employees with these characteristics who were employed in traditional employment.

Education

The educational level of workers is shown in Tables 2.7 and 2.8. A larger percentage of contingent workers than noncontingent workers reported having less than a high school diploma. Interestingly, this was also true in 2005 for college education. Within alternative employment arrangements, the percentage of temporary help agency workers pos-

Table 2.7 Distribution of Contingent and Noncontingent Workers, by Educational Attainment, 2005 (%)

	Less than high school diploma	High school graduate, no college	Some college, less than a bachelor's degree	College graduate
Contingent workers	15.5	24.5	23.5	36.6
Noncontingent workers	8.6	29.7	28.5	33.1

SOURCE: Bureau of Labor Statistics, Current Population Survey Supplements: Contingent and Alternative Employment Arrangements, Employed Contingent and Noncontingent Workers by School Enrollment and Educational Attainment, February 2005.

Table 2.8 Distribution of Workers in Alternative Work Arrangements, by Educational Attainment, 2005 (%)

	Less than high school diploma	High school graduate, no college	Some college, less than a bachelor's degree	College graduate
Independent contractors	7.7	27.6	29.1	35.6
On-call workers	13.7	27.8	28.8	29.7
Temporary help agency workers	16.9	29.5	32.4	21.2
Contract firm workers	13.0	19.9	30.5	36.6
Traditional arrangements	8.7	29.8	28.3	33.2

SOURCE: Bureau of Labor Statistics, Current Population Survey Supplements: Contingent and Alternative Employment Arrangements, Employed Workers with Alternative and Traditional Work Arrangements by School Enrollment and Educational Attainment, February 2005.

sessing less than a high school diploma was larger than that of any other employment arrangement. Both contract firm and independent contract employment arrangements had a larger percentage of college-educated workers than did traditional employment. The employment arrangement with the largest percentage of workers in the "some college" category was temporary help agencies, suggestive perhaps of employment in this category being most consistent with continued progression toward degree completion.

Occupation and Industry

Table 2.9 shows that, compared to the distribution of workers in regular (noncontingent) employment, a larger percentage of contingent workers in 2005 was in the occupational categories of administrative support or operators, fabricators, and laborers, and a lower percentage was in professional specialties. Compared to the occupational distribution of workers within traditional employment arrangements, the distribution of independent contractors was more concentrated in a professional specialty (57 percent) and substantially less among administrative support occupations (3.4 percent) (Table 2.10). The occupational distribution of temporary help agency employment was more concentrated in administrative support (24.8 percent) and operators, fabricators, and laborers (37.2 percent) and less in professional specialties (22.4 percent) than was the case in traditional employment. The occupational distribution in contract firms and on-call employment were similar, both with a substantially higher percentage in service occupations and in the opera-

Table 2.9 Distribution of Workers in Contingent and Noncontingent Arrangements, by Occupational Category, 2005 (%)

	Professional specialty	Administrative support	Services	Operators, fabricators, laborers
Contingent	41.6	14.8	15.7	27.8
Noncontingent	47.3	13.9	15.6	23.3

SOURCE: Bureau of Labor Statistics, Current Population Survey Supplements: Contingent and Alternative Employment Arrangements, Employed Contingent and Noncontingent Workers by Occupation and Industry, February 2005.

**Table 2.10 Workers in Alternative and Traditional Work Arrangements,
by Occupational Category, 2005 (%)**

Work arrangements	Professional specialty	Administrative support	Services	Operators
Independent contractors	57.0	3.4	13.7	25.8
On-call	40.0	8.2	22.1	29.6
Temporary help agency	22.4	24.8	15.6	37.2
Contract firm	42.1	4.7	26.2	27.0
Traditional	46.7	14.9	15.5	22.9

SOURCE: Bureau of Labor Statistics, Current Population Survey (CPS) Supplements: Contingent and Alternative Employment Arrangements, Employed Workers with Alternative and Traditional Work Arrangements by Occupation and Industry, February 2005.

tor et al. grouping and less in administrative support occupations than was the case for traditional employment.

There were also differences among industries. Under all three definitional estimates of the contingent workforce, there was a higher percentage of workers in the services industrial classification than in the case of noncontingent employment (Table 2.11). Work in the service sector represented the majority of employment for on-call workers (55.7 percent) (Table 2.12). While the percentage employed in services among independent contractors and temporary help agency workers (44.4 percent and 47.7 percent, respectively) was similar to that of traditional employment (43.4 percent), a substantially lower percentage of contract firm employment (30.9 percent) was in services. Manufactur-

**Table 2.11 Workers in Contingent and Noncontingent Arrangements, by
Selected Industry Grouping, 2005 (%)**

	Services	Wholesale/retail	Manufacturing
Contingent	57.6	8.6	6.4
Noncontingent	43.3	15.6	11.9

SOURCE: Bureau of Labor Statistics, Current Population Survey (CPS) Supplements: Contingent and Alternative Employment Arrangements, Employed Contingent and Noncontingent Workers by Occupation and Industry, February 2005.

Table 2.12 Distribution of Workers in Alternative and Traditional Work Arrangements, by Selected Industry, 2005 (%)

Work arrangements	Services	Wholesale/retail	Manufacturing
Independent contractors	44.4	11.0	3.2
On-call	55.7	7.7	4.8
Temporary help agency	47.7	7.5	28.4
Contract firm	30.9	6.5	14.1
Traditional	43.4	16.1	12.6

SOURCE: Bureau of Labor Statistics, Current Population Survey (CPS) Supplements: Contingent and Alternative Employment Arrangements, Employed Contingent and Noncontingent Workers by Occupation and Industry, February 2005.

ing employment represented less than 5 percent of total employment for independent contractors and on-call workers, in contrast to 12.6 percent of traditional employment, and was a higher percentage of employment among temporary help workers (28.4 percent) than any other form of employment arrangement.

VOLITION IN THE SHADOW WORKFORCE

An important issue in the study of contingent and alternative employment relationships is the extent to which the arrangement reflects employee choice. The CPS supplement lends itself to some exploration of this question in that it asks individuals to report their preference for the current work arrangement, the response options for contingent workers being "prefer noncontingent," "prefer contingent," and "it depends." Across all three contingent employment definitions/estimates, the most frequently stated preference of workers currently employed in contingent employment was that of noncontingent employment arrangements and by a wide margin (55.3 percent preferring noncontingent employment to 35.5 percent preferring contingent employment in 2005 [Table 2.13]). Investigating preference across alternative work arrangements reveals greater differences in attitudes. Independent con-

Table 2.13 Distribution of Contingent Workers, by Preference for Contingent Employment, 2005 (%)

Work preference	Contingent workers
Prefers noncontingent	55.3
Prefers contingent	35.5
It depends	5.7
Not available	3.5

SOURCE: Bureau of Labor Statistics, Current Population Survey (CPS) Supplements: Contingent and Alternative Employment Arrangements, Employed Contingent Workers by their Preference for Contingent or Noncontingent Work Arrangements, February 2005.

Table 2.14 Distribution of Alternative Workers, by Arrangement, 2005 (%)

Work preference	Independent contractors	On-call	Temporary help agency
Prefers alternative	82.3	46.1	56.2
Prefers traditional	9.1	44.6	32.1
It depends	5.2	6.8	6.5
Not available	3.4	2.5	5.3

SOURCE: Bureau of Labor Statistics, Current Population Survey (CPS) Supplements: Contingent and Alternative Employment Arrangements, Employed Workers with Alternative Work Arrangements by their Preference for a Traditional Work Arrangement, February 2005.

tractors expressed little interest in traditional employment (only 9.1 percent), contrasted with significantly larger percentages of temporary help workers (32.1 percent) and on-call employees (44.6 percent) (Table 2.14).

EARNINGS AND ACCESS TO BENEFITS IN ALTERNATIVE EMPLOYMENT RELATIONSHIPS

Median weekly earnings for contingent workers ($405 to $488, depending on operational definition of contingent employment used) were lower than median weekly earnings of noncontingent workers (Table 2.15). The median weekly earnings of independent contractors and contract firm workers were higher than individuals who are on-call or temporary help agency workers (Table 2.16). Perhaps somewhat surprising is that contract firm workers, not independent contractors, show the highest median weekly earnings level in the 2005 survey. The lowest median earnings level was that of temporary help agency workers, with on-call workers earning a higher median weekly income.

In terms of benefits, only 18.1 percent of contingent workers reported access to employer-provided health insurance. 52.1 percent of noncontingent workers and 12.4 percent of contingent workers were eligible for employer-provided pension plans, in contrast to 44.7 percent of workers in noncontingent employment (Table 2.17). We would not expect independent contractors to have access to these benefits, as they are self-employed and responsible for providing their own. Nearly

Table 2.15 Median Usual Weekly Earnings of Contingent Workers, 2005

Contingent worker estimates	Usual weekly earnings ($)
Estimate 1	405
Estimate 2	411
Estimate 3	488

SOURCE: Bureau of Labor Statistics, Current Population Survey (CPS) Supplements: Contingent and Alternative Employment Arrangements, Median Usual Weekly Earnings of Full- and Part-time Contingent Wage and Salary Workers and those with Alternative Work Arrangements by Sex, Race, and Hispanic Origin, February 2005.

Table 2.16 Median Usual Weekly Earnings of Workers with Alternative Work Arrangements, 2005

Alternative worker arrangement	Usual weekly earnings ($)
Independent contractors	716
On-call	519
Temporary help agency	414
Contract firm	756

SOURCE: Bureau of Labor Statistics, Current Population Survey (CPS) Supplements: Contingent and Alternative Employment Arrangements, Median Usual Weekly Earnings of Full- and Part-time Contingent Wage and Salary Workers and those with Alternative Work Arrangements by Sex, Race, and Hispanic Origin, February 2005.

50 percent of employees in contract firms reported employer-provided health insurance, compared to only 8.3 percent of temporary help agency workers (Table 2.18). Similarly, 33.5 percent of contract firm workers were eligible for employer-provided pension plans in contrast to 3.8 percent of temporary help agency workers. In summary, contingent workers had less access to both health insurance and pension benefits than their noncontingent counterparts, and, with the exception of our expectation on independent contractors, the lowest level of health insurance and pension coverage was among temporary help agency workers. Combined, these data paint a complex portrait of the shadow workforce. It is a tapestry of diverse employment arrangements with distinct demographic profiles, differing levels of employee volition, and very different outcomes as measured in earnings and benefits.

To increase understanding of the forces that provide the impetus for the formation and the maintenance of the shadow workforce, we adopt the economist's propensity for demand and supply. We first discuss the demand side, highlighting factors that may motivate organizations to increase their use of contingent workers. We then focus on the supply side, examining why employees choose to work in a contingent capacity. In this examination we concentrate on temporary employees, where research exists to shed light on the question. Logic and evidence suggest that the factors are likely a function of both supply and demand. The chapter ends with an examination of the consequences of contingent worker usage for the organization.

Table 2.17 Access to Employer-Provided Health Insurance and Pension Plans, 2005 (%)

	Contingent	Noncontingent
Health insurance provided by employer	18.1	52.1
Eligible for employer-provided pension plan	12.4	44.7

SOURCE: Bureau of Labor Statistics, Current Population Survey (CPS) Supplements: Contingent and Alternative Employment Arrangements, Employed Contingent and Noncontingent Workers and those with Alternative and Traditional Arrangements by Health Insurance Coverage and Eligibility for Employer-provided Pension Plans, February 2005.

Table 2.18 Workers with Alternative and Traditional Work Arrangements, by Employer-Provided Health Insurance and Eligibility for Employer-Provided Pension Plans, 2005 (%)

Work arrangements	Employer-provided health insurance	Eligible for employer-provided pension plan
Independent contractors	0.0	1.9
On-call	25.7	27.8
Temporary help agency	8.3	3.8
Contract firm	48.9	33.5
Traditional	56.0	47.7

SOURCE: Bureau of Labor Statistics, Current Population Survey (CPS) Supplements: Contingent and Alternative Employment Arrangements, Employed Contingent and Noncontingent Workers and those with Alternative and Traditional Arrangements by Health Insurance Coverage and Eligibility for Employer-provided Pension Plans, February 2005.

ORGANIZATIONAL REASONS TO HIRE CONTINGENT WORKERS

Numerous reasons have been cited in the literature for organizational usage of contingent employees, from filling in for absent permanent employees to avoiding the perception of wage inequity. These reasons can be divided into three general categories: cost reduction, increasing flexibility, and avoiding restrictions/consequences (von Hippel et al. 1997). Although these reasons are presented separately, organizations may rely on the contingent workforce for all of these reasons (Liden, Wayne, and Kraimer 2003).

Cost Reductions

Reducing wage and benefit costs is a major motivation for companies to turn to a contingent workforce. As a rule, most contingent employees do not receive the same wages as permanent employees doing the same work (Coates 1997). Average benefits costs can increase compensation levels anywhere from 25 to 40 percent above the base levels. Consistent with this reasoning, a positive relationship has been documented in a large number of organizations between the average fringe benefit level and the ratio of temporary to total employee use (Mangum, Mayall, and Nelson 1985). In addition, even when pay rates for contingent workers are not necessarily lower, resources can be saved by hiring employees only for a finite period of time. For example, a company may hire temporary executives, such as chief financial officers (CFOs), when unable to afford a permanent hire (Messemer 1994). The temporary CFO can bring key financial stewardship and insight to an organization for a limited time, within a manageable budget (World Future Society 1997).

Use of contingent workers can affect costs other than wages. Organizations may save on training-related costs by hiring contingent workers who were trained elsewhere for the tasks they will be performing (Caudron 1994). Temporary employees in particular also may reduce organizational costs of recruiting and testing. For example, hiring from temporary worker ranks can serve as a screening tool for the organization, and thus lower selection costs (Pfeffer and Baron 1988). This kind of strategy has been employed by organizations such as Hancock Information Group, where 39 percent of its permanent employees began as temporary employees. Similarly, Universal Tax Systems typically brings in 40 temporary employees prior to its busy season, of whom 10 to 20 are hired permanently afterward (Fenn 1995). Indeed, 70 percent of employers in a Robert Half International Survey said that they had hired a temporary employee for a permanent position after having seen the temporary employee "in action" (Financial Management Association 1997). Finally, organizations may save on administrative overhead when the temporary agency is responsible for processing the employee paychecks and attending to paperwork associated with employment (Davis-Blake and Uzzi 1993).

Flexibility

Flexibility is another frequently cited reason for organizations' use of contingent employees. Given our global economy, it is now a truism that output demand fluctuates tremendously over time. These fluctuations may be more effectively managed through the use of a contingent workforce (Kochan et al. 1994). In a survey by the Society for Human Resource Management (1999), respondents indicated that the main reason companies use flexible staffing arrangements is to meet workload or business fluctuations. Such flexibility would be particularly attractive where the corporate culture favors employment security for permanent employees. Rather than laying off permanent workers, the company may rely upon judicious use of contingent workers to respond to transitory fluctuations in output demand (Cappelli and Neumark 2004). Indeed, in a twist on this strategy, Lancaster Laboratories avoids layoffs during the slow season by having their employees work as temporary employees outside the company during their off months (Greco 1997).

The use of contingent workers may also enhance flexibility by enabling the organization to focus permanent employees' efforts on core competencies while having contingent workers perform more peripheral work. This approach has the potential to reduce structural differentiation within the permanent workforce and thereby make integration easier among employees. That is, they develop a shared set of values, orientations, and activities as a result of focusing on the organization's core competencies (Lawrence and Lorsch 1967). This is consistent with the trend to outsource and the focus toward relying upon a small group of higher-paid employees who have firm-specific knowledge. Contingent workers can also facilitate organizational access to skill flexibility by providing highly specialized functions that, while necessary, are infrequently recurring, or for which need is periodic or unpredictable.

Avoiding Restrictions and Consequences

Organizations also may be motivated to use contingent workers to avoid some of the potentially negative consequences of permanence in employment relationships. Organizations can avoid building commitment to a large number of permanent workers and subsequently having to fire unneeded employees by using contingent workers. That is, "contingent workers offer flexibility without long-term commitments" (Grossman 1998), as discussed in Chapter 3. Restrictions that may be avoided include those created by unions, the legal framework, the organizational budget, and internal wage levels.

It has been speculated by union officials that companies may use contingent workers, in particular temporary employees, as an attempt to avoid unionization (Kochan et al. 1994). But in an even broader sense, with the increase in use of temporary workers, unions are concerned that employers are using temporary workers to redefine the employee relationships. To counteract this, unions have moved to reduce the restrictions on organizing temporary workers, thus reducing this organizational rationale for their use (Dreazen 2000). For more information on union responses, refer to Chapter 4.

Companies also avoid various legal restrictions by using contingent workers. Typically, the client organization pays a flat fee to a temporary employment service agency or a leasing company to cover the worker's wages and benefits, as well as overhead to the agency. The client organization is not liable for benefits such as health care insurance, vacation pay, and holiday pay. At the same time, the organization also is relieved of paying unemployment taxes, workers' compensation, and other payroll taxes. This also may provide a strategy for avoiding the requirements of Consolidated Omnibus Budget Reconciliation Act (COBRA) and the Fair Labor Standards Act (FLSA); see Chapters 5 and 6 for more details. Thus, although the company may pay a higher hourly rate for the temporary worker, it eliminates many of the extra costs and risks associated with a permanent employee.

One issue of concern, especially with temporary workers, is that of coemployment, the term used to describe the relationship between the client employer and the worker (Tansky and Veglahn 1995). That is, the temporary worker is employed by the temporary agency but works on-site at the client employer. Under this employment arrangement it is unclear who is legally responsible for the temporary worker. For example, if the temporary worker is sexually harassed while placed at the client employer, does the temporary agency or client employer take legal responsibility? The laws are not entirely precise on these matters. These issues are discussed in more detail in Chapter 5.

In addition, companies may hire contingent workers as a means of avoiding internal budget constraints in place for permanent hires. For example, in many state and federal agencies authorization is necessary to hire a new employee. Moreover, companies often impose hiring "freezes" for budgetary or even public relations reasons. Often, however, these companies or units within the company have discretionary budgets that are not subject to the same kinds of authorizations and constraints. Thus, if a department cannot hire a permanent employee, it may still be able to contract out the work by hiring a contingent worker (Grossman 1998). Additionally, companies may be under pressure to keep their personnel allocations down. By hiring contingent workers they are able to achieve this goal since the costs are not permanently incorporated into the base budget.

Finally, organizations may access the shadow workforce to avoid perceptions of wage inequity among their permanent employees. For example, companies that pay above market wages may contract out those activities that can be staffed at lower relative salaries. Through the use of contingent workers, this may be done without damaging the organization's reputation as a high wage provider. Alternatively, organizations may decide to contract out high-paying activities (e.g., consulting) to avoid pressure to upgrade the current internal wage scale. It has been argued that by cutting overall employment costs, contingent workers can enable organizations to provide permanent employees with greater job security and better compensation (Davis-Blake, Broschak, and George 2003).

INDIVIDUAL MOTIVATION TO WORK AS A CONTINGENT WORKER

Although companies have strong incentives to hire contingent workers, the individuals' motivation to work as a contingent worker may bear little correspondence to these incentives. The desirability of permanent employment has been well ingrained in our culture, and permanent employment provides workers with better salaries, benefits, and a greater level of job security than contingent work (Connelly and Gallagher 2004; Golden and Applebaum 1992). Why, then, would anyone choose to work in a contingent capacity?

Although there are a large number of idiosyncratic reasons why individuals are motivated to work as contingent employees, the research on temporary employees in particular points to a few critical factors. Specifically, temporary employees work in such a capacity because they cannot obtain the kind of permanent position they desire, they want the flexibility that temporary employment offers, they value the variety that temporary employment offers, and/or they seek the skills and training provided in temporary positions (Golden and Applebaum 1992; Mendenhall 1993; Tetrault 1994; von Hippel et al. 1997). At a broader level, one could classify this list of reasons to propose that some people work as temporary employees because they prefer various aspects of the job such as flexibility, variety, and skill enhancement, whereas others work as temporary employees because they have only limited opportunities to do otherwise (Feldman 1995; Nardone 1986). For example, a college student might find temporary employment attractive because of the flexibility it provides. A student can work during the summer months and school holidays, while turning down positions when exams and assignments are pending. In contrast, an employee who has been recently laid off from a downsizing company might be working in a temporary capacity until a permanent position becomes available.

In previous work, the implication of classifying temporary employees in this manner was explored (von Hippel et al. 2000). Specifically, temporary employees were categorized based upon their beliefs about the degree of choice they have to work as a temporary employee. Those employees who perceive themselves as having no choice but to work as a temporary employee were classified as "involuntary" temporaries, whereas those who believed they were with a temporary agency by choice were classified as "voluntary" temporaries (Ellingson, Gruys, and Sackett 1998; Feldman 1995; Feldman, Doerpinghaus, and Turnley 1995; Marler, Barringer, and Milkovich 2002). This classification appears to be meaningful in that voluntary temporary employees were found to have different sources of satisfaction with their work, commitment to their employers, and perceptions of personal control over how they accomplish their work than involuntary temporary employees (von Hippel et al. 2000). Specifically, involuntary temporaries showed increased personal control, satisfaction, and commitment to the degree that they were gaining new skills from their temporary assignments. In contrast, voluntary temporaries showed increased personal control and satisfaction to the extent that they experienced variety in their task assignments. Thus, it seems that voluntary temporary employees are looking for variety in temporary placements, whereas involuntary temporary employees are looking to gain new skills from their temporary placements. To the extent that voluntary and involuntary temporary employees experience these differential characteristics, work-related attitudes are more positive.

Feldman, Doerpinghaus, and Turnley (1994, 1995) propose a similar distinction. They find that temporary employees who work in a temporary capacity by choice have more positive job attitudes than those who believe they have no other option. Temporary employees who work in positions consistent with their expertise, and who are not trying to convert a temporary position into a permanent one, also manifest more positive job attitudes. Ellingson, Gruys, and Sackett (1998) also explore whether temporary employees who work in this capacity voluntarily are more satisfied than their involuntary counterparts. They find that both univariate and multivariate indices of "voluntariness" were comparable in predicting satisfaction among temporary employees. Voluntary temporary employees were more satisfied than involuntary temporaries with temporary work, whereas no differences emerged between voluntary and involuntary temporary employees with regard to growth satisfaction, co-worker satisfaction, or supervisor satisfaction. Finally, Marler, Barringer, and Milkovich (2002), using a similar classification (termed "traditional" and "boundaryless" contingent workers), demonstrate that voluntary temporary employees' performance was more sensitive to job-related attitudes such as satisfaction and commitment compared to involuntary temporary employees.

This research does not speak to contingent workers more generally, however. Interestingly, although statistics indicate that an overwhelming percentage of the workforce is desirous of permanent employment, anecdotal evidence suggests that an increasing number are viewing contingent work positively. For example, in the high-tech area, many individuals move from one company to the next, hiring themselves out for limited projects, or allow themselves to be hired permanently with the knowledge that their stay will be relatively short. This flexibility enables them to continuously offer themselves up to the highest bidder, thus keeping their compensation at or above the market. It also permits them to maintain a skill set that is not company-specific; in so doing, that makes them far more valuable both to the company in which they work and the market in general. Finally, in some sectors of the economy, the growth of individual wealth over the past decade is such that some people, having satisfied many of their extrinsic interests, are free to focus on lifestyle and work and nonwork uses of time. People want to spend time with their families, to work at home, and to have extended periods of not working. Contingent work is enabling insofar as they can select positions aligned with their values and needs, leave positions that impose unacceptable demands on their time, and negotiate for preferential arrangements.

INTERFACE OF SUPPLY AND DEMAND FACTORS

We have approached the utility of contingent workers as main effects from both the demand and supply side, but in the economy of the twenty-first century, it appears as if the interaction of needs is more compelling. The convergence of thinking regarding the utility of contingent workers has been a significant trend that may portend their increasing use. The meeting of the minds regarding contingent workers can best be seen in two areas: the changing nature of the employment relationship and the changing nature of benefits. We will discuss each briefly.

Abundant research suggests that the nature of the employment relationship is changing (Littleton, Arthur, and Rousseau 2000). Specifically, both employers and employees are seeing the benefit of keeping options open; flexibility allows a company to release people it no longer needs, and allows workers to easily leave when a better position becomes available. These examples best illustrate the changing mind-set: the diminishing stereotypes of the laid-off employee and the employee who job hops, the movement to more of a project orientation, and the outsourcing of noncore competencies. First, we all know that there has been a stigma associated with someone who was released from a job or who moves around "too frequently." This stereotype has begun to change from a very negative one—reflected in a general desire to avoid the person—to a neutral or even positive one—an openness to see what the person has to offer, and in the case of someone who has moved around, an attribution that the individual might be highly sought after.

Second, as companies become more project-oriented, they necessarily use permanent employees in a more incidental nature and often need to "backfill" with contingent workers. This project orientation has necessitated frequent reorganizations in existing firms, but more importantly has served to make salient to employees the temporary nature of the work. That is, rather than being job focused and thus having permanence because of the position, work is now seen as transitory, with a finite beginning and end.

Third, the widespread use of outsourcing has led to the deterioration of the traditional companies. Even in the most conventional companies, it is common to see consultants come into the company to assist in areas that fall outside the company's basic expertise. Moreover, when a firm chooses to outsource, efforts are made to treat the individuals who assist as partners, thus blurring the separation between permanent and contingent workers. Finally, when individuals who had previously performed the now outsourced function are replaced, the firm becomes dependent upon the outsourced partners. As a consequence, the contingent workers from the outsourced partner develop a sense of permanence with the organization.

Another area that has seen a convergence of the needs of both companies and employees is benefits. Historically, benefits have rested within the company, so if an employee moved to a different organization, she risked not being covered or having to wait for eligibility. This forced many employees—particularly those who might need to use the benefits—to stay with an organization regardless of their satisfaction. Recently, at least two significant changes have occurred in the nature of benefits that not only facilitate the movement between organizations, but also reinforce the normative nature of movement. First, retirement plans have moved from traditional plans to more portable plans, such as 401(k)s and "cash balance" or "pension equity" plans. These plans—ignoring the problems of the new plans for older workers—are notable for their portability and thus are appealing to young employees who may want to change jobs frequently. With these new plans, employees can move to a different organization at will and can retire at any point of their careers. These plans facilitate flexibility and the kind of restructuring in which dynamic organizations need to engage (Burlingame and Gulotta 1998).

Second, with the spiraling costs of health care, insurance is a requirement and is often the factor that motivates people to work. Stories of "dumping" noninsured patients to other hospitals abound. Although issues of insurability continue to be important, statutes (e.g., authorizing COBRA) now assist people in keeping their insurance when they change jobs.

DIRECTIONS FOR FUTURE RESEARCH

Although the previous discussion provides evidence for the use of contingent workers, a variety of issues remain unexamined. The scope of this chapter does not allow for an exhaustive list of these issues, but we address a few of them here. Specifically, we discuss the implications of a blended workforce, that is, a blend of permanent and contingent workers. Next we examine the changes that occur in company culture when there are large numbers of contingent workers in the workplace. Finally, we address the question of what motivates the contingent worker, focusing primarily on the temporary employee. Other important questions, such as whether public policy changes are required with the increased use of contingent workers, are covered in Chapter 6.

Almost all workforces are blended in some important ways. For example, there often are regional and divisional differences within a company, as well as differences in job description, training level, pay, and demographics. These sorts of blended workforces are unlikely to create the same sorts of problems and opportunities created by a blend of contingent and permanent workers, however, because all of these workers accept and endorse the common in-group identity provided by the company that employs them. In contrast, the blend of contingent and permanent workers brings people together who may share no common in-group identity at all. This lack of a bond between workers has the potential to create prejudice and conflict between groups (as discussed below), which in turn can be exacerbated by the inherent differences in status that exist between permanent and contingent workers (Pettigrew 1998).

The existing research focuses on temporary employees and suggests that they have largely negative effects on permanent employees. Permanent employees often resent the presence of temporary employees, feeling that their work is not up to par, which then forces the permanent employee to compensate for the temporary workers' poor performance (Smith 1994). Permanent employees who work alongside temporary employees also showed decreased trust in and commitment to the organization (George 2003). Not surprisingly then, blended workforces also reduced permanent employees' intentions to remain at their jobs (Davis-Blake, Broschak, and George 2003).

More recent research has started to examine some of the psychological mechanisms underlying these negative consequences of blended workforces (Kraimer et al. 2005; von Hippel 1999). The results of this work suggest that a blended workforce produces negative outcomes when the perceived motives for using temporary employees are deemed inappropriate (e.g., hiring temporary employees as a way to cut costs rather than to increase flexibility or deal with fluctuations in demand), the layoff policy is unfavorable, and/or the relative rank of the temporary worker is equal to or greater than that of the permanent employee. These results further suggest that these conditions lead to negative outcomes because the permanent workers feel threatened by their temporary colleagues. Specifically, perceptions of threat arise, which in turn lead to intergroup biases on the part of permanent employees, causing them to think and act negatively toward their temporary co-workers.

The negative consequences of a blended workforce appear to translate to permanent employees' performance as well. In one study, permanent employees who felt threatened by the presence of temporary co-workers showed lower performance than employees who did not (Kraimer et al. 2005). Further research is necessary to fully understand the effects of a blended workforce, as well as to determine how to prevent these negative consequences and thereby allow companies to reap the full benefits of a blended workforce. Indeed, recent research suggests that temporary workers can also feel threatened by negative stereotypes held by managers and their permanent co-workers (Gallagher and Parks 2001; von Hippel et al. 2005).

Another issue that has not been addressed deals with company culture when a workforce contains a blend of contingent and permanent workers. Most organizations pride themselves on their unique culture, and staffing decisions—hiring, retention, and promotions—often rest on the fit of the individual with the organization (which is to say the culture). With increasing use of temporary, contract, and outsourced partners, two problems may result. First, as organizations are increasingly outsourcing their HR functions, the company's culture becomes increasingly similar to the culture of the company to which it has outsourced the human resource function. Companies try to hire employees who "match" the company culture and image, just as prospective employees try to determine if their values match those of the company. As a consequence, the culture of the organization must take on components of the culture of the partnering groups. The second problem results when a sizeable percentage of the company is composed of contingent workers who come and go frequently. Contingent workers may not stay long enough to detect and assimilate to the client employer's culture. These situations can result in either cultural blending or cultural blandness, depending on how well the employees are managed. These situations may have implications for the company's long-term vitality. If human resources are outsourced or there are too many transient workers, there may be no "unique culture," and thus, the organization's competitive advantage will suffer.

Because contingent workers, by definition, do not share the same sense of "permanence" with employees of the organization, managing their attitudes and performance may be an entirely different process than for permanent employees. Indeed, different antecedents and interrelationships among temporary employees' attitudes and behaviors have been described in recent years (Moorman and Harland 2002; Parker et al. 2002; Slattery and Selvarajan 2005). Some new methods of managing contingent versus permanent employees have also been proposed. Through two case studies, Koene and van Riemsdijk (2005) have demonstrated the benefits organizations reap through careful management of temporary employees in distribution centers. When temporary employees are "carelessly managed" they are treated as expendable, socialization is nonexistent, and training is minimal. In this particular distribution center there was a standing joke whereby permanent workers would not tell a temporary employee their names until the temporary employee had been working for six weeks. It was believed that providing your name before this time was pointless since temporary employees typically did not last six weeks—no wonder! Contrast this approach with the second distribution center, where temporary workers were given extensive training, socialization, and support. Although temporary employees in this firm were treated differently from the permanent employees, this treatment was no worse (nor better, just different). As a consequence, this careful management resulted in lower rates of sickness, minimal "no shows," and increased tenure compared to the "careless" approach.

As this chapter has demonstrated, however, contingent employees are not a homogeneous group, and thus not all management strategies are likely to be equally effective with this diverse population. For example, von Hippel et al. (1997) show how human resource practices for temporary versus permanent employees vary according to the business philosophy regarding temporary employees (e.g., as strategic partners or a necessary evil) and by human resource functional area (e.g., staffing, development, compensation). Additionally, as discussed previously, the management of contingent workers is likely to differ depending on whether the contingent workers are working as such voluntarily or involuntarily. For example, when managing voluntary temporaries, managers can try to provide a number of different tasks for workers to enhance feelings of variety. In contrast, a skills focus should be adopted when managing involuntary temporary employees, given the role that learning new skills plays in their levels of satisfaction, commitment, and personal control.

CONCLUSION

The shadow workforce is a sizeable, heterogeneous group. If it was ever the case, researchers certainly cannot now lump such workers into a single grouping category. There is also significant heterogeneity in motivation on the employing side of the labor exchange. Researchers and policymakers must distinguish among types of contingent work and contingent workers or risk simplistic analyses with simplistic solutions. Articulation of the construct of contingent worker is required, as sweeping generalizations ignore critical differences inherent in this group of workers. This chapter demonstrates the diversity in demographic profiles, levels of employee volition, different job outcomes, and occupational and industry representations among categories of contingent workers. The old stereotypes of the contingent employee must be reconceptualized and replaced with new understandings.

References

Bridges, W. 1994. "The End of the Job." *Fortune* 130(6): 62–74.
Bureau of Labor Statistics. 2001. "Contingent and Alternative Employment Arrangements, February." News release May 24, USDOL 01-153.

Burlingame, H.W., and M.J. Gulotta. 1998. "Cash Study: Cash Balance Pension Plan Facilitates Restructuring the Workforce at AT&T." *Compensation and Benefits Review* 30(6): 25–31.

Cahill, M. 1996. *The Downsizing of America.* New York: Times Books.

Callaghan, P., and H. Hartmann. 1991. *Contingent Work: A Chart Book on Part-Time and Temporary Employment.* Washington, DC: Economic Policy Institute.

Cappelli, P., and D. Neumark. 2004. "External Churning and Internal Flexibility: Evidence on the Functional Flexibility and Core-Periphery Hypotheses." *Industrial Relations* 43(1): 148–183.

Carré, F., and P. Joshi. 2001. "Looking for Leverage in a Fluid World: Innovative Responses to Temporary and Contracted Work." In *Nonstandard Work: The Nature and Challenges of Changing Employment Arrangements,* F. Carré, M.A. Ferber, L. Golden, and S.A. Herzenberg, eds. Champaign, IL: Industrial Relations Research Association, pp. 313–339.

Caudron, S. 1994. "Contingent Work Force Spurs HR Planning." *Personnel Journal* 73(7): 52–54.

Church, G.J. 1993. "Jobs in an Age of Insecurity." *Time* 142(22): 32–40.

Coates, J.F. 1997. "Temporary Work—A Permanent Institution." *Employment Relations Today* 24: 19–22.

Cohany, S.R. 1998. "Workers in Alternative Employment Arrangement: A Second Look." *Monthly Labor Review* 121(11): 3–21.

Connelly, C.E., and D.G. Gallagher. 2004. "Emerging Trends in Contingent Work Research." *Journal of Management* 30(6): 959–983.

Davis-Blake, A., J.P. Broschak, and E. George. 2003. "Happy Together? How Using Nonstandard Workers Affects Exit, Voice, and Loyalty among Standard Employees." *Academy of Management Journal* 46(4): 475–485.

Davis-Blake, A., and B. Uzzi. 1993. "Determinants of Employment Externalization: A Study of Temporary Workers and Independent Contractors." *Administrative Science Quarterly* 38(2): 195–223.

Dennard, H.L. 1996. "Governmental Impediments of the Employment of Contingent Workers." *Journal of Labor Research* 17(4): 595–612.

Dreazen, Y.J. 2000. "Regulators Probe U.S. Reliance on Temporary Workers—Expected Lifting of Restrictions on Organizing Temps Would be a Coup for Unions." *Wall Street Journal,* Eastern edition. August 7, A:2.

Ellingson, J.E., M.L. Gruys, and P.R. Sackett. 1998. "Factors Related to the Satisfaction and Performance of Temporary Employees." *Journal of Applied Psychology* 83(6): 913–921.

Ettore, B. 1994. "The Contingency Workforce Moves Mainstream." *Management Review* 83(2): 10–16.

Feldman, D.C. 1995. "Managing Part-Time and Temporary Employment Relationships: Individual Needs and Organizational Demands." In *Employees, Careers, and Job Creation: Developing Growth-Oriented Strategies and Programs*, M. London, ed. San Francisco: Jossey-Bass, pp. 121–141.

Feldman, D.C., H.I. Doerpinghaus, and W.H. Turnley. 1994. "Managing Temporary Workers: A Permanent HRM Challenge." *Organizational Dynamics* 23(2): 49–63.

———. 1995. "Employee Reactions to Temporary Jobs." *Journal of Managerial Issues* 7(2): 127–141.

Fenn, D. 1995. "When Temps Become Permanent." *Inc.* 17(14): 112.

Financial Management Association. 1997. "Temping a Popular Route to a Permanent Job." *Financial Management* 75(1): 6.

Freedman, A. 1985. "The New Look." In *Wage Policy and Employee Relations*. Conference Board report no. 865. New York: Conference Board.

Gallagher, D.G., and J. McLean Parks. 2001. "The Contemporary Work Environment." *Human Resource Management Review* 11(3): 181–208.

George, E. 2003. "External Solutions and Internal Problems: The Effects of Employment Externalization on Internal Workers' Attitudes." *Organization Science* 14(4): 386.

Golden, L., and E. Applebaum. 1992. "What Was Driving the 1982–88 Boom in Temporary Employment? Preference of Workers or Decisions and Power of Employers." *American Journal of Economics and Sociology* 51(4): 473–493.

Greco, S. 1997. "How Can I Avoid Layoffs during Our Slow Season?" *Inc.* 19(12): 109.

Grossman, R.J. 1998. "Short-Term Workers, Long-Term Issues." *HR Magazine* 43(5): 80–90.

Hipple, S. 1998. "Contingent Work: Results from the Second Survey." *Monthly Labor Review* 121(11): 22–35.

Kochan, T.A., M. Smith, J.C. Wells, and J.B. Rebitzer. 1994. "Human Resource Strategies and Contingent Workers: The Case of Safety and Health in the Petrochemical Industry." *Human Resource Management* 33(1): 55–77.

Koene, B., and M. van Riemsdijk. 2005. "Managing Temporary Workers: Work Identity, Diversity, and Operational HR Choices." *Human Resource Management Journal* 15(1): 76.

Kraimer, M.L., S.J. Wayne, R.C. Liden, and R.T. Sparrowe. 2005. "The Role of Job Security in Understanding the Relationship between Employees' Perceptions of Temporary Workers and Employees' Performance." *Journal of Applied Psychology* 90(2): 389–398.

Lawrence, P.R., and J.W. Lorsch. 1967. *Organization and Environment.* Boston: Graduate School of Business Administration, Harvard University.

Lenz, E.A. 1996. "Flexible Employment: Positive Work Strategies for the 21st

Century." *Journal of Labor Research* 17(4): 555–566.

Liden, R.C., S.J. Wayne, and M.L. Kraimer. 2003. "The Dual Commitments of Contingent Workers: An Examination of Contingents' Commitment to the Agency and the Organization." *Journal of Organizational Behavior* 24(5): 609.

Littleton, S.M., M.B. Arthur, and D.M. Rousseau. 2000. "The Future of Boundaryless Careers." In *The Future of the Career,* A. Collin and R. Young, eds. New York: Cambridge University Press, pp. 101–114.

Mangum, G., D. Mayall, and K. Nelson. 1985. "The Temporary Help Industry: A Response to the Dual Internal Labor Market." *Industrial and Labor Relations Review* 38(4): 599–611.

Marler, J.H., M.W. Barringer, and G.T. Milkovich. 2002. "Boundaryless and Traditional Contingent Employees: Worlds Apart." *Journal of Organizational Behavior* 23(4): 425–453.

Mendenhall, K. 1993. *Making the Most of the Temporary Employment Market.* Cincinnati: Betterway Books.

Messemer, M. 1994. "A Match Made in Heaven." *Management Review* 83: 26–29.

Moorman, R.H., and L.K. Harland. 2002. "Temporary Employees as Good Citizens: Factors Influencing Their OCB Performance." *Journal of Business and Psychology* 17(2): 171–187.

Nardone, T.T. 1986. "Part-Time Workers: Who Are They?" *Monthly Labor Review* 109(2): 13–19.

Nollen, S.D. 1996. "Negative Aspects of Temporary Employment." *Journal of Labor Research* 17(4): 567–582.

Parker, S.K., M.A. Griffin, C.A. Sprigg, and T.D. Wall. 2002. "Effect of Temporary Contracts on Perceived Work Characteristics and Job Strain: A Longitudinal Study." *Personnel Psychology* 55(3): 689–719.

Pettigrew, T.F. 1998. "Intergroup Contact Theory." *Annual Review of Psychology* 49(1): 65–85.

Pfeffer, J., and J.N. Baron. 1988. "Taking the Workers Back Out: Recent Trends in the Structuring of Employment." *Research in Organizational Behavior* 10: 257–303.

Polivka, A., and T. Nardone. 1989. "On the Definition of 'Contingent Work.'" *Monthly Labor Review* 112(12): 9–16

Slattery, J.P., and T.T.R. Selvarajan. 2005. "Antecedents to Temporary Employee's Turnover Intention." *Journal of Leadership and Organizational Studies* 12(1): 53.

Smith, V. 1994. "Institutionalizing Flexibility in a Service Firm." *Work and Occupations* 21(3): 224–247.

Society for Human Resource Management. 1999. "Alternative Staffing Survey." *Bergen County Record*, November 15.

Tansky, J.W., and P.A. Veglahn. 1995. "Legal Issues in Co-Employment." *Labor Law Journal* 46(5): 293–300.

Tetrault, S. 1994. "The Permanent Temporary." *Legal Assistant Today* 11: 56–61.

von Hippel, C. 1999. In-Groups and Out-Groups in the Workplace: The Impact of Threat on Permanent Employees' Interactions with Temporary Co-workers. PhD dissertation, Ohio State University.

von Hippel, C., D.B. Greenberger, S.L. Mangum, and R. Heneman. 2000. "Voluntary and Involuntary Temporary Employees: Predicting Satisfaction, Commitment, and Personal Control." In *Research in the Sociology of Work*, R. Hodson, ed. Greenwich, CT: JAI Press, pp. 291–309.

von Hippel, C., S. Mangum, D. Greenberger, R.L. Heneman, and J. Skoglind. 1997. "Temporary Employment: Can Organizations and Employees Both Win?" *Academy of Management Executive* 11(1): 93–104.

von Hippel, W.H., C.D. von Hippel, L. Conway, K.J. Preacher, J.W. Schooler, and G.A. Radvansky. 2005. "Coping with Stereotype Threat: Denial as an Impression Management Strategy." *Journal of Personality and Social Psychology* 89(1): 22–35.

World Future Society. 1997. "Execs for Rent." *Futurist* 31(2): 64.

Part 2

Workplace Policy Issues
for Employers and Unions
in the United States

3
Employer Perspectives

Competing through a Flexible Workforce

Douglas J. Miller
University of Illinois, Urbana–Champaign

Jay B. Barney
Ohio State University

More than 4 percent of workers in the United States are in some form of alternative employment arrangement. Most large businesses now have a permanent budget category for temporary workers (*CPA Journal* 1998).

Evidence suggests that employer demand—not labor supply—is driving contingent work. Firms apparently want the cost savings and flexibility of hiring workers with no expectation of permanent employment (Golden 1996; Golden and Applebaum 1992). Companies hired more temporary workers as the last two decades progressed, although there was not a corresponding increase in workers willing to take contingent jobs (e.g., young people, married women, and older workers).

In this chapter we explain how forces external to a company operate to increase the demand for a flexible workforce and summarize evidence on how employers use contingent workers to manage labor and related costs. We then argue that, in many situations, creating a flexible workforce through investment in permanent employees may be a feasible alternative to the use of contingent workers and can be expected to lead more readily to a sustainable competitive advantage. This argument employs the concept of "real options" to link labor and related costs with decision making under uncertain conditions. It then combines the real options approach with the resource-based view of the firm to provide additional insights into the use of flexible permanent employees as a competitive strategy for organizations. This resource-based view contends that competitive advantage results from appropriately managing resources that are valuable, rare, difficult to imitate, and combined uniquely within an organization. We also provide suggestions for future research.

WHY DO EMPLOYERS USE CONTINGENT WORKERS?

An employer wishing to determine the economic value of any employee's contribution compares the costs associated with hiring and employing a worker relative to the additional production expected (labor productivity).[1] Firms also need to consider how to plan to achieve the flexibility desired to manage variable and uncertain future economic conditions. Distinguishing between ongoing costs and transaction costs is important when explaining why employers use contingent workers.

Ongoing Costs: Wages and Benefits

Firms may wish to use contingent workers to lower wages or benefits. According to the 1999 Current Population Survey (CPS) by the U.S. Census Bureau, the median weekly earnings for a full-time, adult male contingent worker were only 80 percent of earnings for a comparable noncontingent worker. Women in contingent work earned less than 72 percent of comparable noncontingent workers. The discrepancy holds across all levels of education, age, and race (von Hippel et al. 1997). Contingent workers are eligible for employer-sponsored health insurance or pension coverage less than half as often as noncontingent workers (pp. 20–23). Efforts by temporary employees to demand better pay and benefits—such as lawsuits filed by oil field workers against ARCO and by independent contractors against Microsoft—highlight the differential compensation offered to contingent workers (Eisenberg 1999; *Training* 1999).

On average, contingent workers receive lower wages than equivalent, noncontingent employees. Workers employed through temporary service agencies (TSAs) make approximately 7.7 percent lower wages than long-term employees in similar jobs (Segal and Sullivan 1997).

However, according to the 1999 CPS supplemental survey, full-time contingent workers in some occupations, such as "precision production, craft, and repair" and "construction," earn nearly the same or higher median weekly earnings than noncontingent workers. However, wage comparisons may be deceiving because employers pay other costs, such as a markup to the TSA or the expenses of a self-employed consultant. On the other hand, a TSA could substitute for the employer's internal human resources personnel, so not all of the markup should be attributed to wages.

Several published studies support the claim that firms use temporary workers to save on fringe benefits.[2] The growth of the temporary help supply industry is positively related to the ratio of quasi-fixed labor costs to variable costs (Golden 1996). Quasi-fixed labor costs, such as health insurance and pension contributions, are associated with a particular worker rather than with hours worked. At the firm level, a higher level of benefits as a percentage of total payroll is correlated with increased use of temporary agency or call-in employees (Mangum, Mayall, and Nelson 1985). Firms may contract out for services to skirt the need to pay all workers the same high rate because of union pay scales or because workers believe equal pay is fair.[3]

Transaction Costs

Unlike wages and benefits, many costs associated with employees are not ongoing. Costs that are incurred each time an agreement is formed between two parties are called *transaction costs,* such as time spent interviewing job candidates and processing paperwork, the expense of training new employees in firm-specific skills, the loss of goodwill during negotiations, and strategies to protect core workers.

Using temporary employees generally would be expected to increase transaction costs since temporary employees come and go more often than permanent workers. Some costs are borne by the human resources budget, such as advertising, conducting interviews, or paying for travel. Time spent interviewing applicants can be a substantial investment for firms with high turnover. Another important transaction cost is the time and money spent on training new workers, especially when a job requires idiosyncratic skills or knowledge. Consequently, hiring new workers frequently entails high transaction costs.

Also, a less obvious transaction cost is that of continuing to employ the same workers under short-term contracts. Most employees develop some experience and information that is of more value to the current employer than to anyone else. This stock of knowledge, skills, and abilities (called firm-specific human capital) develops over time.

Because there is usually some uncertainty surrounding the particular tasks the worker should do, human capital often develops in ways that are not specified in the original employment contract. Thus, at the end of a short-term contract, the employee may wish to renegotiate the terms of employment to reflect his or her new perceived value to the firm. Likewise, the employer may argue that the worker cannot transfer that firm-specific human capital to another company and should be satisfied with remuneration that only reflects what the market will pay for generic skills, regardless of the fact that the employee truly can add value to the current firm. Even if the employer and worker agree to split the value created, reflected in some small raise at the time of renegotiation, the time spent in the negotiation process and the potential for hard feelings and loss of goodwill impose real costs on both parties. Consequently, rather than renegotiate every time the situation changes, an employer often will prefer to sign the worker to a long-term employment contract. The long-term contract gives the employer the right to alter the worker's use of the knowledge or skill as necessary to respond to unanticipated changes; it also protects the worker from an employer using bargaining power to renegotiate rewards downward. Particularly when a job requires substantial firm-specific training, the employer will prefer to hire permanent workers, even if it has to keep them on during slack periods when productivity is low (Williamson 1985).

The amount of firm-specific training may be decreasing as standard tools such as computer software make firms' processes more similar (Szabo and Negyesi 2005). If so, temporary and contract agencies may have an economy of scale in training workers. For example, Manpower Inc. introduced a Web-based learning center (www.manpowernet.com), which allows its employees and applicants access to technical training material. The free information technology training is particularly attractive to people trying to enter computer fields, precisely the level of workers Manpower typically places, but it also benefits Manpower's own full-time employees. Manpower's knowledge of clients and workers allows it to track which skills are most in demand. Delivery of training over the Internet is ideal for technology workers (Cole-Gomolski 1999). Even in professions with more stable skill requirements, temporary employment agencies may have the opportunity to train more workers in a given profession than most businesses. Client firms may be willing to give up some of their firm-specific training preferences to hire temps with strong generic skills. (See Cappelli and Crocker-Hefter [1996]. The authors cite examples of how flexible business strategies match well with outside development of employee competencies.)

On the other hand, if workers receive minimal training, the key transaction cost surrounding employment may be the bureaucratic system of the employer. For a firm using generic labor in a seasonal business, the administrative and legal costs of hiring and firing temporary workers can be prohibitive. Furthermore, the legal doctrine of "employment-at-will," which allows an employer to dismiss an employee for almost any reason, has been weakened by federal regulation, thereby increasing the cost of firing a permanent worker (Lee 1996).[4] In this case, the transaction costs associated with contingent workers are less than those associated with permanent workers. Moreover, a temporary agency has an economy of scale in processing workers. John Bowmer, CEO of TSA Adecco, cites the firm's move to acquire Olsten's staffing unit as a response to the importance of information technology, which makes size important (Studer and Stern 1999). Larger TSAs can spread the costs of central computers and software over more placements. Adecco pioneered interactive "Job Shop" kiosks in public areas, linked to the Internet via Monster.com (Sunoo 1999). Such efforts reduce the transaction costs related to contingent workers.

Another kind of transaction cost relates to the firm's reputation with its core workers. The more frequent the layoffs, the more workers that the firm hopes to keep will look elsewhere for employment. By clearly identifying some jobs as temporary, firms can buffer their core workers from layoffs. The resulting loyalty of key employees can offset minor productivity losses that come from using day laborers or other contingent workers.[5] Respondents to a minisurvey from *Compensation and Benefits Review* noted that temporary workers allow the respondents' companies to cover the work performed by full-time workers when they take time off or to complete special projects (Jefferson and Bohl 1998).

The alternatives—requiring other employees to work overtime when someone goes on sick leave, or hiring extra programmers with no promise to recognize seniority after the project is over—would be more detrimental to the firm's core workers. For example, Bell Atlantic used an interim marketing staff for its move into the long-distance marketplace. If the venture failed, no long-term Bell Atlantic Corp. employees would be affected. If the market opened up, the company could transfer or hire permanent employees to handle the increased work (Keenan 1999).

EMPIRICAL RESEARCH ON TRANSACTION COSTS

Empirical research supports the importance of transaction costs in the management of hiring decisions. Research has investigated how firms respond to temporary increases in workload, the role of firm-specific training, and the impact of bureaucracy and firm size.

A nationwide survey of employers in the early 1980s, as well as archival and interview data, showed how different kinds of employers respond to temporary increases in workload (Mangum, Mayall, and Nelson 1985). In general, the researchers conclude that the use of temporary agencies lowered transaction costs related to temporary workers by eliminating various employer costs for a fixed fee paid to the agency, fulfilling an economic role similar to the union hiring hall. The study finds that the use of temporary employees from an agency, "call-ins" (occasional workers on a list maintained by the company itself), or "limited duration hires" (day workers or others whose employment is for a brief, specific time) is more likely when

- a firm has a high level of benefits (not true for call-ins),
- the firm's employment level is changing,
- the firm is large, or
- the skills involved are less specialized.

Another study using employer survey responses defines transaction costs primarily in terms of firm-specific training (Davis-Blake and Uzzi 1993). In general, the findings support the hypotheses that, in addition to employment costs and external economic forces, skill requirements, organizational size, and bureaucratization affect the use of temporary workers, leased workers, and independent contractors. When a job requires training, the position is less likely, albeit slightly, to be "externalized" (filled by someone not on the permanent payroll). The effect is statistically significant but extremely modest. A job that involved over seven months of training was only one-half of 1 percent less likely to be externalized than a job that required no firm-specific training. This result argues against transaction costs being the driving factor in the decision. On the other hand, this measure actually includes all hours of formal training, informal training by managers, and informal training by co-workers for the typical incumbent in that job. It reflects at least some industry-specific training and possibly occupational training as well. Only some of this training is truly firm-specific, so this measure may underestimate the true impact of this type of training. Also, since the survey asked managers to consider the last position they filled, there is a selection bias toward hard-to-fill jobs. In order to fill a difficult position, firms may be more likely to hire a worker who lacks prior training.

In the same study, the authors measure the amount of paperwork necessary to fire an employee at each firm. The assumption is that some firms are more bureaucratic than others. Based on the argument in the previous section, one might predict that the administrative costs in a bureaucratic organization would create more demand for temporary workers. However, the hypothesis here is that workers undergo a particular kind of firm-specific training in a highly bureaucratic firm: the orientation to the bureaucratic system. Since temporary workers may be less able to follow rules without direct management, bureaucratic firms should use fewer temporary workers.

Firms with more employees tend to have more bureaucracy and can avoid layoffs in any business unit more easily by spreading jobs around. Therefore, the hypothesis is that firm size should vary inversely with the use of temporary workers. In contrast, contract workers generally manage themselves apart from the rules of the host firm. Since the diversified firm may need access to specialized skills occasionally, it should be more likely to use contract workers. As predicted, larger firms and those with higher levels of bureaucracy are less likely to hire temporary workers and more likely to use contract workers. Apparently, the transaction costs of actually hiring and firing are outweighed by the transaction costs of orienting an employee to a bureaucratic organization.

The disadvantage of having temporary employees on site who have difficulty following rules is a cost of integration, even though the integration is only temporary. The same dynamic can work with contract workers in certain settings. For example, contract employees in the petrochemical industry have less safety training than permanent workers (Kochan et al. 1994). Since the contract company supervises their employees, the host firm reduces its transaction costs. However, the host firm and its employees may be harmed if the safety problems caused by contract workers go beyond accidents that injure contract employees. Thus, it may be in the best interest of the host company to offer further safety training and oversight to contract employees to avoid accidents. This effectively increases the transaction costs associated with contract employees, which may still be outweighed by the transaction costs associated with hiring and firing permanent employees.

PRODUCTIVITY

From the employer's perspective, the decision to define a task as contingent work or noncontingent work employs a standard cost-benefit analysis. The value of the expected contribution from either type of employee is productivity minus costs. Thus, if contingent workers are just as productive at a certain task as permanent employees, firms will hire contingent workers if the total cost is less. The total cost includes both ongoing and transaction costs. That is,

Value created = Productivity – Total cost

Total cost = Ongoing costs + Transaction costs.

In the same job over the same duration, contingent workers may be slightly more or less productive than noncontingent workers. Most academic research on direct productivity comparisons has studied entry-level employees because their tasks are generally the same across firms and settings. For instance, two case studies of data entry operators found that the productivity of part-time contingent workers was at least 7 percent below that of core workers. Considering the relative wages, benefits, and training costs, the use of contingent employees did not seem to be cost effective, but the use of agency-provided temporaries did provide savings. The biggest difference between the two categories of contingent workers was that the agency temps required much less training (Nollen and Axel 1996). Contingent workers in professional and technical fields, such as independent contractors of engineering services, may be at least as productive as a firm's own workers (see Jarmon, Paulson, and Rebne [1998]. A survey of managers in six high-technology settings found that the perceived performance of contractors was similar to employees).

Thus, the relative productivity of contingent and permanent employees depends on the circumstances. If an organization implements a new data entry system using off-the-shelf software, agency temps who have used the package at other establishments may be more efficient and accurate than the company's own workers who are just learning the system. Regarding professional workers, hiring an attorney who specializes in the particular legal issues currently facing the firm may be preferable to keeping one attorney on retainer who is a generalist. It may be impossible to hire permanent workers who are able to handle every contingency or to pay them full time when the work is seasonal.

Returning to the Bell Atlantic example, another reason the company decided to outsource may have been to access marketing people with skills related to the specific market or project. Many self-employed, independent contractors offer specialized expertise that employers need only on occasion. An extreme example is the U.S. Census Bureau, which hires thousands of workers for each decennial census (Potok and Holdrege 1999). The contingent work arrangement can provide an employer with flexibility to maintain high productivity, even when circumstances change.

USING "REAL OPTIONS" TO EXPLAIN
FLEXIBILITY PLANNING

A flexible workforce is one that can create value under various conditions of production. There are two ways to achieve a workforce that can adapt over time to perform different tasks. One way is to hire different workers over time through contingent arrangements, including hiring into the firm with no long-term commitment. The other way is to hire and develop flexible permanent employees with either a broad range of skills or the ability and willingness to learn and adapt with the organization over time. In terms of the value equation above, a simple approach is:

Productivity = (Productivity under one condition × Probability of
              that condition)
              + (Productivity under another condition × Probability
              of that other condition).

If there are only a few possible conditions, and if an employer can anticipate their probabilities accurately, then it is possible to write those expectations into an employment contract. However, as the variety of potential tasks increases or the business environment becomes more unpredictable, it becomes impossible to work out every possible scenario ahead of time. Then, flexibility is helpful not only because productivity is increased under various conditions, but also because negotiations are simplified. Uncertainty, not just variability, makes flexibility valuable. But how does one estimate the value of flexibility?

Mathematically, the employer can estimate probabilities and conduct a more complete cost-benefit analysis than discussed above. Theoretically, one could even generate expected cash flows resulting from the worker's contribution. Standard financial analysis would use those cash flows discounted appropriately over time to produce a measure of net present value (NPV). Of course, realized cash flows may differ substantially from the expectation. Thus, a financial analyst will usually check to be sure conclusions do not change substantially if assumptions (e.g., the interest rate) change slightly. This "sensitivity analysis" considers not only the mean of the distribution of potential returns, but also the variation around the mean. For example, one can use a mathematical formula to estimate the value of mineral rights based not only on the expected price of the mineral and the costs of extraction, but also the possible drift in price in the future (Copeland, Koller, and Murrin 1995, Chapter 15). The right to drill for oil can be worth much more than might be revealed through a simple NPV analysis, because the owner only has to invest in extraction if the price of oil is high.

Similar logic underlies the large market for financial options. A call option, for instance, gives the investor the right to buy a stock at a specified price at a future date. If the stock price drops, the investor loses only the initial purchase price of the option, which is usually a few dollars for each share of stock. But if the stock price rises, the investor's gain is potentially huge. The investor can buy the stock at a preset, low price and sell at a high price. If the stock price is certain, options do not matter much; but if a stock price varies widely, an option is highly valuable.[6] The value of the option comes from the fact that the investor will only exercise the right to buy the stock if circumstances are favorable.[7]

The prevalence of financial options has led financial analysts to apply the term "option" to other kinds of investment under uncertainty. For example, the right to drill for oil is considered a "real option." The term "real" comes from the fact that this option involves investment in a real asset such as real estate rather than a financial asset such as stock. Also, the additional value not captured in the simple NPV calculation is sometimes called the "option value."

A real option usually will be reflected in a series of small, staged investments rather than a single, large investment, which is aimed at the same goal but is less flexible.[8] For example, firms entering highly uncertain new markets appear to invest in joint ventures rather than wholly owned subsidiaries because a joint venture embodies an option (Chi and McGuire 1996; Kogut 1991). For a relatively small investment, the firm can 1) learn more about the market and its potential partners, 2) wait to see if the market develops in some unpredictable manner, and 3) get out of the deal if necessary without damaging its reputation. The essential characteristic of a real option is that it allows the owner to make a claim when conditions are favorable, with limited downside risk. When change is likely but its direction is unpredictable, the firm may have different requirements than if the current environment is expected to continue.

Hiring temporary workers is a type of real option because the employer can switch labor inputs as conditions fluctuate (Foote and Folta 2002). While this arrangement does not have a written purchase price or exercise period, there are parallels to financial options. The purchase price of the real option may be lower productivity, higher transaction costs, or even higher wages. The option may only be good for a certain period, either because temporary workers can be expected to move on to other employers more likely to offer permanent positions, or because government regulation prevents keeping workers contingent forever. Transaction costs incurred in switching from one set of contingent workers to another, such as the cost of firm-specific training, represent a price paid when the option is exercised. Using real options logic in the employment context does not negate the importance of costs, but it allows consideration of flexibility as well. Therefore, under high uncertainty, the option value may flip the decision from hiring inflexible permanent workers to hiring contingent workers.

On the other hand, investing in full-time employees can create a different real option in which the firm secures the right to ask the employee to vary activities. The purchase price is the cost of inducing the employee to develop firm-specific human capital, perhaps through a company-sponsored training program. The exercise period depends on the outside job market as well as the person's age and ability to learn. There may be some further cost to exercise the right. For example, the manager may have to give some attention to restructuring work relationships, and the employee may not be at optimal productivity in the new setting right away. Both of these real options hedge against the same kinds of risks, and the value of both increases with higher uncertainty. Of course, just as there are different kinds of transaction costs, there also are many kinds of uncertainty to consider.

Factors Creating Uncertainty

There are three important categories of uncertainty: demand, technological, and measurement. Any change in demand can increase or reduce the number of labor hours (and therefore workers) a firm requires. These changes can result from shifts in buying power, consumer preferences, competition, or other factors. Moreover, cyclicality of consumer demand can lead to increased demand for temporary workers, even if that cyclicality is perfectly predictable, as in the case of the decennial census of the United States. Given uncertainty about demand, a firm would prefer to collect more information and wait before hiring permanent employees. The greater the degree of the uncertainty, the more tenuous the desired commitments to employees become. If it were costless to hire and fire permanent employees, dishonest managers might offer "permanent" jobs when needed, and simply lay off people to match fluctuating demand. However, the costs of such actions include the loss of company reputation and the breakdown of the internal labor market (e.g., people performing their best to get a promotion).

In fact, the specific type of job influences the response to demand uncertainty, according to a study of contract services (Abraham and Taylor 1996, pp. 411–412). Organizations in industries with seasonal or cyclical workloads contract out significantly less of their janitorial and machine maintenance work. Cyclical firms also seem to contract out fewer engineering and drafting services, but more of their accounting work. The researchers offer a caveat that they had to construct seasonality and cyclicality measures from employment data at the industry level since they did not have access to that information for each establishment. A different study used establishment-level data to construct a measure of employment variability over a two-year span prior to the survey. This measure, which blends seasonality, cyclicality, and trend effects, is positively related to the use of temporary workers, as expected, confirming the value of flexibility under variability in demand (Davis-Blake and Uzzi 1993, p. 207).[9]

Similarly, if a firm is uncertain about what technology will be the most efficient, it will be difficult to specify what tasks employees will do in the future. The greater the degree of technological uncertainty, the more problematic it is to commit to a group of employees with set skills. Any change that affects the labor supply—equipment purchases, worker education, job process reengineering, or other factors that change the productivity of labor or the specific skills required to best implement production—can impact not only what tasks a worker performs, but also what that worker must be able to learn. A computer software designer can probably learn another programming tool. However, a company that moves from a business plan based on lean production to one based on customer service may desire employee competencies that were not required previously.

Measurement uncertainty arises because an employee's productivity in any specific task is never fully verifiable. The resulting possibility of shirking work or other opportunistic behavior creates agency costs. Either the employer has to pay for someone to monitor the employee, the employee has to pay (perhaps in the form of self-financed education) to give assurance he can do the job, or the employer has to be willing to live with the potential losses. These agency costs are primarily characteristic of the task, not the employee. Some jobs are more difficult to monitor. Therefore, it is difficult to predict the impact of measurement uncertainty on the use of contingent workers. A permanent, internal employee may be more trusted, and can be rewarded based on long-term performance. On the other hand, using a contract worker or leased worker may allow a firm to share some of the agency risk with the contracting firm. A temporary employment agency might have an economy of scale or develop a particular skill in monitoring its employees or training them to a minimal degree of productivity. Also, externalized workers may have less opportunity to shirk duties if their assignments are more specific. To the extent that employers believe workers differ in their propensity to be opportunistic (and vice versa), temporary employment can be an effective screening device prior to a permanent hire.

To summarize, real option theory generally would propose that, under high uncertainty, companies should desire a more flexible workforce than required under low uncertainty. Flexibility can be achieved in two ways. One way is to employ more flexible permanent employees. In the face of demand uncertainty, companies will want to hire workers who will accept overtime hours and pay. If technological uncertainty makes it impossible to fully define the skills required in an employee, companies should aim to recruit employees with multiple competencies. The increased value of the flexible permanent workers would then require higher overall compensation. Moreover, the transaction costs and agency costs associated with flexible employees would likely be higher than for focused employees, but the value of their productivity under various scenarios will outweigh the increased costs as uncertainty increases. The firm will only invest in such human capital if it can retain the right to exercise the option at its discretion. Thus, these flexible employees should be bound with contractual agreements that protect the firm's options, such as long-term contracts and "do not compete" clauses.

Alternatively, firms could achieve flexibility through the structure of the workforce: outsourcing work, or using leased or temporary employees (Foote and Folta 2002). In the case of demand uncertainty, the firm can hire temporary employees as needed. When technological uncertainty is high, the firm can hire contingent workers with different skill sets, and hire permanently only those it needs. Or, the firm can hire the workers it needs today and replace them in the future with workers with other skills. As technological uncertainty increases to very high levels, it would be impossible to hire permanent workers with the ability or desire to learn every possible skill required. The flexibility inherent in any one person is limited. When measurement uncertainty is present, firms may use temporary employment as a screening device. Firms can learn about specific employees and reduce the uncertainty involved in offers of permanent employment.[10] For example, the company could put temporary workers through a brief training program to see which are best suited to the company. Furthermore, certain firms may be able to hire these workers permanently at wages lower than for employees who did not temp first, because the temporary relationship convinced the worker that the company is a good place to work. The permanent hiring of temporary workers depends on the uncertainty being resolvable. In the extreme, hypercompetitive environment, a firm will desire to maintain the contingent relationship so it can swap skill sets as needed.

EVIDENCE FROM THE CURRENT POPULATION SURVEY

Existing research has tested for the importance of various determinants of demand for contingent labor. Unfortunately, studies to date have typically focused on one type of contingent work, or have measured only whether a form of contingent work is used at all, not the extent to which it is used. Gathering data on wages, benefits, transaction costs, and productivity for the same set of workers has been difficult.

However, to distinguish the economic importance of the various factors, they must all be included in the same statistical model.[11] The biennial supplements to the Current Population Survey (CPS) on contingent work offer an initial approach to these issues using a large sample of workers. We offer the following analysis of these data to confirm general facts and to point to issues deserving more rigorous research.

The February 1995 supplement to the CPS was the first to focus on contingent workers, whom Polivka and Nardone (1989) define as "workers who have no implicit or explicit contract for ongoing employment." The survey pertained to the worker's length of expected service as well as work arrangement. Respondents are categorized as contingent according to three definitions and their associated employment estimates. Estimate 1 includes wage and salary workers who have been in their jobs for up to one year and expect their jobs to last no more than an additional year. Estimate 2 includes those workers plus self-employed or independent contractors whose length of service matches definition 1. Estimate 3 includes wage and salary workers who believe their jobs to be temporary, without a specific time frame, plus all self-employed and independent contractors.[12] Thus, a worker is not defined as contingent simply because he or she works for a temporary agency, for example. Temporary agencies have permanent employees, and some firms that hire from temporary agencies also maintain their own pools of on-call workers. Using definition 3, 66.5 percent of workers paid by temporary help agencies in 1995 were contingent workers, and 3.6 percent of workers in traditional arrangements were contingent workers (Cohany 1996).

Each estimate reflects worker responses rather than a formal description by a human resources person at the company. It captures all employment arrangements in which contingency is understood even if not recorded in a written contract. Moreover, it reflects all different kinds of contingent relationships, which is important since these relationships can be substitutes for each other. The percentages of each estimate have remained similar in subsequent surveys.[13] Thus, 400,000 workers employed by temporary agencies see their positions lasting as long as they wish, while nearly 4 million workers employed directly by a firm consider their jobs more or less temporary.

Our analysis of data on 2,568 workers answering the 1995 CPS supplement reveals several important determinants in the choice of the relative importance of contingent and noncontingent jobs in the employment structure.[14] The model presented here assumes managers go to the labor market and identify prospective employees who are willing to accept a given level of compensation for their skills, experience, and education. Managers then choose whether to offer a contingent or noncontingent position based on the costs and benefits associated with those workers available to fill each kind of position.[15] This is a model of labor demand, not supply, so no conclusions should be drawn regarding workers' choices of positions. Furthermore, this model contains no information on worker productivity. The implicit assumption is that contingent workers and noncontingent workers perform the same. These simplifying assumptions are clearly unrealistic to some extent, and make the results given in this section exploratory. However, clarifying the assumptions also can help identify what kind of data would better untangle the interrelationships between factors.

All data in the discussion that follows are based on Estimate 1. Results are similar for the other definitions of contingency, except the impact of fringe benefits decreases when self-employed workers are included in the contingent ranks. The evidence shows the importance of ongoing costs, transaction costs, and flexibility in the decision to make a position contingent.

The current legal and cultural environment allows firms to offer, on average, lower wages and fewer benefits to contingent workers than to permanent workers. Our evidence confirms previous findings that employers hire contingent workers to reduce ongoing costs. The higher the level of weekly pay, the less likely a worker is contingent. Furthermore, if the employer provides health insurance or a pension in conjunction with the job, the worker is less likely to be contingent.

The CPS supplement did not ask about hours of training or other indicators of transaction costs. No information is given on the employer, other than the industry. However, if temporary agencies and contracting firms reduce transaction costs through economies of scale in processing and training workers, then firms should hire more contingent workers when these agencies are available and can achieve economies of scale. Thus, jobs in metropolitan areas should be more likely to be filled by contingent workers. The CPS identifies the worker by census tract into three categories: central city, nonmetropolitan, and other (e.g., suburban). Indeed, we find that workers in nonmetropolitan areas are 2.59 percent less likely to be contingent than workers in other areas.

Firms can achieve workforce flexibility either through more flexible permanent employees or through the use of specialized, contingent workers. More flexible workers will therefore be less likely to be contingent employees. Age, education, and willingness to work nontraditional hours may all relate to worker flexibility. First, older workers have had more time to acquire a range of knowledge, skills, and abilities, including human capital specific to the firm. From the supply side, older workers also should be less willing to enter some contingent arrangements (such as temporary work) because their expected return on additional investments in human capital, such as learning new skills or acquiring new firm-specific knowledge, is limited by the time period available to benefit from the return. On the other hand, older workers may be more willing to be self-employed to take full advantage of their experience or take part-time jobs to enjoy more leisure. Second, a worker with more schooling should be more capable of learning new tasks, so we control for education level. Third, workers who work more than 40 hours a week provide a buffer against demand variation and uncertainty. However, part-time workers may be a substitute for contingent workers as defined in the CPS supplement. Firms may use workers for fewer hours each week on a permanent basis, rather than hiring full-time workers for short durations.

Including age in the model lessens the effect of pay, which makes sense since a worker's earnings usually increase throughout his or her career. A change in age from 30 to 40 reduces the probability that a worker is contingent by 5.7 percent. However, education does not seem to make a difference. Considering raw correlation statistics, having a bachelor's or graduate degree appears to be negatively related to contingent status. However, in a full model including the other factors, education has no effect.[16] The more overtime hours a person works, the more likely he or she is to be a permanent employee of the firm. Part-time status has no effect after controlling for wage and other variables.

Finally, firms facing higher uncertainty or variability should be more likely to hire contingent employees than firms facing lower uncertainty. Since firm-level data are not available due to privacy concerns, an industry-level measure is used. This measure is the mean variation in stock returns over a two-year period for each three-digit SIC code, matched to the industry codes used in the CPS. Only industries with at least five actively traded firms were included. Aggregating over the industry creates a proxy for changes that affect total demand and the technology shared by the members of that industry.[17] We find that industry-level variability has no bearing on the use of contingent workers. It may be that the option value is more closely tied to firm-level uncertainty, or that achieving flexibility through investment in permanent workers is a close substitute for hiring temporary workers.

Overall, contingent positions pay less in wages, offer health insurance and pension coverage less often, and are more likely to be located in a city and not in a rural area. Contingent positions are less likely to be filled by older workers and those who worked overtime hours in the previous week. These broad correlations reinforce the tabulated results released by the U.S. Bureau of Labor Statistics.

COMPETITIVE ADVANTAGE THROUGH A FLEXIBLE WORKFORCE

As explained above, employees add value to an organization, and this value varies according to different conditions. We have argued that firms desire a workforce that can adapt quickly and effectively, especially as the pace of change in technology, international competition, and other dynamic environmental forces require increased flexibility. Furthermore, the employer can adjust the mix of contingent work arrangements and flexible permanent employees to address demand, technological, and measurement uncertainties. These two means of achieving flexibility can often substitute for each other. The key to gaining a competitive advantage is whether one firm can achieve flexibility that competitors cannot. Employers pursue strategic human resource management (SHRM) to compete effectively in these uncertain conditions. The primary theoretical perspective being used in studies of SHRM is the resource-based view of the firm.[18] In this approach, an organization gains competitive advantage from managing resources that are valuable, rare, difficult to imitate, and organizationally implemented (Barney 1991; 1997, Chapter 5).

A resource or capability has *value* to the extent that it enables the firm to cut costs, increase price, or otherwise allow the firm to pursue a strategy in product markets. A resource or capability is *rare* when only one or a few competitors employ it in their strategies. Standard microeconomic approaches usually assume that competitors all have access to the same resources and will adjust prices or quantities until the earnings from the resource are just enough to cover the risk involved in its purchase. However, this "perfect competition" rarely, if ever, occurs. Some industries or geographic markets have only a few participating companies and, in emerging markets, a first mover may be able to gain high returns on its product while competitors try to catch up. Therefore, ongoing rarity is a function of how difficult a resource or capability is to *imitate*.

One reason a competitor may not be able to imitate a resource is that it was acquired at a unique point in history that cannot be repeated. For example, pharmaceutical companies that already valued basic science research in the 1970s were able to adopt new "science-driven" drug discovery procedures that led to highly profitable blockbuster drugs, whereas those companies that had relied on more random testing of existing chemicals to solve medical problems were unable to hire the scientists and create the culture needed to imitate them (Cockburn, Henderson, and Stern 2000).

A second obstacle to imitation is that someone outside the organization may not be able to distinguish the resource that is making the difference. Even if the competitor knows which capability to imitate, it may be hard to achieve since value is often created by teams of people working together in ways that are difficult to manage. Of course, those same management struggles affect the firm that already has the resource, so creating and maintaining an organization to get the best out of the resources is the final condition for competitive advantage. We now apply these concepts to the case of a flexible permanent workforce, with an emphasis on the issue of imitation.

The Flexible Permanent Workforce

For several reasons, a flexible permanent workforce built from training and rewarding permanent employees will be more difficult to imitate than a flexible workforce using contingent workers. First, creating a flexible permanent workforce takes time, whereas creating a flexible contingent workforce can be done more quickly, particularly with the aid of large-scale temporary service agencies. A permanent worker's flexibility may increase naturally over time as the employee changes jobs within the organization, encounters different customers, or communicates with other workers about their jobs. Also, an employee's long tenure often includes times when the employee sacrifices for the benefit of the firm, and other times when the company rewards that service by giving the employee extra consideration. The repeated reciprocity builds trust and encourages the worker to be flexible again in the future. Since knowledge and trust are rooted in a particular history, it would be difficult for a competitor to quickly reproduce that kind of relationship. When a change in demand or technology occurs, the capabilities must be already in place to be effective. In contrast, adjusting the workforce with contingent workers happens at the time of the change. A competitor can implement the same plan from scratch, assuming the purpose of the plan is apparent and does not rely on either reconfiguring the physical assets the contingent workers will use or redesigning jobs.

The second argument for a flexible permanent workforce is that employment policies focused within the firm are less transparent to observers than are relationships with external parties. Temporary service agencies, contract agencies, or independent contractors may reveal the parameters and proposed benefits of their relationship with one firm to entice another firm to use their services. Competitors can even ask contingent workers how their previous employers used them. The flow of information makes the market for contingent workers fairly efficient: any employer should have to pay about the same amount to contract for similar services. However, matching cost is not the only aspect of benchmarking. Even more important is the issue of whether the resource or policy under consideration is central to the firm's success. With a relatively minor investment, a competitor can investigate an employer's contingent work practices and determine whether they are the source of the firm's competitive advantage or merely a convenient way to staff a firm that really gains its superiority from other factors besides human resources (e.g., its well-known brand name). On the other hand, an employer's relationship with its permanent employees is harder to benchmark. A large organization follows complicated selection procedures, conducts numerous training programs, transfers employees between departments, and offers various incentives.

Part of what makes human resource systems so hard to understand is that they are very complex, involving informal communication and relationships. This complexity also makes it difficult to duplicate such systems, even when the key components are well understood. Competitors thus find it difficult to determine which policies and practices have the desired effect. It is possible that an employer uses an outside consultant to determine salaries or off-the-shelf software to train personnel. In that case, a competitor could use the same methods. However, if the key aspect of firm-specific human capital is something less obvious, such as the personal commitments of team members to one another, implementing all the standard solutions will be ineffective in matching the successful firm. For example, HR practices that target employee development can speed organizational learning, increase quality, and enhance the flexibility of manufacturing systems.[19] So, does a firm's manufacturing quality come from its proprietary machinery, used by merely competent line workers, or from highly involved workers who make constant suggestions for ongoing improvement to the machinery? The answer to this question could lead a competitor to invest in new equipment, new HR policies, or both.

The third explanation for why it can be more difficult to imitate a flexible permanent workforce than one created through contingent workers is that the imitator firm's own history and capabilities impede transfer of best practices from elsewhere. A small misunderstanding can have a large impact on employees' loyalty and productivity. Firms must select, train, compensate, and commit to employees to create learning synergies—just one of those aspects probably is not enough. The difficult nature of implementing such systems may explain why many firms do not adopt "high-performance" work systems, and why many of these systems die off quickly (Pfeffer 1994). An important aspect of the complexity in workforce flexibility is the relationship between a plant or division and company headquarters. Employees will only welcome some practices (e.g., merit pay) if they are universally applied. Likewise, staff may establish uniform policies in order to simplify record keeping and avoid mistakes. Both pressures will work against the manager of a particular plant trying to benchmark to a competitor whose practices differ from the policies of his parent corporation. However, the harder a strategy is to implement, the more likely the successful firms will have a source of sustainable advantage. A workforce that creates value through flexibility will remain rare only if there exist barriers to imitation. The challenge for managers is to create an organizational structure and culture that is consistent with the strategy, but not so formal or simple as to allow for easy benchmarking.

Combining the Resource-Based and Real Options Frameworks

We have presented two frameworks for understanding flexible employment. Real options help managers know under what conditions flexibility is important for any organization. The real option approach also explains why contingent workers and flexible permanent employees are substitute methods of creating value under uncertainty. The resource-based view clarifies that gaining flexibility through permanent employees is more likely to sustain that value in the face of competition. Bringing the two frameworks together can generate some additional insights into how managers can use real options to gain competitive advantage. The resource-based descriptions of markets, uncertainty, and competitive advantage fit well with the type of economic framework represented by financial options and real options. Three keys to the use of financial options are information, complementarity, and efficiency, and the same aspects exist for the real option of a flexible workforce.

Financial investors trade stocks based on *information* about the magnitude, timing, and direction of profits and price movements. Financial options can be a less expensive way to profit from stock price movement. For the price of one share of stock, an investor could purchase dozens of options that will also appreciate if the stock goes up. It is even possible to make money on financial options solely by having superior information about the amount of variability a stock's price will exhibit over time. For example, a certain combination of call options and put options may gain value if the stock price begins to move more erratically over time. An investor does not need to know whether the stock is going up or down, just whether world events or other factors will cause the company's cash flows to be less predictable in the future. Likewise, purchasing and exercising real options can lead to competitive advantage if a firm has superior information.

Certain kinds of superior information may enable a firm to hire employees at an advantage. Suppose a firm has superior information about which knowledge and skills will be in greatest demand in the near future. Competitors may be recruiting workers with broad skills, perhaps paying a premium for intelligence and industry experience. But the firm with superior information is able to select relatively inflexible workers with just the right skills. While other firms are paying higher transaction costs for churning through contingent workers, this firm can hire once.

Also, the *complementarity* between financial options and the underlying assets determines the value for each investor. The value of financial options depends on the other assets in the investor's portfolio, often because investors use financial options to hedge against exposure to specific risks. For example, an American company doing business in Europe will earn revenues in euros, and will want to hedge against changes in the exchange rate of the euro versus the dollar. A purely domestic U.S.-based company would have no need to hedge against currency risk. Even though traders and companies have sometimes been hurt by speculative investment in options, the market for them continues to be strong because they are a low-cost way to hedge against specific risks. On the individual level, an investor who already owns shares of stock can sell call options on those shares to lock in a limited profit; the call option thus serves as a form of insurance. Similarly, different real options will be worth more to some companies than others because of the uncertainty each faces and the resources under its control.

A firm with a particular resource may find investment in a flexible permanent workforce to be more valuable to it than a similar investment would be to its competitor. For instance, a firm with a distinctive culture, brand name, managerial know-how, or location may be able to leverage that resource into greater profits by hiring more flexible permanent employees at lower cost or with greater productivity than their competitors. Consider an organization with superior proprietary technology that allows a single worker to coordinate production of multiple items. For competitors, the same production requires multiple workers supervising multiple machines. The firm with the advantage can afford to bid more than its competitors for the workers with the best learning ability, and still be able to make an abnormal profit from their efforts. The reverse is also possible. A firm may use distributed manufacturing to meet demand as it arises. Because machines and systems are simple or standardized, the company can hire temporary workers for a relatively low cost. A competitor committed to one large production facility may have expensive overhead even during downtimes.

Finally, the U.S. stock market is still highly efficient in the sense that the mechanisms of trade are not costly (e.g., stocks trading in penny increments) and do not automatically bias prices one way or the other. The *efficiency* occurs despite the fact that the information available to investors is sometimes clouded by corporate misinformation (e.g., Enron's off-balance-sheet accounting), and some risks cannot be anticipated (e.g., a terrorist attack). On the other hand, the markets for resources that create real options are not necessarily efficient. Firms do not frequently trade or sell real options, and managers may discount the value of flexibility if it means trying something new.

Any input for sale in an efficient market will not be a likely source of competitive advantage. Competing firms should bid up the price of the resource to its fair market value. The market for contingent workers, at least in large metropolitan areas, is fairly efficient. Temporary service agencies, contract agencies, and independent contractors generally provide their services at the same price to each employer. Likewise, if every potential employer knows that certain potential employees are more flexible, the cost of engaging those workers on a permanent basis should rise to a level that equals their value contribution. Many seemingly different job abilities are highly correlated, at least as commonly measured (Campion 1989). Entering the market for flexible employees, an organization may find that everyone is its competitor, not just the other firms in its industry. Thus, although a flexible permanent workforce can be achieved through the structure of work and the selection of workers, such processes are likely to cost a firm the full price of the flexibility. Structure and selection can bring the average firm to competitive parity, but not competitive advantage.

On the other hand, in order to gain or extend a competitive advantage through investment in permanent employees, a company must only have superior information relative to its employees. Companies typically have a better understanding of what a job requires than does the prospective employee. The difference in information allows the firm to hire the worker at a fair market price, but less than the full value the individual will create within the firm over time. Then, continued investment in firm-specific human capital can create more value to be shared between the employer and an employee. The employee is willing to learn from the employer because of the employer's superior information and resources. Even skilled workers who know more about their tasks than any manager will find it easier to prove their value to the organization by listening to how their tasks fit within the overall strategy, rather than trying on their own to unpack complex interactions among other workers. The agreement between the employer and employee is not an efficient market, but rather a negotiation, even if it takes place within the structure of a union contract.

This is not to argue that all firms would do equally well to invest in permanent employees. Managerial skill, teamwork, distinctive reward systems, partnerships with universities, or other resources could create a superior environment for developing the right kind of employee flexibility. An optimal strategy for any given firm may be to invest in real options through some permanent employees and some contingent workers. Periodically integrating outsiders can invigorate organizational learning and facilitate change, even in businesses relying primarily on core workers.[20] Similarly, firms with good reason to employ many contingent workers may need to invest in a few key employees who can coordinate the constant flow of workers. Nevertheless, the resource-based view clarifies that a flexible permanent workforce may be a more sustainable source of competitive advantage than a contingent workforce, and the real options logic highlights the importance of information about industry conditions, firm-specific risks, and how an employee can become part of a complex system to create value.

CONCLUSION AND DIRECTIONS FOR FURTHER RESEARCH

Current research suggests that increasing rates of change in the economic environment and uncertainty have driven demand for contingent workers. Temporary supply agencies, independent contractors, and other organizational forms have arisen to take advantage of economies of scale and reduce transaction costs related to hiring workers with a particular, identifiable skill. Contingent work situations are diverse and they are designed to address different costs and benefits. A multivariate regression analysis using CPS data confirmed that employers are likely to hire contingent workers to save on wages, health insurance, and pension contributions, and to take advantage of the availability of large-scale agencies located in metropolitan areas. However, more flexible workers, such as those who have had more experience or are willing to work overtime, are less likely to be in contingent positions, which implies that employers also recognize the possibility of gaining a flexible workforce through hiring and training permanent employees. The resource-based view of the firm and the real options approach to valuing flexibility clarify that a company relying on multiskilled permanent employees to adapt to change may be in a better position to gain and sustain a competitive advantage than a company using contingent workers to handle uncertain labor demand.

Future research should shed light on two main areas. First, what are the most important factors driving demand for contingent workers? Second, under what circumstances is it preferable to invest in flexible permanent employees rather than using contingent workers? To answer both questions, there is a need for research designs that will measure all relevant costs and employee productivity. These studies would do well to move beyond studies of low-skilled temporary workers to consideration of the kind of high-skilled and professional occupations that are more central to value creation in a business. The measurement of particular risks in each firm's environment is necessary to test whether firms create the right real options.

An appropriate case study to address both questions might compare two firms that face ongoing technology changes, the timing of which is unpredictable. One firm might make a commitment to its existing full-time workers, promising to train them in any new skill required. The other firm might cut back to a core of full-time employees and fill the other positions with temporary workers. When the change occurs (e.g., when a new time-saving computer technology is released), the first company pays to train its employees and may have to fire or offer early retirement to some who cannot make the adjustment, but it retains people with years of firm-specific experience. The second firm can move more quickly to hire temps with the newly required skills, assuming they are available in the labor market, or rely on the agency to train workers. The company using temporary workers ramps up to full productivity more quickly and inexpensively, but perhaps the eventual peak productivity is less than at the firm using its own employees. After the fact, one could assess which firm had higher overall productivity. But such examples are hard to find. Managers facing the same uncertainty often follow similar strategies, and estimating costs of training, turnover, and benefits is difficult.

Such research would require detailed personnel data, as well as integrated theories. The worker's own assessment of knowledge, skills, abilities, and motivation is relevant, as well as the employer's evaluation of the environment, the firm's strategy, and the worker's productivity and costs. Transaction costs are important, but theories also accounting for firm-specific resources and the need for flexibility must be tailored to specific industry and occupational contexts.

Finally, economy-wide evaluations of supply and demand for contingent work should be replicated at the level of the industry and firm. The CPS supplements have helped to define contingent work and its impact for the overall economy. However, new data sets at a more detailed level would allow tests of models considering worker and employer motivations. An understanding of both labor supply and demand is necessary to untangle the multiple factors driving contingent work.

Notes

1. This discussion builds on a review of workforce practices that concludes organizations use temporary employees to cut costs, avoid restrictions/consequences, and increase flexibility. See von Hippel et al. (1997).
2. The exception is a major study of employment externalization finding no relation between likelihood of a job being temporary and the level of fringe benefits. However, data on fringe benefits were only available at the industry level (2-digit SIC code), whereas the dependent variable is at the job level. This acknowledged mismatch might have diluted the statistical and economic impact of the benefits factor (Davis-Blake and Uzzi 1993).
3. This argument relies on empirical research that questions whether the dual internal labor market exists. Full-time employees may not believe managers who claim temporary workers are not competing for the same jobs (Abraham and Taylor 1996).
4. The major exception is dismissal based on discrimination such as gender or race discrimination.
5. While the distinction between core and periphery workers is intuitive, some empirical evidence questions whether employing contingent workers actually provides any buffer against involuntary turnover among permanent workers (Capelli and Neumark 2004). Further research is needed on the effects of employing both contingent and permanent workers under different conditions.
6. The Black-Scholes model is the most famous example of a mathematical formula to estimate the value of a financial option. The formula takes into account the option's purchase price, exercise date or period, and exercise price. The formula also considers the amount of uncertainty about the price of the stock.
7. This is why many executives who received stock options as compensation during the Internet stock boom of the late 1990s made so much money.
8. For a helpful categorization of real options, see Trigeorgis (1996).
9. Also, Abraham (1998) finds differences in mean use of staffing arrangements between firms with and without seasonality and cyclicality.
10. The first published paper to apply real options logic to employment decisions was Malos and Campion (1995). The authors explain the up-or-out promotional systems in professional service firms as creating a real option that mitigates uncertainty about employee productivity.
11. We use logistic regression analysis, which allows us to investigate the impact of independent variables on the probability that a position is contingent. Logistic regression is an extension of standard ordinary least squares analysis that is appropriate when the dependent variable is of a yes/no nature. Technical details and tables of results can be obtained from the first author.
12. See Chapter 2 of this volume for a more detailed discussion of these three estimates and the CPS definition of "alternative work arrangements" as distinct from contingent work.

13. By 1999, the numbers had changed slightly to 60.7 percent and 2.9 percent, respectively (DiNatale 2001, Table 6).
14. We report results from our analysis of the 1995 data because little has changed over time in the CPS variables employed in this study.
15. Managers and employees make decisions about the duration of a position, the compensation for the position, and the attributes of the workers simultaneously. To appropriately estimate all the relationships between these variables would require a system of equations. However, if employers can choose to save money on wages and benefits by hiring contingent workers, this choice implies that the employers are price takers.
16. Using Estimate 3 of contingent work, with self-employed and independent contractors included and the time frame restriction removed, those workers with some graduate work are 12 percent more likely than other workers to be contingent. Well-educated people are apparently more likely to start their own businesses.
17. In fact, Dixit and Pindyck (1994) argue that aggregate measures are superior to firm-level data at capturing technological risk because shocks should affect all industry users of the same technology.
18. Articles discussing theoretical approaches to strategic human resource management include Barney and Wright (1998); Gerhart, Trevor, and Graham (1996); and Snell, Youndt, and Wright (1996).
19. Several researchers have considered whether bundles of human resources practices are more effective than individual practices at creating value through people. Influential papers include Youndt et al. (1996); MacDuffie (1995); Becker and Huselid (1998); and Arthur (1992). An interesting and readable study is Upton (1995), in which the author finds that flexible manufacturing requires flexible employees.
20. Case studies show that the benefits of using contingent-knowledge workers can outweigh the costs (MacDougall and Hurst 2005). For a thorough discussion of how to use contingent workers to accumulate and disseminate knowledge, see Matusik and Hill (1998).

References

Abraham, K. 1998. "Flexible Staffing Arrangements and Employers' Short-Term Adjustment Strategies." In *Employment, Unemployment, and Labor Utilization*, R.A. Hart, ed. Winchester, MA: Unwin Hyman, pp. 288–311.

Abraham, K., and S. Taylor. 1996. "Firms' Use of Outside Contractors: Theory and Evidence." *Journal of Labor Economics* 14(3): 394–424.

Arthur, J.B. 1992. "Effects of Human Resource Systems on Manufacturing Performance and Turnover." *Academy of Management Journal* 37(3): 670–687.

Barney, J.B. 1991. "Firm Resources and Sustainable Competitive Advantage." *Journal of Management* 17(1): 155–171.

———. 1997. *Gaining and Sustaining Competitive Advantage*. Reading, MA: Addison-Wesley.

Barney, J.B., and P. Wright. 1998. "On Becoming a Strategic Partner: The Role of Human Resources in Gaining Competitive Advantage." *Human Resource Management* 37(1): 31–46.

Becker, B.E., and M.A. Huselid. 1998. "High Performance Work Systems and Firm Performance: A Synthesis of Research and Managerial Implications." In *Research in Personnel and Human Resources Management*, G.R. Ferris, ed. Greenwich, CT: JAI Press, pp. 53–101.

Campion, M.A. 1989. "Ability Requirement Implications of Job Design: An Interdisciplinary Perspective." *Personnel Psychology* 42: 1–24.

Cappelli, P., and A. Crocker-Hefter. 1996. "Distinctive Human Resources are Firms' Core Competencies." *Organizational Dynamics* 24(3): 7–22.

Cappelli, P., and D. Neumark. 2004. "External Churning and Internal Flexibility: Evidence on the Functional Flexibility and Core-Periphery Hypotheses." *Industrial Relations* 43(1): 148–182.

Chi, T., and D.J. McGuire. 1996. "Collaborative Ventures and Value of Learning: Integrating the Transaction Cost and Strategic Option Perspectives on the Choice of Market Entry Modes." *Journal of International Business Studies* 27: 285–307.

Cockburn, I.M., R.M. Henderson, and S. Stern. 2000. "Untangling the Origins of Competitive Advantage." *Strategic Management Journal* 21(10–11): 1123–1145.

Cohany, S. 1996. "Workers in Alternative Employment Arrangements." *Monthly Labor Review* 119(10): 31–45.

Cole-Gomolski, B. 1999. "Recruiters Lure Temps with Free IT Training." *Computerworld,* August 2, 10.

Copeland, T., T. Koller, and J. Murrin. 1995. *Valuation: Measuring and Man-*

aging the Value of Companies. New York: John Wiley & Sons, Inc.

CPA Journal. 1998. "Temps Have Permanent Place in Staffing Budgets." January, 11.

Davis-Blake, A., and B. Uzzi. 1993. "Determinants of Employment Externalization: A Study of Temporary Workers and Independent Contractors." *Administrative Science Quarterly* 38: 195–223.

DiNatale, M. 2001. "Characteristics of and Preference for Alternative Work Arrangements, 1999." *Monthly Labor Review* 124(3): 28–49.

Dixit, A.K., and R.S. Pindyck. 1994. *Investment under Uncertainty.* Princeton, NJ: Princeton University Press.

Eisenberg, D. 1999. "Rise of the Permatemp." *Time* 154(2): 48.

Foote, D.A., and T.B. Folta. 2002. "Temporary Workers as Real Options." *Human Resource Management Review* 12: 579–597.

Gerhart, B., C. Trevor, and M. Graham. 1996. "New Directions in Employee Compensation Research." In *Research in Personnel and Human Resources Management*, G.R. Ferris, ed. Greenwich, CT: JAI Press, pp. 143–203.

Golden, L. 1996. "The Expansion of Temporary Help Employment in the U.S., 1982–1992: A Test of Alternative Economic Explanations." *Applied Economics* 28: 1127–1141.

Golden, L., and E. Applebaum. 1992. "What Was Driving the 1982–88 Boom in Temporary Employment? Preference of Workers or Decisions and Power of Employers." *American Journal of Economics and Sociology* 51(4): 473–493.

Jarmon, R., A. Paulson, and D. Rebne. 1998. "Contractor Performance: How Good are Contingent Workers at the Professional Level?" IEEE *Transactions on Engineering Management* 45(1): 11–19.

Jefferson, F., and D. Bohl. 1998. "CBR Minisurvey: Part-Time and Temporary Employees Demand Better Pay and More Benefits." *Compensation and Benefits Review* 30(6): 20–24.

Keenan W. Jr. 1999. "Can You Use a Temporary Marketing Manager?" *Industry Week,* May 17, 18.

Kochan, T., M. Smith, J. Wells, and J. Rebitzer. 1994. "Human Resource Strategies and Contingent Workers: The Case of Safety and Health in the Petrochemical Industry." *Human Resource Management* 33(1): 55–77.

Kogut, B. 1991. "Joint Ventures and the Option to Expand and Acquire." *Management Science* 37: 19–33.

Lee, D.R. 1996. "Why Is Flexible Employment Increasing?" *Journal of Labor Research* 17(4): 543–553.

MacDougall, S.L., and D. Hurst. 2005. "Identifying Tangible Costs, Benefits, and Risks of an Investment in Intellectual Capital." *Journal of Intellectual Capital* 6(1): 53–71.

MacDuffie, J.P. 1995. "Human Resource Bundles and Manufacturing Performance: Organizational Logic and Production Systems in the World Auto Industry." *Industrial and Labor Relations Review* 48: 197–221.

Malos, S., and M. Campion. 1995. "An Options-Based Model of Career Mobility in Professional Service Firms." *Academy of Management Review* 20(3): 611–644.

Mangum, G., D. Mayall, and K. Nelson. 1985. "The Temporary Help Industry: A Response to the Dual Internal Labor Market." *Industrial and Labor Relations Review* 38(4): 599–611.

Matusik, S., and C.W.L. Hill. 1998. "The Utilization of Contingent Work, Knowledge Creation, and Competitive Advantage." *Academy of Management Review* 23(4): 680–697.

Nollen, S.D., and H.A. Axel. 1996. *Managing Contingent Workers*. New York: ANACOM.

Pfeffer, J. 1994. *Competitive Advantage through People: Unleashing the Power of the Work Force*. Boston: Harvard Business School Press.

Polivka, A., and T. Nardone. 1989. "On the Definition of 'Contingent Work.'" *Monthly Labor Review* 112(12): 9–16.

Potok, N.F., and M.A. Holdrege. 1999. "Contingent Staffing: Lessons from Census." *Public Manager,* Spring, 23–26.

Segal, L.M., and D.G. Sullivan. 1997. "The Growth of Temporary Services Work." *Journal of Economic Perspectives* 11(2): 117–136.

Snell, S.A., M.A. Youndt, and P.M. Wright. 1996. "Establishing a Framework for Research in Strategic Human Resource Management: Merging Resource Theory and Organizational Learning." In *Research in Personnel and Human Resources Management*, G.R. Ferris, ed. Greenwich, CT: JAI Press, pp. 61–90.

Studer, Margaret, and Gabriella Stern. 1999. "Swiss Temp Firm Shoots to No. 1 Spot in U.S.—Adecco Agrees to Acquire Olsten's Staffing Unit in a $840 Million Deal." *Wall Street Journal*, August 19, A:10.

Sunoo, B.K. 1999. "Temp Firms Turn up the Heat on Hiring." *Workforce* 78(4): 50–54.

Szabo, K., and A. Negyesi. 2005. "The Spread of Contingent Work in the Knowledge-Based Economy." *Human Resource Development Review* 4(1): 63–85.

Training. 1999. "Court Rules against Microsoft in Temp Worker Case." 36(8): 18.

Trigeorgis, L. 1996. *Real Options: Managerial Flexibility in Strategy and Resource Allocation*. Cambridge, MA: MIT Press.

Upton, D.M. 1995. "What Really Makes Factories Flexible?" *Harvard Business Review* 73(July/August): 74–84.

von Hippel, C., S. Mangum, D. Greenberger, R. Heneman, and J. Skoglind. 1997. "Temporary Employment: Can Organizations and Employees Both Win?" *Academy of Management Executive* 11(1): 93–104.

Williamson, O. 1985. *The Economic Institutions of Capitalism*. New York: The Free Press.

Youndt, M.A., S.A. Snell, J.E. Dean, and D.P. Lepak. 1996. "Human Resource Management, Manufacturing Strategy, and Firm Performance." *Academy of Management Journal* 39(August): 836–866.

4

Union Responses to the Challenges of Contingent Work Arrangements

M. Catherine Lundy
Michigan State University

Karen Roberts
Michigan State University

Douglas Becker
Visteon Corporation

There are several terms for contingent work and the activities surrounding the use of contingent workers. Some of the most common terms are strategic staffing, market-mediated work, temporary help, and alternative work arrangement. Furthermore, contingent employment arrangements take many forms, including agency temporaries who are paid by temporary employment agencies, contract workers whose services are contracted out by their employer, per diem or on-call day workers, part-time employees, independent contractors, and the self-employed.

We use the term *contingent work* in this chapter because it best characterizes the challenge this shift in the employment relationship poses for unions. The term *contingent workers* was coined by Audrey Freedman in 1985 to refer to employees whose work is contingent on the variability of employers' need for them (Nollen and Axel 1996b). This description expresses the essential problem for unions: the use of alternative work arrangements is largely an employer-driven phenomenon that will result in employment and earnings instability for many employees working under these arrangements.

Several measures of contingent work are available. What they have in common are the characteristics of short-term work, variability in work schedule, absence of either an implicit or explicit contract, and lack of worker attachment to a particular employer (Nollen and Axel 1996a).[1] Additional characteristics often are noted, such as the involuntary nature of such arrangements, inferior pay and benefits, absence of promotion opportunities, and lack of opportunity to build human capital (Barker and Christensen 1998, p. 223).

Why Use Contingent Workers?

There are a variety of reasons for employers to use contingent work arrangements. Contingent workers can fill temporary vacancies, work during peak periods, and provide specialized skills needed for brief periods (Roberts and Gleason 1999). However, from the perspective of workers the use of contingent workers allows employers to pass on to workers the economic insecurity associated with changing product markets, new technologies, and the business cycle (Tilly 1992, p. 23). This is clearly antithetical to union goals of protecting worker earnings and job security. Historically, this goal has meant negotiating for long-term, stable employment for full-time employees, with little attention paid to part-time or other work arrangements (Cobble and Vosko 2000).

The use of different kinds of contingent work arrangements represents two broad strategies by employers to gain greater flexibility in their production methods. One is the very short-term, often ad hoc strategy of using individuals to fill particular jobs or accomplish specific tasks. Often workers under these arrangements are working side by side with traditional full-time workers. Examples of these arrangements include using workers from temporary employment agencies, casual day workers, and perhaps part-time workers. The other strategic use of contingent work typically involves a relatively large-scale, long-term reorganization of how work is done and who does it, and frequently is associated with efforts to reduce labor costs. Usually this results in work being moved off site. Examples of these arrangements include subcontracting portions of work previously done internally, the use of leased workers, and privatization in the public sector. From a union perspective, both of these strategies represent a common threat: the removal of work from the bargaining unit. This creates two serious problems: the workers are no longer subject to contractual protections, and the union is weakened by reduced membership.

How Do Unions Respond to Contingent Employment Arrangements?

The analysis in this chapter is based on the review of standard contract language in the industrial and service sectors and the public and private sectors. The assumption underlying our methodology is that collective bargaining agreements represent the negotiated resolution at a point in time of the classic conflict between management desire for full discretion in the use of labor and the union goal of protecting the welfare of its members. Even when unions and management are working relatively cooperatively, a tension exists between management desire for unfettered authority over labor and the union objective to protect workers from management discretion (Sloane and Whitney 1994, p. 458). Consequently, the content of the agreements is the operational articulation of that tension.

Unions can respond to the use of contingent work by pursuing a strategy of exclusion or inclusion of contingent workers as reflected in the language of the contract. A strategy of exclusion entails deliberately excluding contingent work arrangements from the bargaining unit and attempting to limit the employer's use of workers outside the bargaining unit. The strategy of inclusion seeks ways to include contingent workers in the bargaining unit and attempts to negotiate good wages and working conditions for those workers while protecting traditional full-time union members, thus eliminating the cost advantage of nontraditional workers.

In this chapter, examples of each strategy are discussed for temporary employees, part-time employees, leased employees, and other categories of employees. We review union responses to employer efforts to remove significant numbers of workers from the bargaining unit through the use of subcontracting, outsourcing, privatization, and independent contractors. We present mechanisms for inclusion of contingent workers in the unit and the protection of their seniority rights and other benefits, and identify the issues that organized labor will face in the future. We conclude with a discussion of future research questions.

HOW CONTINGENT WORKERS GAIN UNION REPRESENTATION: THE DEFINITION OF THE BARGAINING UNIT

When unions decide to follow an inclusionary strategy, they can either include contingent workers in the bargaining unit, which is the most common approach, or negotiate separate contracts for traditional and contingent workers (Sloane and Whitney 1994, p. 21).

Selecting the Strategy of Exclusion or Inclusion

Our review of contract language suggests that the way in which a union responds to the threat of contingent work depends in part on whether the employer is a goods producer or a service producer. The language in the contracts of industrial or goods-producing employers is more likely to address subcontracting and the use of leased employees. These unions have pursued a strategy of exclusion which contractually excludes alternative work arrangements and attempts to limit management rights to subcontract bargaining unit work. Contract language in manufacturing, for example, tends to address the conditions under which work can be assigned outside the bargaining unit and when the employer can outsource. There is little language limiting the ad hoc use of individuals with the exception of fairly standard language about the number of days a temporary worker can work before becoming a permanent employee and a dues-paying member of the bargaining unit.

In contrast, service sector contract language is more likely to address issues regarding the ad hoc use of individual contingent workers. In general, service sector unions tend to agree to include some types of contingent workers in the bargaining unit. As a result, the contract language must address a variety of issues clarifying the rights and uses of traditional and contingent workers in the same bargaining unit. These issues include distinguishing between different types of employees included in the bargaining unit, the differential accumulation of seniority by employee category, and prorating benefits. One prominent exception to this service sector approach is privatization efforts by public sector employers. Over the last two decades, there has been an effort on the part of some state and local governments to privatize government functions. Privatization is the public sector analogue to private sector outsourcing, since work is taken out of the bargaining unit and given to a separate organization. Depending on how the bargaining unit is defined, it is possible for privatization to effectively eliminate the unit (DuRivage, Carré, and Tilly 1998).

Deciding which approach to take is complicated by the fact that, in some instances, a contingent work arrangement meets the needs of union members (SEIU 1993). There are workers who prefer a flexible work schedule so they can manage family demands, return to school, or for some other reason. According to the American Staffing Association (2001), 28 percent of the temporary employees placed by their member agencies prefer temporary work to gain flexibility for nonwork interests, and 43 percent chose temporary work for family reasons. In its 2001 survey, the Bureau of Labor Statistics (BLS 2001) found that 39 percent of workers in contingent arrangements preferred these arrangements to traditional work. Furthermore, 14.9 percent of full-time and 6.8 percent of part-time workers are union members, suggesting that part-time workers are an important union constituency. These figures suggest that a union taking a doctrinaire approach advocating the elimination of contingent work would not serve all of its members.

Defining the Bargaining Unit

Organizing activities and the representation of contingent employees in the public and private sectors generally are governed by the National Labor Relations Act (NLRA). (Some exceptions occur in states with separate legislation for public employees and in the few states that offer no collective bargaining rights at all. See SEIU [1993]). For contingent workers to have the right to collectively bargain with their employer, there must be a union able to represent them. As is the case with traditional workers, union representation is obtained through a union organizing drive.

Unions build their memberships through organizing campaigns that are regulated by federal or state agencies. Only one union can represent a group of workers at a time. Unions may specialize in the workers they attempt to organize. For example, some unions operate only in the public or private sectors, while others are organized along industrial, service, or craft lines. In general, unions determine their preferences for who should be included in the bargaining unit based on the membership most likely to be successfully organized. During an organizing drive the union will determine the preferred bargaining unit membership and file a petition with the National Labor Relations Board (NLRB) or the state agency governing public sector industrial relations in that state. The relevant agency will determine if these workers are an appropriate unit for the purposes of collective bargaining. The composition of the unit is extremely important to both the employer and the union because this will be the electorate that determines the outcome of the election. Typically, each group attempts to create the bargaining unit that will best support its objectives.

The NLRB refers to the "community-of-interest principle" when establishing the appropriate bargaining unit, which refers to what the employees within the potential bargaining unit have in common with regard to wages, working conditions, and regularity of hours (DuRivage, Carré, and Tilly 1998). The more homogeneous the employees are according to these criteria, the more likely it is that the board will find that they have a community of interest and are thus an appropriate unit for bargaining. Using the community of interest principle, the NLRB rulings have identified general principles or guidelines governing the inclusion of various types of workers within the bargaining unit (SEIU 1993).

If workers in contingent employment arrangements pass the community of interest test and other guidelines for inclusion, they may be included in a bargaining unit. Contract language suggests that unions address three types of contingent work arrangement: temporary employees, part-time workers, and leased workers. Other categories of employees also may be covered in some contracts such as student employees in university contracts. Unions must determine which aspects of the contract will apply to contingent workers.

Temporary Employees

According to the NLRB, *temporary employees* can be included in the bargaining unit when they are hired or employed for an indefinite period. The NLRB uses a "date to certain" test, meaning that a temporary employee should be included in the unit if no certain date has been set for termination of employment.[2] As discussed above, union strategies vary in the handling of temporary employees. Our review suggests that, typically, although not always, service sector unions are more likely to use contract language that includes specific definitions of employee categories. However, some service sector unions use exclusionary language and limit the hours of work of temporary employees. Industrial unions generally bargain for exclusionary contract language.

Contracts with both Sparrow Hospital in Lansing, Michigan, and Mercy Hospital of Buffalo, New York, provide examples of inclusive language. The Sparrow contract specifically includes regular part-time and per diem employees in the professional bargaining unit.

> The Hospital recognizes the Union as the sole and exclusive representative of its full-time, regular part-time and per diem professional employees employed by the hospital for the purpose of collective bargaining with the respect to rates of pay, wages, hours of employment and other conditions of employment.[3]

Because it covers such a broad spectrum of workers, the Sparrow agreement includes long descriptions of each category of employment. These descriptions are necessary to define precisely the duties and rights of each job classification. This agreement includes explicit definitions for three types of temporary workers (External Temporary Employees, Union Temporary Employees, and Float Employees) as well as Full-Time and Regularly Scheduled Part-Time (Core) employees. Each of these descriptions details the number of hours available to be worked and is explicit about when an employee in each of these categories becomes a dues-paying regular employee.

In the agreement between Mercy Hospital of Buffalo and the Communications Workers of America (CWA) the categories of employment also are specified carefully. The categories as defined in Mercy and CWA provide an example of the explicit specification of employee types:

> Article 15, Purpose – A. Flexible employee is one who is hired for a specified number of hours per week . . . Flexible Employees respond to variations in workload created by increases or decreases in census and/or acuity. Flexible employees also provide general staffing relief for planned and unplanned absences (e.g. Paid Time Off).
> Article 16, Section 1 – A Per Diem Employee is one who works on a day to day as needed basis without a guarantee of set hours per week and without benefits.

> Article 17, Section 1 – A temporary employee is an employee des-
> ignated as such, hired for a specific job of limited duration not
> exceeding six (6) months. This period may be extended for up to
> another six (6) months by mutual agreement of the Hospital and
> the Union.[4]

However, not all service unions take an inclusive approach. Some
unions exclude temporary employees from their bargaining unit and
then try to limit the encroachment of temporary workers through contract language. Kaiser Hospital in Portland, Oregon, is a good example of this. First, they exclude temporary workers from the bargaining
unit.

> Temporary or irregularly scheduled employees shall be excluded
> from this agreement so long as they are not used to deprive regular
> employees of work time. All regular employees must be working
> before temporary or irregularly scheduled employees are used. It is
> further agreed that such employment will not result in any reduc-
> tion in the number of persons employed in the bargaining unit or
> in the number of regular hours of employment of any employee in
> the bargaining unit.[5]

Second, a limit is placed on the period of time the services of temporary workers can be used.

> A temporary employee is one who is hired from outside the Bar-
> gaining Unit to work for a specific period of time not to exceed
> three (3) consecutive months, or to replace a permanent employee
> not to exceed (6) months or to replace an employee on Union-re-
> lated leave not to exceed twelve (12) consecutive months. Specific
> exceptions to provide for an additional and limited time period in
> a temporary status may be made by mutual agreement in writing
> by the parties.[6]

This explicit limitation on the number of hours a temporary worker
can work is seen relatively frequently in service agreements, suggesting
that the use of short-term temporary workers is a strategy commonly
used by service sector employers.

Most industrial contracts use the exclusionary approach. One tactic
is defining normal hours of work to ensure that only full-time, regularly scheduled workers are used. A typical example is LTV Steel and
the United Steelworkers of America agreement. The hours of work are
defined as

[t]he normal work day shall be any regularly scheduled consecutive twenty-four (24) hours of work comprising eight (8) consecutive hours of work and sixteen (16) consecutive hours of rest except for such rest periods as may be provided in accordance with practices heretofore prevailing in the Works of the Company. The normal work pattern shall be 5 consecutive workdays beginning on the first day of any 7-consecutive-day period.[7]

This language limits the use of nontraditional employees by restricting how hours of work will be assigned to employees.

Part-Time Employees

According to the NLRB, regular part-time employees can be included in a bargaining unit and are entitled to vote in an election. An employee is included in a unit if the employee works a sufficient number of hours on a regular basis to have a substantial interest in the wages, hours, and working conditions in the unit.[8] Thus, an employee who works only one day a week every week as a weekend relief can be included in the bargaining unit.

Unions pursuing a strategy of inclusion generally have used one of three tactics: including part-time workers in the bargaining unit as regular part-time employees, including language converting part-time jobs to full-time jobs, or negotiating separate contracts for full-time and part-time workers. For example, the language in the Sparrow Hospital and Michigan Nurses Association contract cited earlier includes part-time workers in the bargaining unit. Similarly, the language in the contract between Mercy Hospital of Buffalo and Communications Workers of America, Service, Technical, and Clerical Employees also includes these workers.

Article 4, Categories of Employees; Section 2 – A regular part time employee is defined as one who is regularly scheduled to work less than thirty-four (34) hours per week but fifteen (15) hours or more per week.[9]

A third example is the contract between the United Food and Commercial Workers, Local 951, and Meijer, Inc.

The Employer recognizes the Union as the collective bargaining agent for all full-time and regular part-time Grocery, Meat, Produce, General Merchandise, Warehouse and Property Services employees at the covered units, excluding any employees of any lease operation, employees of any existing or future operations which are either not physically attached to a covered unit or are not operated within the same premises as a covered unit, Manger Trainees, Store Directors, Line Managers, Department Managers, Property Services Supervisors, Distribution Center Supervisors, Working Supervisors and the management to which such Managers report, Auditors, Registered Pharmacists, Pharmacy Technicians, Professional, Confidential, Office, Clerical, Systems Monitors, Managerial employees, Security employees and other Guards and Supervisors as defined in the Labor Management Relations Act as amended and all other employees.[10]

The tactic of converting part-time jobs to full-time jobs is illustrated by the 1997 and 2002 contracts between the United Parcel Service (UPS) and the Teamsters. The 1997 Teamsters strike against UPS was an example of an aggressive approach to limiting employer use of part-time workers. During this strike the Teamsters were able to generate public support in part because part-time work symbolizes reduced job security and benefits to much of the American public (Tilly 1998). The UPS-Teamsters contract clearly committed UPS to slowing the increase in the number of part-time jobs and beginning to convert part-time into full-time jobs.

The 1997 contract was emphatic that full-time and part-time workers would be included in a single bargaining unit:

All employees, Unions and the Employer covered by this Master Agreement and the various Supplements, Riders and Addenda thereto, shall constitute one (1) bargaining unit. It is understood that the printing of this Master Agreement and the aforesaid Supplements, Riders and/or Addenda in separate agreements is for convenience only and is not intended to create separate bargaining units.[11]

It was also clear that the purpose of including part-time workers in the bargaining unit was to facilitate their movement to full-time employment.

The parties agree that providing part-time employees the opportunity to become full-time employees is a priority of this Agreement. Accordingly, the employer commits that during the life of this Agreement, it will offer part-time employees the opportunity to fill at least twenty thousand (20,000) permanent full-time job openings throughout its operations covered by this Agreement.

The result of contract renegotiation in 2002 was a UPS contract that has been described as "the richest contract in Teamster history" (LRA 2002). In this contract UPS agreed to bring in-house nearly 10,000 sub-contracted, nonunion jobs to create a pool of union jobs that would go to current part-timers. Thus, the Teamster agreement helped to reduce the gap between full-time and part-time workers by reducing wage differentials and providing more job mobility, job security, and retirement security for both part-time and full-time workers.

A third tactic unions use is to negotiate separate contracts for full-time and part-time workers. Marriott Management Services and the United Catering, Restaurant, Bar, and Hotel Workers negotiated separate contracts for workers providing food service to the Ford Motor Company, thereby creating two separate bargaining units. The two contracts are virtually identical except for the provisions for hours of work and costs of benefits to employers.[12]

In the industrial sectors, the contract language is more likely to be exclusionary. One tactic to eliminate part-time workers from the bargaining unit is to define the hours for shift work so that part-time employment is prohibited. This strategy is illustrated by LTV Steel contract.

> The normal work day shall be any regularly scheduled consecutive twenty-four (24) hour period comprising eight (8) consecutive hours of work and sixteen (16) consecutive hours of rest except for such rest periods as may be provided in accordance with practices heretofore prevailing in the Works of the Company.[13]

Leased Employees

Leased employees are workers on the payroll of one employer (the leasing firm) who are supplied to another employer (the client employer) based on a contract negotiated between the two employers. Leased employees can be included in the bargaining unit of the client employer if the client employer and leasing company are deemed to be "joint employers." Joint employment occurs if the two employers share and co-determine matters governing the essential terms and conditions of employment. The essential terms and conditions of employment typically include hiring, firing, discipline, supervision, direction, and scheduling of work. To establish joint employer status, one must show that both employers meaningfully affect some or all of these matters relating to the employment relationship.

The NLRB has found that two employers are joint employers where regular and leased employees have the same supervision, perform essentially the same tasks, have functionally integrated work, and receive the same wages (Jenero and Spognardi 1995). Joint employment provides limited protection to workers because the NLRA does not prohibit the client employer from failing to renew a subcontract, thus eliminating the leased workers from the bargaining unit (DuRivage, Carré, and Tilly 1998). However, leased employees included in the bargaining unit are eligible to vote in NLRB elections to determine whether they are represented by a union. Consequently, leased employees who traditionally receive fewer benefits than regular employers would have the right to unionize as a means of improving their terms and conditions of employment.

Other Employee Categories

Unions also may seek to include other categories of employees in collective bargaining contracts to manage contingent work. For example, students may be included in a bargaining unit depending upon their communities of interest. A student working after school on a regular schedule can be included in the unit as a regular part-time employee.

The inclusion of students in an agreement is illustrated by the contract between the Board of Regents Montana University System and the Montana Faculty Association. Since students are a major part of the university labor force, the union has included them as a tactic to control this form of employment.

> Any student who is employed as a "temporary" employee on a "full-time" basis for seven hundred (700) or more hours in any one fiscal year, and is doing work within the position description of a classified position within a bargaining unit, or doing work which is within the described scope of work of a bargaining unit, shall be required, as a condition of continued employment, to pay the equivalent of initiation fees and/or monthly dues, or a service fee in lieu of dues, to the union in accordance with Article 11, Section A of this agreement.

Furthermore, the contract includes language that specifies under what circumstances the university can use students as employees.

> In keeping with the federal and state policies of providing employment for students to provide economic opportunity to obtain further education, and in order to make available to students the benefits of state and federal work-study and financial aid programs, the employer shall continue to employ students.[14]

However, the contract makes certain that student workers will not encroach on protected union positions.

> Students shall not be hired into any position, which would result in the displacement of any employee.

In the LTV Steel and the United Steelworkers of America contract student employment also is addressed. In an appendix to the contract on student employment in the summer, language establishes limitations on the period of employment and protects core jobs from being filled by student workers.

> During the term of the labor agreement, the probationary provisions of the Labor Agreements shall be modified as follows for students hired for summer employment on or before May 1 provided those students terminate their employment on or before September 15 of the same year.[15]

Other types of nontraditional employees also may be included in the bargaining unit under specified circumstances. On-call employees may be included in a bargaining unit if the employee works regularly, such as those needed by a large employer that has regular absences to be filled. Seasonal workers, such as resort or agricultural workers, may be included in a bargaining unit of regular full-time employees if the seasonal workers have a reasonable expectation of returning each season. Retirees who work regularly may be included in the bargaining unit even if working a limited number of hours.

The NLRB uses a test to determine whether a *trainee* who might become a supervisor or fill a management position is eligible to vote. This eligibility is determined by: 1) the kind of work being done, 2) whether work is done under the same conditions and for the same pay as other employees, 3) whether special training is required, 4) whether there is an eventual guarantee of a top management job, and 5) the length of the training period (Schlossberg and Scott 1983, p. 250). In a recent decision concerning a Massachusetts teaching hospital, the NLRB overruled a long-standing precedent about doctor trainees who are now considered employees under federal law. The NLRB found that doctor trainees were employees because they were involved in a master-servant relationship that provided services for the hospital, received compensation for working in the physician-training program, and received fringe benefits similar to other employees. This change in board opinion opens up a new area for union organizing (Ruskin Moscou Faltischek, P.C. 2003).

Probationary employees with a reasonable expectation of completing their probationary periods and being permanently hired also are included in a bargaining unit.

UNION EFFORTS TO LIMIT USE OF CONTINGENT WORK: RESPONSES TO SUBCONTRACTING, PRIVATIZATION, AND INDEPENDENT CONTRACTORS

The two major large-scale contingent work arrangements used by employers are subcontracting and privatization. Subcontracting, also called outsourcing, is the contracting out of a portion of the employer's work that was previously done in-house, such as janitorial services. It can occur in both the private and public sectors. Privatization is giving to private individuals or corporations the assets or functions that were previously performed by state or local government employees. It occurs only in the public sector (Bilik 1990). An example is contracting with a private company to run a correctional institution. In addition, employers in both the private and public sectors also use independent contractors. All of these contingent work arrangements are perceived by unions as eroding the strength of the bargaining unit and consequently reducing unions' ability to protect their members.

Subcontracting

One major goal of collective bargaining for industrial unions is to negotiate language that continues the work of the bargaining unit and limits the use of outside workers. Traditionally this has been done by negotiating language that excludes contingent workers from the bargaining unit and blocks or limits the ability of management to subcontract work to outside companies and vendors. However, in recent years unions such as the United Automobile Workers (UAW) have recognized the importance of helping the employer remain competitive in a global market. As a consequence, unions have used different tactics, such as negotiating early involvement in outsourcing planning, to limit the impact of subcontracting on the job security of their members.

Under the NLRA, contractual limits on the employer's ability to use contingent workers are a mandatory subject of bargaining. This means that the union may bargain over these issues to the point of impasse and then, if necessary, strike to obtain an agreement from the employer. The NLRB has ruled that if the type of subcontracting clause sought by the union is lawful, an employer has an obligation to bargain with the union over the issue of subcontracting unit work when subcontracting will adversely affect the bargaining unit (Helper 1990).

The variations in the strength of the contract language indicate that some unions have been more successful than others in negotiating limitations on subcontracting. One example of strong language limiting the use of subcontracting is seen in American Axle and Manufacturing, Inc. and the UAW contract.

> In no event shall any seniority associate who customarily performs the work in question be laid off as a direct and immediate result of work being performed by any outside contractor on the plant premises.[16]

The agreement between the United Steelworkers of America (USWA) and LTV Steel is an example of weaker language that provides management the latitude to use subcontractors while generally acknowledging a spirit of limiting the use of subcontracting. Although the USWA contract states that the guiding principle should be to keep work in the bargaining unit, many areas are left to the discretion of management.

> The parties have existing rights and contractual understandings with respect to contracting out. These include the existing rights and obligations of the parties which arose before the parties included specific language in their collective bargaining agreements, the arbitration precedents which have been established before and since the parties included specific provisions addressing contract-

ing out in their collective bargaining agreement, and the agreements resulting from the review of all contracting out work performed inside or outside the plant under the provisions of the Interim Progress Agreement dated January 31, 1986. In addition, the following provisions shall be applicable to all new contracting out issues arising on or after the effective date of this agreement.

The General Motors Corporation and the International Union of Electronic, Electrical, Salaried, Machine & Furniture Workers AFL-CIO contract is another example where management retains considerable discretion in the use of subcontracting. The contract includes a general acknowledgment that management will not use outside workers unless necessary.

> The corporation states that it will make a reasonable effort to avoid contracting out work which adversely affects the job security of its employees and that it will utilize various training programs available to it, whenever practicable, to maintain employment opportunities for its employees consistent with the needs of the corporation.[17]

However, there is additional contract language that includes a provision requiring management to provide advance notice in writing of its intention to subcontract: "In all cases, except where time and circumstances prevent it, Local Management will hold advance discussion with and provide advance written notice to the Chairperson of the Shop Committee."[18]

A loophole remains for management in the words "where time and circumstances prevent it." Nevertheless, the inclusion of a written justification for subcontracting is a significant limitation on management.

More recently unions have used tactics to ensure their early involvement in planning for subcontracting to limit its impact and protect the job security of their members. For example, the 1996 contract language from the UAW and General Motors negotiations is very explicit about the tendency toward subcontracting while demonstrating the ability of the union to limit that trend. This language ensures income security protection for workers by involving the union in the process.

> During the life of the current Agreement, the Corporation will advise, in writing, the Union members of the Sourcing Committee of the Labor Policy Board meeting results relative to sourcing recommendations, including the number of potential jobs affected. Addi-

> tionally, data regarding incoming and outgoing work will be given to the International Union in a quarterly meeting. (The Corporation will provide inquiry access to the International Union through the use of a computer terminal.) In this manner, the parties can judge the success of mutual efforts toward improved job security. The Corporation agrees to incorporate the procedures and structure outlined herein when making sourcing determinations during the current Agreement.[19]

The language reflects not only union concerns about job security but also its respect for management concerns about productivity. This is an important shift in position for the UAW since it reflects the recognition of the need for the employer to be economically competitive. It also provides the union with the opportunity to demonstrate its support of improvements in productivity by creating a cooperative labor relations environment.

This contract also addresses the extent to which management can use outside vendors for equipment maintenance.

> Employees of any outside contractor will not be utilized in a plant covered by this Agreement to replace seniority employees on production assembly or manufacturing work, or fabrication of tools, dies, jigs and fixtures, normally and historically performed by them, when performance of such work involves the use of Corporation-owned machines, tools, or equipment maintained by Corporation employees.[20]

This language ensures protection for senior employees by limiting the duties open for subcontracted work. It also restricts contract workers from using GM equipment, thereby limiting the use of contract workers on the shop floor. But the next section of the agreement builds in flexibility for management to contract out repair work:

> The foregoing shall not affect the right of the Corporation to continue arrangements currently in effect; nor shall it limit the fulfillment of normal warranty obligations by vendors nor limit work which a vendor must perform to prove out equipment.[21]

This language provides a loophole for management to continue the use of outside vendors but also indicates that the union will attempt to place some conditions on management.

A separate UAW-GM contract provides another example of the recognition by the unions of the need to support productivity improvements.

The UAW has developed programs to provide income security and encourage union locals to form "productivity coalitions" to compete for work that management might otherwise outsource. One such program, referred to as the Job Opportunity Bank Security (JOBS) Program, has been negotiated between the UAW and the Big Three automakers. The General Motors Corporation and UAW contract language provides an example of increased job security through a JOBS Program, while not explicitly prohibiting the use of subcontractors. It "protects eligible employees against layoff for virtually any reason except volume-related market conditions."[22]

Unions have consistently argued that their membership can do most of subcontracted work if given the proper equipment. Language such as that for the JOBS program provides a formal mechanism for them to demonstrate their productivity.[23] Implied in this language is the guarantee that core employees will not be replaced due to subcontracting as long as they meet productivity standards.

The above examples of contract language range from strong statements prohibiting subcontracting to full management discretion over subcontracting decisions. In a few cases the union has been able to entirely prohibit the use of subcontractors. However, in general most contracts indicate that management retains this right to varying degrees. The effectiveness, therefore, of these provisions varies with the strength of the union local and the intransigence of management. The most promising resolution of this tension between the employer's need for flexibility and the union's need for job security appears in the UAW-GM JOBS Program. This program gives the union the opportunity to demonstrate the productivity of its workers and their ability to do jobs that would otherwise be subcontracted outside the company.

Privatization

Similar to private sector unions, public sector unions are facing a variety of actions on the part of employers to reduce their workforces. By reclassifying and relocating positions, public sector unions are moving work beyond the reach of bargaining agreements and personnel policies. While the term "subcontracting" is used in the private service and manufacturing sectors, "privatization" refers to the same actions in the public sector.

In the current antigovernment environment, where limiting the size and power of government is a popular bipartisan goal, the privatization of government services often is advocated as a way to provide these services more efficiently. However, privatization removes unionized employees from the public sector union. This erosion of public sector bargaining units is especially troublesome to unions in the United States because the public sector has been the only economic sector in which union membership has grown over the past quarter century. In 2001, 37.4 percent of government workers were members of unions, compared to 9.0 percent among private sector employers (BLS 2001).

Unions have two major concerns about privatization: 1) that privatization will undermine wage and benefit standards and reduce the number of full-time public sector jobs, and 2) that privatization will result in the deterioration of the quality of public services since these will be delivered by organizations motivated by profit and cost control rather than a service orientation.

A wide range of state services have been privatized, including mental health, parks and recreation, employment security, education, data processing, police, vehicle registration, corrections, and airport services (Bilik 1990). Mirroring their private sector counterparts seeking to control subcontracting, public unions have developed proactive strategies to counteract privatization, such as identifying the early signs of privatization efforts in order to bargain, strong contract language prohibiting or limiting privatization, and legislative solutions. In addition, many unions also are using legal remedies as an ongoing tactic. An example is seeking court injunctions to stop employer actions opposed by the union.[24]

One example of the use of legal solutions is seen in the actions of Michigan State Government Local UAW 6000 in its opposition to the privatization of the Michigan Department of Corrections Health Care Unit. The department concluded a bidding process aimed at examining the feasibility of subcontracting health care unit staffing at five facilities to a private sector company (Michigan Department of Corrections 1999). The union opposed this measure because it would put the Department of Corrections' health care system under the jurisdiction of a private company and remove the current health care providers from the bargaining unit. UAW Local 6000 representatives testified before the Michigan Senate Committee on Corrections Allocations stating that

[t]he department wants to make physicians and PA's the gatekeep-
ers of managed care systems. There seems to be a clear and direct
conflict of interest, when the gatekeeper of a system is an employee of that same system. Local 6000 strongly urge you to stop
the privatization of physicians and physicians' assistants. (Rivera
2000)

The union also contended that it is better to keep jobs within the
system to ensure the quality of the service. It further argued that there
is no conclusive research to document that privatization will result in
cost savings (Rivera 2000). The Department of Corrections' action is
currently being grieved before the State Civil Service Commission.

Independent Contractors

Another employer tactic is the conversion of current employees
into independent contractors (Coalition for Fair Worker Classification
1994). Independent contractors are excluded from the definition of employee under Section 2(3) of the NLRA and therefore are considered
part of the contingent workforce. Independent contractors are generally distinguished from employees based on the amount of control the
employer exercises over how a person does the work. However, there
is often confusion about who is truly an independent contractor. Consequently, misclassification has been a frequent problem, as discussed in
more detail in Chapter 5.

The impact of misclassification on employees is illustrated by the
experience of reporters and photographers working for the *Philadelphia
Inquirer*. The 175 employees who covered the news in the city's suburban bureaus were assigned stories and deadlines by managing editors.
However, for many years the *Inquirer* classified the city reporters and
photographers as full-time employees, while classifying the suburban
workers as "independent contractors." As a consequence the suburban
workers did not qualify for health or pension benefits and were responsible for paying their own employment taxes. It was not until the suburban employees joined the Newspaper Guild/Communications Workers
in 1997 that they were classified as *Inquirer* employees.

The AFL-CIO has responded at a national level by backing federal legislation making misclassification more difficult. Under current
law, a 20-factor IRS formula is used to determine whether a worker

is classified as an employee or independent contractor. The Independent Contractor Classification Act of 2001 addresses the worker-classification issue by creating a new section 3511 of the Internal Revenue Code to simplify the criteria used to distinguish between employees and independent contractors. It requires employers to reclassify as full-time employees many workers currently considered independent contractors (AFL-CIO 2002). The act reduces the classification test to three criteria. Workers will be considered independent contractors if 1) their employers have no right to control them, 2) they can make their services available to others, and 3) they have the potential to generate profit and bear significant risk of loss.

BARGAINING ON WAGES, SENIORITY, AND BENEFITS FOR CONTINGENT WORKERS

Once employees in a workplace have voted to be represented by a union, an employer is required by law to bargain with the union as the sole representative of the workers. The duty to bargain imposed by the NLRA entails a requirement of the employer to bargain in good faith on hours, wages, and conditions of work, which generally includes seniority and nonwage benefits. The union, on the other hand, is obligated by the "Duty of Fair Representation" to represent the interests of all of its members (Feldacker 1990, p. 352).

During contract negotiations unions consider the advantages, disadvantages, and effects on the different groups in its membership of the various clauses being discussed for inclusion in the collective bargaining agreement. Typically the union will have to make some decisions that favor some bargaining unit employees over others. However, as long as the union does not act in an arbitrary, capricious, discriminatory, or perfunctory manner, its legal obligations are fulfilled. Because of the differing interests within the bargaining unit, some negotiated language may have an adverse effect on contingent workers. Important issues regularly negotiated that affect contingent workers are wages, seniority, and nonwage benefits, including medical care, disability coverage, and sick leave.

Wages

Unions use two strategies to raise wages for contingent workers. The first and most direct strategy is the inclusion of these workers in the bargaining unit so the discussion of their wages is included in negotiations. Examination of recognition clauses in collective bargaining agreements suggests that this approach is most often used for part-time workers. More rare is language covering wages for non–bargaining unit workers. The Teamster-UPS agreement settled in July 2002 (discussed earlier) was an example of a union using a strike to achieve considerable gains for part-time members.

> While full-time workers will receive wage increases of $5 per hour over the life of the six-year agreement, part-time workers will receive $6 per hour over the life of the agreement, achieving a long-term Teamster goal of reducing the gap between full-time and part-time wages. (LRA 2002)

In a 2002 settlement, the Service Employees International Union (SEIU) negotiated a contract for janitors in downtown Boston with wages equal to the hourly rate of full-time workers (Bureau of National Affairs 2002).

Another union strategy is to support public policy changes and living wage ordinances to improve wages for all contingent workers (Carré and Joshi 2000). The Association of Community Organizations for Reform Now (ACORN), the oldest and largest grassroots organization of low- and moderate-income people, is an example of this type of support. ACORN, which has 100,000 members in over 30 cities, argues that when public dollars are used to subsidize employers, these employers should not be permitted to pay their workers less than a living wage (ACORN 2003).

Seniority

Seniority is a defining principle of unionism. Employees with the longest period of service with the organization receive the greatest job security, improved working conditions, and frequently greater entitlement to employee benefits (Sloane and Whitney 1994). Under most collective bargaining agreements, seniority is the basis for determining pay, job opportunities and assignments, the right to paid time off, recalls after layoffs, overtime options, and other nonmonetary aspects of work. An employee's relative seniority status in the company usually depends on three basic considerations: when seniority begins to accumulate, the effect of changes in work assignments on seniority, and the effect of interruptions in employment on seniority.

Determining whether and how seniority can be accumulated for contingent workers remains a challenge to unions. Due to the importance of seniority in determining the economic welfare of full-time workers, many unions are reluctant to grant seniority rights to temporary workers. However, when seniority rights have been successfully negotiated for contingent workers, these rights generally are accrued on a prorated basis. One common feature of contract language governing part-time workers is that they never accumulate more seniority than full-time workers. This approach is illustrated by the United Food and Commercial Workers, Local 951, and Meijer, Inc. contract.

> 7.3—Seniority shall be of two (2) types, full-time and part-time. Full-time seniority shall be convertible to part-time. Full-time seniority shall not accumulate during periods of part-time jobs, and part-time seniority shall not be convertible to full-time seniority if a part-time employee becomes full-time. Part-time seniority shall not be lost by transfer to full-time work. In no case will part-time employees accumulate seniority over full-time employees.[25]

In the American Red Cross and Service Employees International Union contract, per diem employees are allowed to accumulate seniority but at a slower rate than full-time workers.

> Per diem nurses shall be placed on the seniority list calculated on fifty percent (50%) of length of service with the Employer as a per diem nurse plus any seniority earned within any other classification covered by the Agreement.[26]

This language ensures that for the purposes of layoff and recall these employees are the last on the list to be returned to work.

Sparrow Hospital and the Michigan Nurses Association allow temporary workers to accumulate seniority if they convert to either full-time or part-time status. Their seniority date is the date they convert to permanent status, not the date on which they began as temporaries.

> Section 10.4—Employees hired for a limited period of time not to exceed a total of six (6) months shall be classified as temporary employees. Such temporary employment may be extended by the

Human Resources Director or designee if such extension is necessary. A temporary shall be treated as a probationary employee
under this agreement. In the event a temporary employee is reclas-
sified to full time to part-time status, the date of hire in the new
classification shall be the date of hire as a temporary employee.[27]

These examples indicate that unions clearly favor their full-time
members with continuous service over those who work under contingent arrangements. It also suggests, however, that unions are trying to
negotiate the protection that comes with seniority for contingent workers, although on a less preferential basis.

Benefits

When unions include contingent workers in their membership,
there are two reasons to negotiate benefits for their contingent members. First, these benefits enhance worker welfare, which is a central
union objective. Second, one important strategic response to the use by
employers of contingent workers is to try to eliminate the cost advantage of contingent work arrangements. The closer the cost of noncore
contingent workers to the cost of employing traditional core workers,
the less attractive contingent work is to management. The types of benefits commonly included in contracts are health care and dental insurance, paid time off, including disability pay and sick leave, and holiday
pay. Our review suggests that prorated health care benefits are offered
to contingent workers more often than other types of benefits.

The Sparrow Hospital contract is among the most generous in its
treatment of contingent workers to support the recruitment and retention of registered nurses. It provides benefits to both full- and part-time
employees. As seen in the language below, the employer pays the full
medical health care premium for all workers and only prorates dental
benefits.

Flexcare Plan

Section 33.1—Purpose. To provide full-time, part-time, and per
diem employees with tax-free reimbursement for health care and
dependent care expenses incurred on behalf of Plan participants,
spouses, and dependents, and to allow participants to provide for
additional expenses on a pre-tax basis through voluntary wage/sal-
ary reductions.[28]

Dental Insurance

Section 32.1—All full and regular part-time employees (normally scheduled to work 32 or more hours per pay period) are eligible to enroll for dental insurance.

Section 32.2—The Employer will pay 100% of the premium for single coverage and 90% of the premium for applicable dependent coverage for eligible full-time employees. The Employer will pay 100% of the premium for single coverage for part-time employees. Eligible part-time employees pay the full cost for dependent coverage.[29]

The agreement between 1199W/United Professionals for Quality Health Care and the State of Wisconsin is more typical in the health care coverage provided to part-time workers (referred to here as project workers).

Article VI–Employee Benefits, Section 1, Health Insurance:
The Employer agrees to pay 50% of the above listed contributions amounts for insured employees in permanent part time or project positions defined under 230.27, who are appointed to work at least 600 but less than 1,044 hours per year.[30]

Another example of a contract providing health care coverage is in the United Food and Commercial Workers, Local 951, and Meijer, Inc. contract. Benefits for part-time workers are not as extensive as those given to full-time employees, but the union did negotiate partial health care insurance for its part-time workforce.

Article 11: Employee Benefits:
Part-time employees are eligible for benefit coverage for the Comprehensive 200 Medical Plan (COMP200).
Medical Plan (including prescription drug coverage), the Dental/ Optical Plan, and the required weekly pre-tax contribution rates for health coverage are set forth in this subsection 11.1J.[31]

Although there is some variation in the generosity of the health benefits, these examples suggest that, when unions include contingent workers in the bargaining unit, they are able to negotiate at least partial medical benefits for them. To the extent that the contracts reviewed here are typical, they indicate that unionized contingent workers receive better health care coverage than nonunionized workers (BLS 2001).

Contracts also vary in how generously they provide for paid time off, including disability pay and sick leave, and holiday pay. The University of Michigan nurses contract with the University of Michigan allows part-time workers to receive long-term disability benefits.[32]

Sick leave benefits also are provided to part-time employees in the agreement between American Red Cross, Southeastern Blood Services Region, and the Michigan Council of Nurses and Health Care Professionals, Service Employees International Union, Local 79.

> Employees will earn sick leave benefits at the rate of one and two-thirds days per month of service. Employees may accrue up to ninety days of sick leave. Part-time employees shall receive the proportion of sick leave, which the average days worked per week bear to the full-time employees' five-day week.[33]

Unlike full-time employees, part-time union members generally are unable to receive time and a half or double time for working on holidays. This can be seen in the language from two contracts shown below. The agreement between Sparrow Hospital and the Michigan Nurses Association shows that contingent workers are only paid for holidays if they work and only then at straight-time hourly rates.

> Article 35, Holidays
> Section 15.2 B. Part-time and per diem employees receive the base rate of pay for each hour actually worked on each of the six holidays as they occur. Holiday pay is paid for hours worked in excess of a full shift (i.e. 8 hours, 10 hours, or 12 hours).[34]

In the Kroger and United Food and Commercial Workers, Local 951, Western Michigan Clerks agreement, contingent workers do receive some holiday pay if they have worked as scheduled both before and after the holiday. However, this limits their ability to take extended time off during holidays without losing pay.[35]

FUTURE CHALLENGES FOR UNIONS

The discussion in this chapter has highlighted the challenges unions face in their efforts to contain or manage the use of contingent work arrangements by employers. These approaches, particularly those used by industrial unions, still reflect a historical orientation toward traditional employment arrangements (Zalusky 1986). As a result, most unions remain structured to protect job and income security for full-time workers, particularly male workers in blue-collar jobs such as manufacturing, mining, construction, and transportation, whose relative importance in the economy is declining.

If unions want to grow in membership numbers and relative importance in the labor force, they must find ways to meet the needs of a workforce that is about 50 percent female—three-quarters of which is working in the service sector. Furthermore, with a 76 percent labor force participation rate among women between the ages of 25 and 54 who worked in 1998 and 62 percent of women working with children under the age of six, flexibility and alternative scheduling arrangements must be addressed (Fullerton 1999; Hayghe 1997). Worker demands for family-friendly policies and flexible schedules combined with employers' desire for workforce flexibility are forcing unions to rethink their adherence to the traditional employment relationship as the sole mechanism for gaining economic security (Nussbaum and Meyer 1986). As discussed earlier, some unions in the service sector have already begun the process of adapting to the changing demographic characteristics of the labor force by including contingent workers in their bargaining and negotiating their wages and prorated benefits.

Unions will continue to be concerned about the negative impact of part-time and alternative employment arrangements on all aspects of economic welfare. However, unions must address these concerns in an environment in which some employers have legitimate needs for alternative arrangements and some workers prefer them. In facing these challenges, unions cannot afford to take an exclusionary approach that protects only the "haves" of the workforce.

DIRECTIONS FOR FUTURE RESEARCH

Using the lens of negotiated contract language, this chapter has reviewed strategies for inclusion and exclusion used by unions to cope with the challenges created by contingent work. What is clear from this review is that organized labor has not devised a consistent strategy for handling contingent work. Research can explore four important questions that will provide guidance to unions on appropriate future strategies for managing contingent work.

First, investigation has rarely focused on why union locals pursue an exclusionary or inclusionary strategy and the factors influencing this decision. It is necessary to analyze the impact of factors such as the demographic characteristics of the workforce and member preferences for nontraditional work schedules, as well as the internal politics of the union, in the decision to exclude or include part-time workers. For example, evidence indicates that women are more likely to work part time or in some form of alternative work arrangement to balance work and family responsibilities. The greater concentration of women in service occupations may partially explain the contract language negotiated by service sector unions.

The American Federation of Teachers (AFT) executive council has long been concerned about the use of part-time faculty employment. The AFT notes that the use of part-time faculty jeopardizes the quality of education and is used to threaten full-time faculty. The union argues that these part-time positions

> . . . provide the cheap, no-strings-attached labor which makes it unnecessary to declare regular positions open, enables an institution to staff classes even though faculty are denied tenure, reduces the proportion of a department entrusted with decision-making, and intensifies the burden of committee work and departmental governance for full-time faculty. (AFT Higher Education 2000)

A detailed case study can help unions understand why there have been so few examples of successful union activities on behalf of part-time faculty. It has been argued that success has been limited in part because neither universities and colleges nor their full-time faculties have been willing to make equity for part-time faculty a negotiating priority (Leatherman 2000). In July 2002, the UAW won the right to represent more than 4,000 part-time faculty members at New York University, creating the largest adjunct-only union in the nation at a private university (Smallwood 2002b). Adjunct faculty at the University of Massachusetts at Boston, assisted by the local chapter of the Chicago Coalition of Contingent Academic Labor (COCAL), pressured the local union to negotiate for higher pay and greater equity. With this success, COCAL would like to move beyond this campus to the other 58 colleges and universities that lie within a 10-mile radius of Boston (Leatherman 2001).

A second related research topic is determining the effectiveness of various forms of language in protecting bargaining unit work while meeting the needs of the membership for flexibility. It is sometimes argued that contingent work actually protects "good" jobs by insulating core workers from market variability (Mitchell 1986). However, a careful evaluation of this argument is needed.

A third area for investigation by researchers is the successes and failures in unionizing part-time and other contingent workers in other countries, which can provide guidance for future negotiating and organizing strategies in the United States. For example, Japanese unions are faced with the same dilemma as unions in the United States. In 2000 their membership fell by 2.8 percent, partially because they concentrated their attention on regular full-time employment and failed to adjust to the diversification of employment arrangements toward more part-time and other nonregular forms of employment (Euroline 2002a). The Canadian experience contrasts with that of Japan. Zeytinoğlu (1992) conducted a survey of 188 employers in Ontario, Canada, who had collective bargaining contracts covering both "full-time and part-time workers who are in the same occupation and who perform the same or substantially similar tasks." This survey found that the major reason employers included both groups in their contracts was the desire for flexibility in scheduling work that part-time workers make possible. Research on collective bargaining practices in other countries that identifies lessons learned will be useful to U.S. unions.

Finally, future research should explore how public policy can be integrated with collective bargaining to protect part-time workers as well as those in other alternative work arrangements. Experiences in other countries can provide useful insights and models for the United States. For example, in the European Union (EU), some legislation and collective bargaining agreements have been designed to regulate part-time work in a complementary fashion. The European Trade Union Confederation (ETUC) believes that part-time work should be made more attractive and acceptable for workers while also providing the assurance of "decent social protection" (Euroline 2002b). If unions want to rebuild their memberships, they must find ways to unionize part-time workers. The research outlined in this chapter should provide insights into the appropriate strategies for success.

Notes

The authors wish to express their sincere thanks to Danny Hoffman, specialist in the Michigan State University Labor Education Program, and Sharon A. Riviera, secretary/treasurer of UAW Local 6000, for their time and support; and appreciation to the participants in the Michigan State University and University of Illinois Labor Education Programs National Conference for Labor Representatives in the Health Care Industry, April 2–4, 2000, in Lake Buena Vista, Florida, for their comments about the current state of unions and contingent work.

1. The Bureau of Labor Statistics (BLS) biennially collects information on contingent employment and alternative work arrangements. The definitions used by the BLS are discussed in detail in Chapter 2.
2. The NLRB considers several factors in determining the existence of a community of interest, including whether the employees:

    - Perform similar types of work and have similar training and skills, such as craft work, clerical work, or production and maintenance work;

    - Work in the same location and/or interchange and have regular work contact with each other;

    - Perform integrated production or service functions;

    - Enjoy similar working conditions, such as working the same hours or shift schedules, using the same locker room and cafeteria facilities, or being subject to the same personnel policies or work rules;

    - Have similar wage and benefits schedules; and

    - Have common supervision or centralized control over personnel policies or day-to-day operations (Feldacker 1990, p. 46).

3. Sparrow Hospital and the Michigan Nurses Association, Collective Bargaining Agreement, 2004–2007, Article 1. Recognition, 2.
4. Mercy Hospital of Buffalo and Communications Workers of America, Service, Technical and Clerical Employees, Collective Bargaining Agreement, 2004–2008, Article 4, Categories of Employees, 14.
5. Kaiser Foundation Hospitals, Kaiser Foundation Health Plan of the Northwest, and Oregon Federation of Nurses and Health Care Professionals, Local 5017 AFT-FNHP-AFL/CIO, Collective Bargaining Agreement, 2005–2010, Article 7, Section D, p. 4.
6. Ibid., 12.
7. LTV Steel and the United Steelworkers of America, Collective Bargaining Agreement, 2004–2008, Section X, Coverage, p. 94.
8. At one time the board held that an employee had to work a certain percentage of the workweek to be classified as a regular part-time employee, but that rule is no longer followed. See Feldacker (1990, p. 52).

9. Mercy Hospital of Buffalo and Communications Workers of America, Service, Technical and Clerical Employees, Collective Bargaining Agreement, 2004–2008, p. 12.
10. United Food and Commercial Workers, Local 951, and Meijer, Inc., Collective Bargaining Agreement, 2003–2007, Article 2, Coverage, R-2.
11. United Parcel Service and International Brotherhood of Teamsters Collective Bargaining Agreement 2002–2008 and Michigan Supplemental Agreement, August 1, 2002.
12. Marriott Management Services and the United Catering, Restaurant, Bar and Hotel Workers Local Union 1064, R.W.D.S.U., AFL-CIO, Collective Bargaining Agreement, 1998–2001 (1998), p. 10.
13. See Note 7.
14. The Board of Regents Montana University System and the Montana Faculty Association, Collective Bargaining Agreement, 2003–2005, Article I Section B – Student Workers, p. 45.
15. LTV Steel and the United Steelworkers of America, Collective Bargaining Agreement, 2004–2008, Section X, Coverage, p. 117.
16. American Axle and Manufacturing, Inc. and UAW, Collective Bargaining Agreement, 2004–2008, (183)(e), p. 107.
17. General Motors Corporation and the International Union of Electronic, Electrical, Salaried, Machine & Furniture Workers AFL-CIO, Collective Bargaining Agreement, 1996–1999, p. 201.
18. Ibid., Appendix B, 220.
19. Ibid., Appendix L, 233. In addition to this language the contract also has five letters of understanding about specific subcontracting issues.
20. Ibid., (183) (a), 134.
21. Ibid., (183) (b).
22. Ibid., 345.
23. Interview with D. Hoffman, Specialist, Michigan State University Labor Education Program, April 2000.
24. Interview with S.A. Rivera, Secretary/Treasurer for UAW Local 6000, April, 2000.
25. See Note 10.
26. American Red Cross, Southeastern Michigan Blood Services Region and Michigan Council of Nurses and Health Care Professionals, Service Employees International Union, Local 79, Collective Bargaining Agreement, 1993–1996, Article X, p. 21.
27. See Note 3.
28. Ibid.
29. Ibid.
30. 1199W/United Professionals for Quality Health Care and the State of Wisconsin, Collective Bargaining Agreement, 2002–2005, Article VI, Employee Benefits, 2002–2005, p. 22.
31. See Note 10.

32. The Regents of the University of Michigan and the Michigan Nurses Association, Collective Bargaining Agreement, 2001–2004, p. 118.
33. See Note 26.
34. See Note 3.
35. Kroger and United Food and Commercial Workers, Local 951, Western Michigan Clerks, Collective Bargaining Agreement, 1995–2000, p. 10.

References

AFL-CIO. 2002. *Curbing Corporate Greed: Winning Full-Time Rights for Part-Time Workers.* http://www.aflcio.org/corporateamerica (accessed August 28, 2002).

American Federation of Teachers (AFT) Higher Education. 2000. *Statement on Part-Time Faculty Employment.* http://www.aft.org/higher_ed/publications/statement.html (accessed February 13, 2000).

American Staffing Association. 2001. *Staffing Facts.* http://www.natss.org/aboutasa/staffingfacts.shtml (accessed June 6, 2001).

Association of Community Organizations for Reform Now (ACORN). 2003. *ACORN's Living Wage Web Site.* http://www.livingwagecampaign.org (accessed July 29, 2003).

Barker, K., and K. Christensen. 1998. "Controversy and Challenges Raised by Contingent Work Arrangements." In *Contingent Work: American Employment Relations in Transition,* K. Barker and K. Christensen, eds. Ithaca, NY: Industrial and Labor Relations Press, pp. 221–225.

Bilik, A. 1990. "Privatization: Selling America to the Lowest Bidder." *Labor Research Review* 15: 1–5.

Bureau of National Affairs. 2002. "Health Care for Some Part-Time Janitors Negotiated by SEIU Boston Cleaning Firms." *Collective Bargaining Bulletin* 7(23): 101.

Carré, F., and P. Joshi. 2000. "Looking for Leverage in a Fluid World: Innovative Responses to Temporary and Contracted Work." In *Nonstandard Work: The Nature and Challenges of Changing Employment Arrangements,* F. Carré, M.A. Ferber, L. Golden, and S.A. Herzenberg, eds. Champaign, IL: Industrial Relations Research Association, pp. 313–339.

Coalition for Fair Worker Classification. 1994. *Projection of the Loss in Federal Tax Revenues Due to Misclassification of Workers.* http://www.dol.gov/oasam/programs/history/reich/reports/dunlop/section5.htm (accessed August 8, 2006).

Cobble, D.S., and L.F. Vosko. 2000. "Historical Perspectives on Representing Nonstandard Workers." In *Nonstandard Work: The Nature and Challenges of Changing Employment Arrangements*, F. Carré, M.A. Ferber, L. Golden, and S.A. Herzenberg, eds. Champaign, IL: Industrial Relations Research Association, pp. 291–312.

duRivage, V., F. Carré, and Chris Tilly. 1998. "Making Labor Law Work for Part-Time and Contingent Workers." In *Contingent Work: American Employment Relations in Transition*, K. Barker and K. Christensen, eds. Ithaca, NY: ILR Press, pp. 263–280.

Euroline. 2002a. *2001 Industrial Relations in EU, Japan and USA*. Dublin. http://www.eiro/eurofoundie/print2002/12/feature/tn (accessed March 2, 2002).

———. 2002b. *Working Time Developments and the Quality of Work*. Dublin. http://www.eiro.eurofound.ie/2001/11/study/TN0111143S.html (accessed August 16, 2002).

Feldacker, B. 1990. *Labor Guide to Labor Law*. 3rd ed. Englewood Cliffs, NJ: Prentice Hall.

Fullerton, H., Jr. 1999. "Labor Force Projections to 2008: Steady Growth and Changing Composition." *Monthly Labor Review* 122(11): 19–32.

Hayghe, H. 1997. "Developments in Women's Labor Force Participation." *Monthly Labor Review* 120(9): 41–46.

Helper, Sue. 1990. "Subcontracting: Innovative Labor Strategies." *Labor Research Review* 9(1): 89–99.

Jenero, K.A., and M.A. Spognardi. 1995. "Temporary Employment Relationships: Review of the Joint Employer Doctrine under the NLRA." *Employee Relations Law Journal* 21(Autumn): 127–137.

Katz, H.C., and T.A. Kochan. 2000. *An Introduction to Collective Bargaining and Industrial Relations*. 2nd ed. Boston: McGraw-Hill.

Labor Research Association (LRA). 2002. "Highlights of the Teamsters-LPS Agreement." http://www.iraonline.org/print.php?id=212 (accessed August 23, 2002).

Leatherman, C. 2001. "Part-Time Faculty Members Try to Organize Nationally." *The Chronicle of Higher Education,* January 26, A:12–13.

Longmate, J., and F. Cosco. 2002. "Part-time Instructors Deserve Equal Pay for Equal Work." *The Chronicle of Higher Education,* May 3, B:14.

Michigan Department of Corrections. 1999. *Memorandum to All Bureau Health Care Service Staff on Information on Privatization of Health Care Services.* January 12. Lansing, MI: Michigan Department of Corrections.

Mitchell, D.B. 1986. "The New Contingent Employment: A Calm View." In *The Changing Workplace: New Directions in Staffing and Scheduling*, Bureau of National Affairs, ed. Washington, DC: Bureau of National Affairs, pp. 93–94.

Nollen, S., and H. Axel. 1996a. "Contingent and Alternative Work Arrangements, Defined." *Monthly Labor Review* 119(10): 3–21.

———. 1996b. *Managing Contingent Workers.* New York: AMACOM.

Nussbaum, K., and D. Meyer. 1986. "Marginal Work Means Trouble for Workers, Economy." *The Changing Workplace: New Directions in Staffing and Scheduling.* Bureau of National Affairs Special Report. Washington, DC: Bureau of National Affairs, p. 95.

Rivera, S.A. 2000. Testimony of UAW Local 6000 before the Michigan Senate Committee on Corrections Allocations, Lansing, MI. February 15.

Roberts, K., and S.E. Gleason. 1999. "Workforce Planning for Flexibility: Staffing with Temporary Employees." In *Managing Human Resources in the 21st Century*, E.E. Kossek and R.N. Block, eds. Cincinnati: South-Western College Publishing, Module 12.

Ruskin Moscou Faltischek, P.C. 2003. "NLRB Decision Permits Medical Interns, Residents and Fellows to Unionize." July 30. http://www.ruskin-moscou.com/article-nlrb.htm (accessed January 14, 2004).

Schlossberg, S.L., and J.A. Scott. 1983. *Organizing and the Law.* Washington, DC: Bureau of National Affairs.

Service Employees International Union (SEIU). 1993. *Part-Time, Temporary, and Contracted Work.* Washington, DC: SEIU Research Department.

Sloane, A., and F. Whitney. 1994. *Labor Relations.* Englewood Cliffs, NJ: Prentice Hall.

Smallwood, S. 2002a. "Faculty Union Standards for Treatment of Adjuncts." *The Chronicle of Higher Education,* August 2, A:12.

———. 2002b. "UAW Will Represent Part-Time Faculty Members at New York U." *The Chronicle of Higher Education*, July 19, A:10

Tilly, C. 1992. *Short Hours, Short Shrift: Causes and Consequences of Part-Time Work*. Washington, DC: Economic Policy Institute.

———. 1998. "Part-Time Work: A Mobilizing Issue." *New Politics* 6(Winter): 21–26.

U.S. Department of Labor, Bureau of Labor Statistics (BLS). 2001. *Contingent and Alternative Employment Arrangements*. http://stats.bls.gov/news.release/conemp.nws.htm (accessed December 21, 2001).

Zalusky, J.L. 1986. "Labor's Concerns with the New Directions in Staffing and Scheduling." In *The Changing Workplace: New Directions in Staffing and Scheduling*, Bureau of National Affairs, ed. Washington, DC: Bureau of National Affairs, p. 98.

Zeytinoğlu, I.U. 1992. "Reasons for Hiring Part-Time Workers." *Industrial Relations* 31(3): 489–499.

Part 3

U.S. Public Policy toward the Shadow Workforce

5

No Safe Harbor

A Review of Significant Laws
Affecting Contingent Workers

Thomas A. Coens
Alvin L. Storrs
Michigan State University

There has been an increase in contingent employment arrangements in the United States for more than two decades. This increase has generated much discussion in the legal and human resource practitioner communities, as well as legislative activity and litigation, about how to apply federal and state laws governing these forms of employment. However, many of the key precedents used to apply the laws to contingent employment arrangements have been established already through case law. Consequently, the challenge has been to apply these guidelines to new emerging employment arrangements, such as the growth of employee leasing.

The overriding common purpose of U.S. labor and employment laws for more than a century has been to protect the wage-earning worker hired by an employer. This means that virtually every employment-related statute includes an explicit definition of the terms "employee" and "employer" to determine the coverage of the statute and permit enforcement.[1] As a result, many of the issues related to a given statute can be resolved through reference to guidelines and precedents that have been in effect for decades.[2] Unfortunately, the fact that each law has its own unique definitions and evolving case law, and the lack of generic definitions that may be used interchangeably from one statute to another, can be quite confusing to employers.

This confusion has caused some employers to think that contingent employment arrangements offer an easy escape from the obligations and constraints imposed by these laws, and thus a way to reduce labor costs. With a few notable exceptions, however, this belief is fallacious. Classifying people as independent contractors, placing people in temporary or part-time jobs, or retaining employees through a leasing company does not provide a "safe harbor" for employers.[3] Employers should not assume that their legal liabilities are reduced because they hire contingent workers.[4]

This chapter discusses the basic criteria and provisions of the major workplace laws influencing controversial issues pertaining to the contingent worker. Most of the issues are not new, but rather reflect the challenge of applying them in some new contexts and to a larger number of workers. The discussion focuses on the most critical and broadly applied legal interpretation issues embodied in the employment arrangements of independent contractors, temporary employees, and leased employees.[5] The use of the common-law control test and the economic realities test in the interpretation of the laws is reviewed. The key issues then are discussed as they apply to the federal income tax, employment tax, and retirement benefit laws; wage and hour rules (minimum wage); workers' compensation; and equal employment opportunity laws. In closing, recommendations to improve public policy focused on contingent employment issues and questions for future research are discussed.

VARIATIONS IN TERMINOLOGY AND LEGAL TESTS

The application of employment-related laws by employers to the contingent workforce is clouded by the lack of common or universal terminology used to identify the different types of workers or employers within federal statutes or across state statutes. Furthermore, there is confusion about applications of the legal tests used to interpret the meaning of "employee" and "employer" for each law.

Variations in Terminology

Two variations are important to this discussion: the definition of an employee and the definition of an employer. For example, a person may clearly qualify as an independent contractor based on the definition of an employee in the Internal Revenue Service (IRS) or the National

Labor Relations Board (NLRB) rules, but be classified as an employee under the Fair Labor Standards Act (FLSA) and workers' compensation laws. Thus, because of these differences, an attorney who is asked whether an individual qualifies as an independent contractor can only respond, "Under what law?"

One illustration of the confusing variety of terms for employers is the identification of a temporary agency or employee leasing company.[6] These firms may be referred to as the leasing company, general employer, primary employer, labor broker, lessor, loaning employer, staffing company, or contractor employer. Similarly, the employee placed by a temporary or leasing company may be referred to as a temporary employee, leased employee, borrowed employee (or servant), loaned employee (or servant), coemployee, or joint employee.

However, although these terms are similar, they are not necessarily interchangeable due to differing technical definitions. Also, some laws regulate these categories but do not precisely distinguish them. For example, many employment statutes, such as FLSA and Equal Employment Opportunity (EEO) laws, generally do not distinguish between leased employees and temporary employees per se. However, under other laws, such as worker compensation statutes, these categories are addressed with great specificity.

This chapter will use the terminology commonly associated with the particular law being discussed. In some cases distinguishing features will be noted, but every distinction cannot be articulated.

Common-Law and Economic Realities Tests

Statutes, regulations, revenue rulings, and legal tests are used to interpret issues of worker status (for a more detailed discussion of these tests, see Muhl [2002]). The beginning point in analyzing the relationship between a worker and a company is to determine whether the worker is an employee under a given statute. This question is critical because it determines the responsibilities of the employer for a variety of employment taxes in addition to pay and benefits. If a worker can be classified as an independent contractor instead of an employee, the employer can reduce costs.[7]

Two similar legal tests, or a hybrid of the two tests, have been used by the courts to make this determination: the "common-law control test" and the "economic realities" test.[8] These tests ask multiple questions to evaluate all aspects of the employment situation, and the courts examine each fact pattern independently. Particular attention is paid to who has the right to control the work process, but all factors must be considered to determine the outcome. If the employer has this right, then the person controlled generally will be considered an employee. Consequently, it is the conditions of employment that are key in determining employee status, not the classification of the workers assigned by the employer.

These two legal tests vary in the breadth of the circumstances investigated. The common-law test is the most widely used in federal cases. It is based on the legal concept of agency in which the employee is given authority to act for the employer by the employer. This test generally uses 10 factors to determine who has the right to control the work process.[9]

However, the IRS uses 20 factors to determine the presence or absence of control.[10] Also, when presenting a case before the IRS or courts, taxpayers can introduce other factors beyond the 20 as persuasive evidence negating or establishing control. Moreover, some IRS agents use three types of evidence in determining a worker's classification: behavioral control, financial control, and the relationship of the parties. The intent of the parties, industry custom, independent contractor agreements, and the provision of employee-type benefits are other factors which have been considered by courts.[11]

If a company misclassifies a worker as an independent contractor, the IRS will reclassify the independent contractor as an employee and impose taxes, interest, and penalties that can create large tax bills.[12] In a typical reclassification, the company may be assessed for income taxes that were not withheld and employment taxes; the employment tax liability would include both the employer's and employee's share.

The economic realities test usually is applied where the purpose of the law is to protect or benefit a worker who is financially dependent on an employer. It focuses on the nature of the economic relationship between the employer and the worker. It uses six factors to determine whether a worker depends on the employer for ongoing employment and economic livelihood. Since this test has a broader focus than the common-law test, individuals are more likely to be classified as employees by the court.[13]

The hybrid test also examines all of the circumstances affecting the employment relationship by combining elements from the common-law and economic realities tests. It considers the economic realities particularly critical, but it also considers who has the right to control the work process.

These different tests have resulted in varying interpretations of who is an employee and who is an independent contractor across the spectrum of tax, labor, employment, and retirement benefit laws. As a consequence, a worker in the same job category can be either an employee or independent contractor, depending on the facts and circumstances.[14] For example, in *Consolidated Flooring Services v. United States* (1997), a holding company owned two companies in which workers were installing floor coverings. The workers in both companies were doing the same work but were classified differently due to varying circumstances. One company, Monroe Schneider Associates (MSA), used union employees to install floor coverings while the other company, Consolidated Flooring Services (CFS), contracted with nonunion workers for installation services. The Court applied the common-law test to conclude that the CFS nonunion installers were independent contractors. The Court stated: ". . . where CFS did maintain some control . . . installers retained their independence with respect to the sequence, manner and skill with which jobs were completed. Installers bore the risk of profit or loss on their jobs and controlled their own work force."

FEDERAL INCOME TAX, EMPLOYMENT TAX, AND RETIREMENT BENEFITS LAWS

Identifying a worker as an employee or independent contractor is critical for federal income tax, employment tax, and retirement benefits laws. The determination of employee or independent contractor classification is made by examining statutes, regulations, revenue rulings, and case law. Once it is established that a worker is an employee, then full-time, part-time, temporary, or leased employee status must be ascertained. The full- or part-time status of an employee generally will be decided by the number of hours worked. The arrangement with an outside company will determine whether the worker is a temporary or leased employee instead of an employee of the company for which a worker performs services. The application of the test and the factors used to guide decisions are discussed below.

Federal Income and Employment Tax

Employee or Independent Contractor

The Federal Unemployment Tax Act (FUTA) and Federal Insurance Contribution Act (FICA) are employment taxes.[15] Employers generally prefer to hire independent contractors when appropriate because it reduces both their administrative costs of collecting and paying federal income and employment taxes. In contrast, the IRS prefers to have workers classified as employees so that it can collect the maximum amount of tax revenue.

If the worker is an employee, the company as employer has the responsibility to withhold income and employment taxes (e.g., to pay for the Social Security and Medicare programs supported by FICA) from the compensation of the employee.[16] The payment of one-half of the FICA tax with the accompanying filing and reporting obligations is a primary reason many companies attempt to classify a worker as an independent contractor. In addition, the employer must pay the FUTA tax, which covers the cost of administering the unemployment insurance system and the states' Job Service programs, and provides 50 percent of the cost of extended unemployment benefits when unemployment is high.[17]

In contrast, payments to independent contractors are not subject to withholding of any taxes because the company is not considered an employer of this type of worker. Independent contractors therefore must pay the proper amount themselves in estimated quarterly income tax payments or be subject to penalties and interest.[18] A negative consequence for independent contractors is that they are not covered by unemployment insurance and are not entitled to these benefits if they become unemployed.[19] Similarly, as discussed in Chapter 6, many part-time employees are not eligible for FUTA coverage due to working too few hours.

Coemployment

The determination of the "employer" who is liable for tax and employment law compliance can be particularly perplexing when a company is employing temporary workers provided by a temporary employment agency or leased workers provided by a leasing agency.[20] The issue created by these arrangements is whether the worker can be an employee of *both* the employment agency and the client (customer) organization. This dual status where two or more parties both stand legally as the employer of a single employee is "coemployment."[21]

In the typical one-to-one employment situation, the employer for whom the worker performs services is responsible for income tax withholding. However, in a coemployment situation in which another party has control over the payment of wages, then that party is considered to be the employer. For example, in a case involving the General Motors Corporation, the company was held not to be the employer for employment tax withholding purposes when it contracted with a foreign company to obtain design engineers (*General Motors Corp. v. United States* 1990). The court concluded that regardless of whether the auto company ultimately controlled each design engineer while on the job, the facts supported a finding that the foreign company was responsible for paying the wages of the design engineers. This court focused on which party had control over the payment of wages to determine which company was the employer and therefore responsible for the employment taxes.

Retirement Benefits

A qualified retirement plan offers attractive tax features to employers and employees. Generally, for federal tax purposes, an employer is allowed a deduction when an employee includes the amount in gross income; however, the employer receives an immediate deduction for contributions to qualified retirement plans, even though employees do not have to include the amount of the contribution in gross income.[22] The tax consequences for the employee are deferred until the employee receives a distribution from the qualified plan. Contributions maintained in a trust or other qualified fund accumulate tax free, resulting in an accelerated accumulation of pension funds for employees.

However, a qualified plan must meet a strict set of statutory requirements. Generally, a qualified retirement plan by its design and operation must satisfy standards requiring coverage of a minimum percentage of employees and not discriminate in favor of highly compensated employees in contributions or benefits.[23] The definition of employee is critical in the qualified plan arena.

Employee or Independent Contractor

A specific definition of "employee" for qualified retirement plans is not contained in the Internal Revenue Code (I.R.C.). The Supreme Court applied the common-law test in determining whether a worker was an employee for the purpose of a qualified plan, but did not conclude that the common-law definition must apply in all employee benefit cases.[24]

The continuation of the qualified status of a retirement plan can be dependent on the proper classification of workers. If workers who are actually employees but improperly classified as independent contractors are excluded from a qualified plan, then the minimum coverage or nondiscrimination standard could be violated, resulting in disqualification of the plan. Similarly, the requirement that the plan should be for the exclusive benefit of employees would be violated if an independent contractor was incorrectly classified as an employee and included, and could cause disqualification.[25] Also, the qualified status of the plan may be in jeopardy if a sufficient number of part-time employees who have one year of service have not been allowed to join the plan.[26] Even where the tax-qualified status of a plan is not in jeopardy, the erroneously excluded part-time employee would be entitled to participate in the plan. This would require the employer to make any missed past contributions to the plan on behalf of such improperly excluded employees.

Disqualification of a qualified retirement plan is viewed as the ultimate penalty because of the severe tax consequences on the employer, plan participants, and the plan trust. The IRS has recognized the severity of the plan disqualification penalties and the need to encourage plan sponsors to correct defects by introducing a set of administrative programs that allow many defective plans to correct problems without disqualification.[27]

Leased Employees

Leasing employees may be an attractive option for companies that are concerned with the higher costs associated with full-time permanent employees, such as the payment of retirement benefits. The U.S. Congress was apprehensive that some companies might attempt to reduce their retirement benefit costs by hiring a large number of leased employees who would perform the same services as employees without being eligible to participate in the retirement plan. Congress therefore enacted strict statutory guidelines to provide leased employees with additional qualified retirement plan protection. The statutory guidelines require the leased individual to be treated as the recipient's employee when verifying standards such as coverage and nondiscrimination if

1) the services are provided pursuant to an agreement between the recipient and any other person,

2) the individual has performed services for the recipient . . . on a substantially full-time basis for a period of at least one year, and

3) such services are performed under primary direction or control by the recipient.[28]

As a result, when using leased employees, the employer must track the number of employees in this category to ensure that the stated percentage of employees benefit under the plan's coverage and participation tests. If the company has too many leased employees who are not eligible solely due to their statuses, then the plan will be disqualified for failing the coverage and participation standards.

Coemployment

Two frequently cited cases illustrate the challenges of determining who is the employer in a coemployment situation: *Vizcaino v. Microsoft* (1997) and *Bronk v. Mountain States Telephone and Telegraph, Inc.* (1996). In both cases the workers brought their action under ERISA, but different outcomes resulted due to the differences in the interpretation of ERISA by the courts. In *Vizcaino v. Microsoft* the court ruled that workers were employees for the purposes of participation in a retirement plan, while in *Bronk* the opposite conclusion was drawn.

Microsoft had a practice of supplementing its regular employee pool with workers who were classified as independent contractors or temporary agency employees. In some job categories the regular employees, independent contractors, and temporary agency employees were performing the same work under the direction and control of Microsoft. The IRS, in an employment tax audit, made a determination that the independent contractors should have been classified as employees. Microsoft responded to the IRS audit reclassification by offering jobs to a small number of the independent contractors as regular employees. However, the majority of Microsoft's independent contractors were given the choice of being fired or converting to temporary agency employees. The temporary employment agency merely provided payroll services; the working relationship between new temporary employees and Microsoft remained substantially the same as before the IRS audit.

Former independent contractors then filed an action on behalf of workers who met the definition of employees under the common-law test but who were not allowed to participate in the retirement benefit plan because Microsoft considered them independent contractors or employees of a temporary employment agency. The 9th Circuit Court of Appeals stated: "Even if for some purposes a worker is considered an employee of the agency, that would not preclude his status of common law employee of Microsoft. The two are not mutually exclusive."[29]

The 10th Circuit Court of Appeals in *Bronk* reversed the earlier District Court's holding that employers must include in pension plans leased employees who were considered by the IRS as "employees" based on the common-law test. The Court of Appeals held that the I.R.C. and Treasury regulations governing the tax qualification of retirement plans did not implicitly modify ERISA to require employers to include in their retirement plans those leased employees who had been excluded from the plans because they were not "regular employees." Moreover, the Court of Appeals reasoned that Congressional action would be required to modify the tax qualification provisions of the Code to permit retirement plans under ERISA to require the inclusion of properly excluded leased employees. Thus, some uncertainty remains about how "employee" will be interpreted by the courts as evidenced by the inconsistent decisions in *Vizcaino* (*In re Vizcaino* 9th Cir 1999), the lower court in *Bronk v. Mountain State Telephone and Telegraph Inc.* (1996), and other cases *Abraham v. Exxon Corp.* (1996); *Clark v. E.I. DuPont De Nemours and Co.* (1997).

FEDERAL WAGE-HOUR LAW: THE MINIMUM WAGE LAW

The FLSA is the primary federal wage-hour law.[30] It imposes on covered employers a minimum wage, a requirement to pay overtime pay at time and one-half after 40 hours of work in a week to employees earning less than $24,000 a year, and child labor restrictions applicable to persons under 18 years of age. This law provides nearly universal coverage for full-time and part-time employees with few exceptions other than independent contractors, white-collar exemptions, and trainees.

Employee or Independent Contractor

Historically, the DOL enforcement policy has carefully monitored and limited the use of independent contractor status because it creates a potential escape for employers from wage and overtime obligations.[31] Based on the influence of an early Supreme Court decision in *Rutherford Food Corp. v. McComb* (1947a) the DOL has applied the economic realities test in deciding who qualifies as an independent contractor because, as the Supreme Court cautioned, "there is . . . no definition that solves all problems to the limitations of the employer-employee relationship" (*Rutherford Food Corp. v. McComb* 1947b). The economic realities test is strictly applied to achieve the purposes of the FLSA to ensure that workers are not deprived of protection due to an artifice of making a would-be employee into a contractor.

The official guiding principles applied by the Wage-Hour Division emphasize four factors in the *Field Operations Handbook* (U.S. Department of Labor 2003, p. 10b06).[32] These and additional control factors, considered in combination with economic reality factors, resemble the approach used by the IRS discussed above (U.S. Department of Labor 2003, p. 10b07). Interestingly, the wage-hour guidelines further advise that the method of compensation, the issuance of governmental licenses, the place where the work is performed, and the absence of a formal agreement are immaterial to the determination of contractor status. The exclusion of these four factors may reflect the fact that each can be easily manipulated by employers to create the artifice of an independent contractor status.[33]

In cases with many factors suggesting an employment relationship, the outcomes can vary, as illustrated by two well-known cases from the U.S. Court of Appeals: *Brock v. Superior Care* (1988) and *Herman v. Express Sixty-Minutes Delivery Services* (1998). In *Brock v. Superior Care* the U.S. Labor Department sought to classify nurses working for a nursing agency as "employees" under the FLSA to support the claims of the nurses for unpaid overtime compensation. Superior Care, a provider of temporary health care nurses to individual patients, nursing homes, and hospitals, contended that the nurses were independent contractors. The arguments employing six key factors from the economic realities test are summarized in Table 5.1.

In a two-to-one split decision in *Brock*, the 2nd Circuit U.S. Court of Appeals found that the nurses were employees under the FLSA, overruling the trial court's decision. Noting the closeness of the case, the court found that the integral relationship between the work and the agency's business, the lack of significant investment, and no risk of loss required a finding of an employee. The court further gave weight to the fact that the agency retained "employees" doing work similar to the alleged contractor nurses. However, the dissenting judge opined that the weight of evidence favored an independent contractor determination.

In contrast, in *Herman v. Express Sixty-Minutes Delivery Services* (1998), where the facts of the case were not substantially different from *Brock*, the 5th Circuit U.S. Court of Appeals majority opinion ruled against the DOL in a split decision.[34] The court found that drivers for Express Sixty-Minutes Delivery Service, a courier delivery service, were independent contractors even though they performed work that was integral to the nature of the company. In determining that the individuals were contractors, the court relied on the same tests used in *Brock*.[35]

These two cases demonstrate that the legal tests do not lend themselves necessarily to consistent interpretation and application; even learned judges with the benefit of extensive testimony and thousands of pages of documents cannot agree on the application of the independent contractor factors in the same case. Such uncertainty may encourage prudent employers to classify borderline cases as employees.

Table 5.1 Key Factors in Arguments in *Brock v. Superior Care*

Key factors in economic realities test	Company arguments for independent contractor status for nurses	DOL arguments for employee status for nurses
Degree of control exercised by alleged employer	No control: nurses worked with little supervision; primarily interacted with patients	Nurses' hours and notes were reviewed; worked subject to procedures in extensive manual and received some direction from physicians
Degree to which employee's opportunity for profit or loss is determined by alleged employer	Similar to independent contractor, some nurses paid flat fee per visit	No opportunity for profit and loss; nurses had no independent investment in business
Permanency of relationship	Assignment spanned from a few days to a few months, depending on patient needs; not ongoing	
Skill and initiative required	Highly skilled work requiring exercise of independent judgment and discretion and interactions with physicians and patients, similar to independent contractor	No indication that nurses used skills independently with business like initiative
Dependence on alleged employer for economic livelihood	Permitted to work for other agencies and many did, not dependent on employer for livelihood	Some paid by the hour based on local labor market conditions; had on payroll some nurses doing similar work paid as "employees"
Performing core work of alleged employer		Work performed was integral to business

Coemployment

Joint liability under the FLSA allows either party to be held accountable for the full amount of liability. By making both the staffing contractor and the client company responsible there is a greater likelihood that employees will be paid properly. Also, if one "employer" should go out of business, the other party is responsible for unpaid minimum and overtime wages. Furthermore, this avoids the legal complexities associated with determining which employer is responsible. Consequently, the DOL holds both temporary employment agencies and leasing companies jointly liable with their customer companies for back wages and penalties. In theory, by making both employers liable, the client company may be more careful in choosing responsible staffing providers. Thus, although there are a variety of risks with coemployment, those under the FLSA are potentially the most expensive (Moldover 2005).

The DOL provides this protection to employees by broadly defining coemployment status in its compliance guidelines. The regulation states that two or more employers may be deemed to be coemployers under any one of three circumstances:

1) There is an arrangement between employers to share an employee's services even with separate payrolls.

2) One employer is acting directly or indirectly in the interest of the other employer or employers in relation to the employee.

3) The employers are not completely disassociated with respect to the employment of a particular employee and may be deemed to share control of the employee, whether directly or indirectly.

Client companies using temporary or leased employees may think that the above definitions do not cover them because they do not hire or assign the employee, or discipline or discharge. However, the second criterion extends employer status to them since they act indirectly in relationship to an employee. Typically, the client company pays the staffing company amounts that are based on the hours worked and the hourly wage and benefit costs. The staffing company then acts directly in the interest of its client company with regard to the employment of individuals assigned to work at the client's establishment. Also, the client company typically "directly acts" through supervision of the temporary or leased employee in the performance of the day-to-day work. In many leasing and temporary arrangements, this may hold true even when the staffing company has a personnel administrator on the client's premises to deal with attendance, payroll, disciplinary, and discharge issues. Accordingly, in conventional temporary staffing and leasing arrangements, both the staffing company and client company are jointly responsible for FLSA compliance (see DOL 1969, 1975).

The courts generally have been supportive of the DOL coemployment guidelines. For example, in a 1998 decision, *Baystate Alternative Staffing v. Herman* (1998), the 1st Circuit U.S. Court of Appeals found that a corporate staffing company and its officers were liable for unpaid overtime even though the client employer directed the workers in their day-to-day work. Similarly, in *Hodgson v. Griffin & Brand, Inc.* (1973), the 5th Circuit U.S. Court of Appeals found that a fruit and vegetable company qualified as a joint employer of farm workers who were supplied by independent contractor crew leaders.

WORKERS' COMPENSATION LAWS

The goal of the workers' compensation programs since their creation[36] has been to maximize the social safety net provided for employees when they are injured or disabled in the course of their employment. The program covers the loss of wages and medical expenses resulting from these injuries and disabilities. Except in a few industries such as railroads, air carriers, shipping, and the federal government, workers' compensation is provided through state laws.[37]

Workers' compensation was developed as "no-fault" insurance designed to address quickly the financial effects of inevitable industrial accidents. The "exclusive remedy" doctrine grants employers immunity against personal injury lawsuits brought by employees for work-related injuries except in extremely narrow exceptions. In granting this immunity, state legislatures require employers to participate in workers' compensation plans that cover virtually all work-related injuries regardless of whether the employee is full- or part-time. The basis of payment is the experience rating of each employer: the greater the number of claims, the more the employer pays. Overall, the workers' compensation program is beneficial to the employer because the dollar amount awarded for workers' compensation claims is only a fraction of what would be awarded by a jury if the employee could sue the employer in a personal injury lawsuit. Moreover, the claims adjudication process in workers' compensation largely alleviates much of the costs of litigation.

Employee or Independent Contractor

Because only employees are eligible for workers' compensation coverage, there can be savings from employing "contractors" instead of employees, especially when an employer has an unfavorable injury rating. This situation may tempt employers to classify workers as independent contractors. However, legislatures and workers' compensation agencies have imposed stringent limitations on classifying employees as independent contractors to provide the broadest basis for coverage, so the outcome is nearly identical to that of the FLSA.

The difficulty for multistate employers and insurance carriers is that the economic realities tests used in these cases vary somewhat from state to state. For example, case law refers to a test that has been derived from various Michigan Supreme Court decisions over the years. This list identifies eight issues:

1) What liability, if any, does the employer incur in the event of the termination of the relationship at will?

2) Is the work being performed an integral part of the employer's business which contributes to the accomplishment of a common objective?

3) Is the position or job of such a nature that the employee depends upon the emolument for payment of his living expenses?

4) Does the employee furnish his own equipment and materials?

5) Does the individual seeking employment hold himself out to the public as one ready to and able to perform tasks of a given nature?

6) Is the work or the undertaking in question customarily performed by an individual as an independent contractor?

7) Control, although abandoned as an exclusive criterion upon which the relationship can be determined, is a factor to be con-

sidered along with payment of wages, maintenance of discipline and the right to engage or discharge employees.

8) Weight should be given to those factors which will most favorably effectuate the objectives of the statute (*McKissic v. Bodine* 1972).

The court cautioned that these issues "must be applied as a whole and on a basis of common sense" (*McKissic v. Bodine* 1972).

Other states apply factors similar to the above list with many expansive questions on control, not unlike the IRS 20-factor test. However, the lack of legislative activity on this issue seems to indicate that the courts are applying strict standards for independent contractors since a liberally construed test would open the floodgates for employee lawsuits.

Typically, employers err on the side of caution and carry workers' compensation insurance to cover any independent contractor who ultimately may be determined to be an employee. Absent willful deception on the part of the employer, the employer will be fully covered as though the contractor was an employee. However, the carrier or state agency often will have the right to seek retroactive premiums for any misclassified individuals.

Coemployment Issues

For many decades workers' compensation tribunals and state legislatures have recognized the "borrowed servant" doctrine (see, for example, West Publishing Co. [2002]). This doctrine recognizes that both the general employer (in this context, the temporary agency, leasing company, or staffing company) and special employer (the client company) may be obligated to provide workers' compensation benefits. This doctrine generally has been applied when one employer borrows another's employees or to specialty staffing companies, such as custodial firms, or employees that come with special equipment from the staffing company. However, it has not been consistently applied to temporary and leased employee arrangements. Because of the exclusive remedy provisions there have been inconsistencies in the interpretation of this doctrine for these two categories of workers.

When an employer retains a temporary agency's employee or enters into an employee leasing contract, the working agreement provides that the temporary agency or lessor company will handle all payroll and insurance matters and expressly includes the provision of workers' compensation benefits. When the coemployment doctrine is applied to these arrangements, often the state statute requires or implies that both companies are legally obligated to ensure that workers' compensation coverage is provided. Therefore, if the temporary agency should go out of business without providing this coverage, the employee can seek workers' compensation benefits from the client company that directly supervised the employee in day-to-day work. This generally holds true even when the temporary agency has breached its contract by failing to provide workers' compensation benefits. If the client company brings a lawsuit for breach of contract against the temporary agency, this will not alleviate any of its joint obligations in the workers' compensation system.

However, the courts generally afford the client company immunity from lawsuits when workers' compensation is provided by a temporary agency. For example, in *Sorenson v. Colibri* (1994), a Rhode Island case, an employee who was injured on the job collected workers' compensation benefits from the temporary agency's policy and then filed a lawsuit against the client employer for the same injuries under tort law. Even though the Rhode Island workers' compensation law requires that the "general" employer (the temporary agency) must provide the workers' compensation coverage, it upheld the dismissal of the lawsuit, holding that the client company was immune from employee lawsuits. The court reasoned that extending immunity to the client company was an equitable result because it is presumed that the temporary agency had charged an hourly rate to the client company that was high enough to recover the cost of workers' compensation premiums.[38] In a minority of states, however, different decisions have been made, particularly in the context of leasing arrangements, which do not give exclusive remedy immunity to the client employer.[39]

Concern has been growing among associations concerned with workers' compensation, such as the International Association of Industrial Accident Boards and Commissions and the National Association of Insurance Commissioners, about a relatively new challenge: the use of leasing arrangements by client employers to circumvent their experience ratings.[40] For example, an industrial employer may experience a high injury rate, resulting in a large increase in the price of its workers' compensation premiums. In response it could "terminate" all employees but continue to employ them through a leasing agency, thereby avoiding higher payments for its poor injury experience rating. In contrast, the leasing agency as a separate entity pays a neutral and lower rate for workers' compensation premiums. Also, there may be deliberate misrepresentations or concealments by the employer or its agents of the reported job duties of workers used for workers' compensation underwriting and quarterly earning and payroll reports.[41] Amendments to workers' compensation statutes have attempted to create a basis for using the experience ratings of the client company when employees are leased.

FEDERAL EQUAL EMPLOYMENT OPPORTUNITY LAWS

The challenge for EEO laws is to hold accountable those who are responsible for ensuring equal opportunity and to prevent discrimination in the workplace. Application of the EEO laws to the contingent worker raises issues similar to those raised under wage and benefit laws.

This discussion focuses on the three major federal statutes: Title VII of the Civil Rights Act of 1964 (Title VII), the Age Discrimination in Employment Act of 1967 (ADEA), and the 1990 Americans with Disabilities Act (ADA). The Equal Pay Act (EPA) is part of the FLSA, so liability for equal pay violations generally follows other FLSA applications as discussed above.[42] State fair employment practice or EEO laws usually follow to varying degrees the precedents set in the federal laws.

In 1997 the EEOC assembled what had been a scattering of court decisions, segments of language from various statutes and regulations, and formal guidance letters into one document addressing the applications of Title VII, ADA, and ADEA to the contingent workforce. These enforcement guidelines were provided in an easy-to-follow format illustrated with examples.[43] Although not binding on the courts, the document generally follows the weight of the case law, and may be given "due deference" by the courts. The EEOC focus on contingent work is not surprising in light of the patterns related to race and gender discussed in Chapter 2. The enforcement guidelines expressly note that the employees of temporary employment agencies are disproportionately female and African American, while workers provided by contract staffing firms are disproportionately male (U.S. EEOC 1997a, pp. 1–2).

Employee or Independent Contractor

Employers commonly use the independent contractor status as a defense against EEO claims made by individuals who work with little supervision and are paid on a commission or incentive basis. However, the EEOC has maintained a conservative posture in allowing employers to assert the independent contractor defense. The EEOC has its own unique list of 16 factors that are used to determine independent contractor status, but none of them are controlling.[44] The courts have liberally applied the hybrid test with varied outcomes, based on the facts of each situation.[45]

Coemployment

Like other employment law agencies, the EEOC has applied broadly the definition of employer to achieve the purposes of the laws for which it is responsible. In relationships between client companies and temporary agencies or employee leasing arrangements, the EEOC guidelines place great weight on whether one or both parties are in a position to control the outcome that is the subject of an alleged EEO infraction. For some infractions liability may extend to nonemployers.

Customarily the temporary staffing agency hires the individual and pays her wages throughout her tenure with the client company. The client company supervises the employee, indirectly pays for her wages and benefits, and has the right to terminate the employee and ask the temporary provider to send another worker. Under these circumstances, the EEOC guidelines indicate that both the temporary staffing agency and the client company are "employers" under the civil rights laws (U.S. EEOC 1997, p. 10). In other variations, the gradations in control and lack of control by the respective parties may change the outcome. For example, although a staffing company provides landscaping employees that it trains and supervises, the client company also may legally become an "employer" if it reserves the right to direct the workers to perform particular tasks or otherwise controls the specific manner of performance (p. 11).[46] In contrast, the guidelines indicate that in a leasing arrangement in which the leasing firm merely provides services for wages and benefits administration, the leasing firm would not be considered to be the "employer"for the purposes of Title VII (p. 8).

The EEOC broadly applies the coemployment doctrine even when one party more clearly seems at fault. For example, if a staffing firm providing nurses is asked to provide a "white nurse," and the client firm says that it will only accept white nurses, the staffing firm nonetheless is liable. The firm making a discriminatory request also is liable if it meets the threshold size test for liability (U.S. EEOC 1997, pp. 18–19).[47]

In sexual harassment cases, liability is more closely related to fault. The guidelines provide an example of a temporary agency assigning a receptionist who then is sexually harassed at the work site by her supervisor. The supervisor is an employee of the client company. She complains to the temporary agency and the temporary agency advises the client company. The client company refuses to investigate and asks for another receptionist who is not "a troublemaker." The temporary agency tells the employee that it cannot force the client to investigate and assigns another worker to the receptionist job. The guidelines conclude that, in this situation, both the temporary agency and the client are liable. The temporary agency failed to take adequate corrective action; it should have insisted that the client investigate and asserted that its workers have the right to work free from harassment.

IMPLICATIONS FOR FUTURE RESEARCH

The use of various types of contingent workers and the expansion in outsourcing to fill workforce gaps is predicted to continue in the future (Society for Human Resource Management 2005). However, the complexity of laws, lack of clarity, and potential for adverse economic effects on employers using contingent workers will continue until changes are made. Public policy initiatives designed to reduce those compliance errors that occur despite the good faith efforts of employers and make compliance easier must be balanced against the objectives of the statutes to protect workers or provide benefits to as many workers as possible. Changes pursued jointly by the federal and state governments should include agreements that create greater uniformity and consistency in the terminology, simplify and clarify the legal tests, and improve guidance for compliance.

Greater Uniformity and Consistency in Terminology

One of the major compliance challenges is the lack of a single definition of "employee" that can be used in all work-related laws. This challenge was recognized by the Dunlop Commission when it recommended the adoption of one definition of "employee" and one definition of "employer" for all workplace laws (DOL 2004). This change would greatly simplify employer compliance, particularly for small and medium-sized companies which, unlike large companies, cannot afford to retain legions of lawyers and consultants and employ staffs of dedicated experts in human resource departments. Furthermore, the cost of compliance for large firms is substantial. An economic analysis detailing the time and costs associated with the absence of universal definitions, as well as inconsistent rules and practices, will provide useful insights into these employer costs.

A comprehensive analysis of the compatibility of uniform terminology and definitions for tax, employment, and retirement benefits laws is an important first step. This analysis could help encourage federal and state agencies to reach agreement on the usage of common terms and begin to apply the laws with greater consistency. In some instances, however, this change in approach will require diligent support from legislative bodies.

Such initiatives have already begun in some areas of the law. The development of uniform model laws and practices has been urged or adopted by industry associations. For example, model legislation drafted by the National Association of Insurance Commissioners has been designed to promote a common approach by state legislatures to the licensing of leased employees and to ensure the proper experience-rating of workers' compensation premiums (Employee Leasing Registration Model Act 1997). To achieve optimal results in the interest of public policy, these cooperative efforts should be undertaken not only through the efforts of government, but with participation of the academicians, industry representatives, and technical professionals, such as lawyers.

Simplify and Clarify the Legal Tests

At present each law has a unique definition of "employee" and is interpreted by referring to lists of factors used to evaluate the facts of each situation. These legal tests have been developed over time by government bodies or created by the courts. As a consequence the interpretations of many tax, employment, and benefit laws are needlessly arcane, verbose, and perplexing.

Despite each law having its own particular guidelines, the factors used to evaluate the facts of each situation are remarkably similar. Therefore it is feasible that careful analysis of cases can lead to the development of a uniform test, or perhaps two or three types of uniform tests, to classify workers consistently in all work-related laws. It is likely that greater uniformity can be achieved without significantly sacrificing the enforcement objective of minimizing the number of independent contractors so the maximum number of employees is covered.

Provide Useful Compliance Guidelines

While it is evident that many employers struggle to understand their legal obligations when classifying workers and engaging in coemployment arrangements, governmental agencies have done little to help. Guidelines can be written in a user-friendly, "plain English" style with clear examples and illustrations that employers can easily understand for the various employment laws. An example of this approach is the EEOC's enforcement guidance document (U.S. EEOC 1997). Although the agency enforces many different laws with unique legislative histories and lengthy tests, it has created a single document that presents the full range of contingent work issues with many helpful illustrations. Case-law authority, distinctions in the application of particular EEO laws, and clear explanations of principles in an easy-to-follow, question-and-answer format are provided. More primers of this sort would be helpful to employers to demystify the legal enigmas of contingent employment arrangements.

Notes

Alvin Storrs is indebted to Matthew Rocky-Hawley, a student at Michigan State University Detroit College of Law, for his assistance with the research in this chapter. Although the topic of this chapter is legal in nature, its content is intended solely to facilitate the purpose of general information and learning. Nothing herein is intended to serve as legal advice relative to any specific or general legal question or problem. Legal advice should only be obtained through retained legal counsel who is fully informed of all of the particular facts and circumstances.

1. These include the Federal Insurance Contribution Act (FICA), Federal Unemployment Tax Act (FUTA), Fair Labor Standards Act (FLSA), National Labor Relations Act (NLRA), Title VII of the Civil Rights Act of 1964, Age Discrimination in Employment Act (ADEA), Americans with Disabilities Act (ADA), Family and Medical Leave Act (FMLA), Employee Retirement Income Security Act (ERISA), Occupational Safety and Health Act (OSHA), and state laws governing unemployment and workers' compensation. Citations for the federal statutes in the order listed are: 42 U.S.C. § 410(e); 26 U.S.C. § 3306(a); 29 U.S.C. § 203(e)(1); 29 U.S.C. § 152(3); 42 U.S.C. § 2000(c); 29 U.S.C. § 623(a)(1); 42 U.S.C. § 12111(4); 29 U.S.C. § 2611; 29 U.S.C. § 1002(6); and 29 U.S.C. § 652(6). For an example of state unemployment and workers' compensation laws, see Michigan compiled Code Laws §§ 421.42, 418.161(b).

2. The major exception is the legislation in employee benefits. The tax code amendments in the 1980s and 1990s significantly altered the arena of deferred benefits.

3. In § 530 of the Revenue Act of 1978, Congress provided so-called safe harbor tests, which prevent the IRS from retroactively reclassifying an independent contractor as an employee. This provision is extremely beneficial because it provides retroactive relief for employment taxes, penalties, and interest. A company seeking relief under § 530 must meet these requirements: have a reasonable basis for classifying a worker as an independent contractor; demonstrate consistent treatment of the worker as independent contractor for periods beginning after December 31, 1997; and file all required federal tax returns consistent with classifying the worker as independent contractor. Although the requirements appear to be straightforward, the interpretation has proven to be complex; only a relatively small number of businesses have qualified for relief.

   There are, however, other methods available to mitigate or reduce potentially onerous employment tax penalties and interest. For example, see I.R.C. § 3509 which provides reduced employment tax liability for certain retroactive reclassifications of workers. Form 1099 is a document used to report nonemployee compensation for independent contractors. If Form 1099 is filed for workers, then the employer's tax liability is 1.5 percent of wages for income tax withholding and 20 percent of employee's share of Social Security taxes. If Form 1099 is not filed, the above 1.5 percent is increased to 3.0 percent and the above 20 percent to 40 percent. I.R.C. § 6205 allows a special interest-free adjustment for certain underpayments of FICA and income tax withholding. I.R.C. § 3402(d) provides for retroactive relief from the assessment of income tax liability if the employer can prove that the worker reported the income assessed on the Form 1040 return. Also, in I.R.S. Notice 98-21, 1998-15 I.R.B. 14, the IRS classification settlement program has been extended indefinitely. This program is designed to resolve worker classification issues as soon as possible in the administrative process. If a taxpayer satisfies certain requirements then the taxpayer may pay a reduced employment tax liability.

4. For example, see the summary of the risks of leasing workers in Dunn and Berkery (2005).

5. Part-time and seasonal employees are not discussed in depth. Contrary to popular belief, there is no universal or even prevailing definition of a part-time employee among the various labor, employment, and retirement benefit laws. Many of these laws employ exact definitions determined by the number of hours in a year or in a week that can affect coverage, exemptions, and obligations. Consequently, human resources, employee benefits, and attorney practitioners are cautioned to review carefully how employees are defined relative to the number of hours worked and full-time status in every labor, employment, and retirement benefit law. For example, the Fair Labor Standards Act (FLSA) exempts from overtime certain seasonal employees connected with amusement industries (29. U.S.C. § 213(a)(3)). Eligibility for coverage under statutes such as the Employee Retirement Income Security Act (ERISA) and the Family and Medical Leave Act (FMLA) often is defined in terms of a minimum threshold of a specific number of hours worked in a year or given time period. For example, ERISA requires a minimum threshold of 1,000 hours before existing law mandates that an employee cannot be excluded from participation in a retirement plan on the basis of hours worked. The FMLA does not apply to a worker who has worked less than 1,250 hours during the 12-month period immediately preceding the commencement of the leave.

6. Similarly, the firm contracting its services may be referred to as the lessee, lessee employer, special employer, secondary employer, client employer (or company), customer employer (or company), borrowing employer, or contracting employer. More recently, leasing companies have begun calling themselves professional employer organizations (PEOs) (BPI Communications 1999).

7. For example, in 1999 the U.S. Department of Labor alleged that Time Warner misclassified as many as 1,000 of its 40,000 workers to reduce its employee benefits costs (*Herman v. Time Warner, Inc.* 1999). A similar case occurred with FedEx in California when it classified drivers as independent contractors (Nicholas 2005).

8. The common-law test is used by the IRS and has been applied by the courts to the FICA, FUTA, ERISA, NLRA, and income tax withholding. The economic realities test has been applied by the courts to the FLSA and Equal Pay Act, Title VII, ADEA, ADA, and FMLA. The hybrid test has been applied by the courts to Title VII, ADEA, and ADA (Muhl 2002, p. 6).

9. These 10 factors are 1) right to control, 2) type of business, 3) supervision, 4) skill level, 5) tools and materials, 6) continuing relationship, 7) method of payment, 8) integration, 9) intent, and 10) employment by more than one firm (Muhl 2002, pp. 5–7).

10. The 20 factors are: 1) instructions; 2) integration; 3) right of discharge; 4) right to terminate; 5) services rendered personally; 6) hiring, supervising, and paying assistants; 7) training; 8) payment by hour, week, month; 9) payment of business and/or traveling expenses; 10) continuing relationship; 11) set hours of work; 12) full time required; 13) working for more than one firm at a time; 14) making service available to general public; 15) furnishing of tools and materials; 16) doing work on employer's premises; 17) order of sequence set; 18) oral or written report; 19) significant investment; and 20) realization of profit or loss. See Rev. Rul. 87-41, 1987-1 C.B. 296 for a description of each factor.

11. For example, see *Illinois Tri-Seal Products, Inc. v. U.S.* (1965); *Bonney Motor Express Inc. v. U.S.* (1962); *In re Rasbury* (1991); and *Butts v. Comm'r* (1993).

12. For example, see the following sections of the Internal Revenue Code: 1) § 6651: The penalty for the failure to pay employment taxes has a maximum of 25 percent, which is calculated at 0.5 percent of the unpaid tax each month. This code section also has a penalty for failure to file employment tax returns with a maximum of 25 percent, which is assessed at 5 percent per month; 2) § 6662: It imposes a penalty of 20 percent of the underpayment attributable to negligence; 3) § 6663: If serious abuse is found there is a 75 percent penalty of underpayment due to fraud; 4) § 6656: A failure to deposit penalty can range from 2 percent to 15 percent of the underpaid deposit. This penalty is imposed in addition to failure to pay the penalty; 5) § 6721: A penalty of $15 to $50 per return is charged for the failure to file the correct information return such as a W-2. The maximum penalty is $250,000 with a reduced maximum of $100,000 for small employers; 6) § 6722: If an employer fails to provide timely W-2s to employees, a penalty of $50 per return may be assessed. The maximum penalty is $100,000.

13. The six factors are 1) integration, 2) investment in facilities, 3) right to control, 4) risk, 5) skill, and 6) continuing relationship (Muhl 2002, pp. 6–9).

14. Artists – Compare Rev. Rul. 57-155, 1957-I C.B. 333 with Rev. Rul. 65-262, 1965-2 C.B. 391; Loggers – Compare Rev. Rul. 71-273, 1971-1 C.B. 286 with Rev. Rul. 71-274, 1971-1 C.B. 287; Repairers – Compare Rev. Rul. 55-248, 1955-1 C.B. 117 with Rev. Rul. 55-370, 1955-1 C.B. 122.

15. I.R.C. §§ 3301–3311 (FUTA); 3101–3128 (FICA).

16. The Social Security tax is imposed at a rate of 12.4 percent on a changing wage base, while the Medicare tax is 2.9 percent on all wages. These taxes are imposed half on the employer as an excise tax and half on the employee in the form of a withholding tax collected from the employee's wages by the employer.

17. The FUTA tax is imposed solely on employers at a rate of 6.2 percent on the first $7,000 of the employee's wages. Generally, a credit is allowed against the FUTA tax for amounts paid into state unemployment funds. This credit cannot exceed 5.4 percent of first $7,000 of wages. If the maximum credit of 5.4 percent is allowed, the FUTA tax rate after the credit is 0.8 percent.

18. Compensation paid to independent contractors is subject to the Self Employ-
    ment Contributions Act (SECA) tax. The self-employed tax rate is 15.3 percent
    (I.R.C. §§ 1401–1403). The independent contractor pays an amount equal to the
    employee plus the employer portion of the FICA tax. In an attempt to mitigate a
    double tax burden, the independent contractor is allowed to deduct one-half of
    self-employment taxes as an adjustment to gross income and for SECA purpos-
    es (I.R.C. §§ 164(f)(1); 1402(a)(12)). The same definition of employee used in
    FICA also applies for SECA to exclude individuals who are not subject to SECA
    tax (I.R.C. § 1402(d)).
19. Two recent cases in Idaho illustrate that this classification problem continues to
    create enforcement challenges. See the discussion of the problem of classifying
    workers at Excell Construction, Inc. (Idaho Supreme Court Reviews Test for
    Independent Contractor Status [2005]).
20. A temporary employee is sometimes defined as one who is retained with an ex-
    pectation of being employed for one year or less and who has worked for the
    current employer for less than one year. There are two categories of temporary
    employees: 1) employees of an organization in a "temporary" status with no
    expectation of continued employment and 2) employees who are hired, referred,
    and sometimes supervised in part by a temporary employment agency. See Hip-
    ple (1998).
    The terminology "leased workers" is somewhat new. However, the con-
    cept of "borrowed servant"—when one employer borrows the employees of
    another—can be traced at least to the 1930s and the early years of workers'
    compensation laws. An entire industry known as "employee leasing" emerged
    in the United States during the 1980s and early 1990s. Setting aside the various
    statutory definitions, in this discussion the term "leased employees" refers to
    employees who are hired, referred, assigned, and in some respects supervised by
    an outside firm (leasing agency) with an expectation of employment longer than
    one year, but the assignment can be indefinite. Thus, a leased employee is differ-
    ent from a temporary employee since the latter is assigned with the expectation
    of employment for one year or less.
21. It also may be referred to as "joint employment" or "dual employment."
22. I.R.C. § 404.
23. I.R.C. §§ 410(b) and 401(a)(4).
24. See *Nationwide Mutual Insurance Co. v. Darden* (1992), where the court used
    only 12 factors in making the decision. See also *Hensley v. Northwest Permanete
    P.C.* (2001), in which it was determined that the plan administrator did not err
    when interpreting the undefined term "employee" in a pension plan by using the
    W-2 definition and not the common-law definition.
25. I.R.C. § 401(a)(2).
26. The definition of one year of service is a 12-month period during which an em-
    ployee works at least 1,000 hours. I.R.C. § 410(a)(l)(a)(ii) & (3). Careful moni-
    toring of hours worked is required to ensure that part-time employees expected
    to work less than 1,000 hours are included if they in fact work more than 1,000
    hours.

27. See Rev. Proc. 2003-44, 2003-C.B. where the administrative program is called the Employee Plans Compliance Resolution System (EPCRS) and includes the following corrective programs: Self-Correction Program (SCP), Voluntary Correction Program (VCP), and the Audit Closing Agreement Program (Audit Cap).

28. I.R.C. §§ 414(n)(3)(a) and 414(n)(2). However, there is a statutory exception that provides that the recipient organization will not be required to include the leased employees for testing purposes if the leasing organization maintains a money purchase plan which meets certain requirements and no more than 20 percent of the non-highly-compensated employees of the recipient are leased. The money purchase plan must provide: 1) a minimum contribution of 10 percent of compensation; 2) immediate participation in the plan; and 3) 100 percent vesting in benefits at all times (I.R.C. § 414(n)(5)). However, it is unusual for a leasing organization to maintain such a generous qualified retirement plan.

29. The protracted *Vizcaino v. Microsoft* litigation spawned appellate victories for independent contractors and Microsoft. See *Vizcaino v. Microsoft Corp.* (1996, 1997). Microsoft, as part of the settlement for the case, changed its worker classification practices. This resulted in 3,000 of the litigants being hired as regular employees entitled to participate in the retirement plans. A similar case occurred in Massachusetts (*Langone v. USCO Distribution Services, Inc.* 2005). See Barran (2005).

30. The FLSA is enforced by the Wage-Hour Division of the U.S. Department of Labor. While state laws also regulate wages and hours and impose similar and additional obligations, this discussion is limited to the FLSA. The FLSA regulations were revised to add income tests effective August 23, 2004. 1938 law, as amended (*Fair Labor Standards Act* 2003).

31. A recent example of a company misclassifying street sweepers in California as independent contractors is seen in *Garces v. Cannon Pacific Services* (October 4, 2005) (Cole 2005).

32. The four factors are 1) the extent to which the services in question are an integral part of the employer's business, 2) the amount of the alleged contractor's investment in facilities and equipment, 3) the alleged contractor's opportunities for profit *and* loss, and 4) the amount of initiative, judgment, or foresight in open market competition required for the success of the enterprise.

33. The courts do not consider the wage-hour guidelines as controlling, although the weight of the case law is largely consistent with the guidelines. Some courts have amplified the tests with factors such as the skill level of the alleged contractor and the contractor having other clients. For example, see *Brock v. Superior Care, Inc.* (1988).

34. In a five-page dissenting opinion, Judge King concluded that the workers were employees. The majority opinion, he said, erred in departing from a long line of cases followed in that circuit.

35. The five tests used were 1) Control: Even though the individuals were required to wear uniforms and attend a special training session, the court found that they could control their own hours, days of work, and reject any delivery without re-

taliation. 2) Opportunity for profit and loss: Drivers were paid on a commission basis, but the majority opinion found that profit and loss was nonetheless driven by worker's ability to cut costs and understand the courier business. 3) Permanency of relationship: The court observed that most of the drivers only worked for the company for a short period of time and were able to work for other companies. No noncompete agreement was required. 4) Skill and initiative required: The court found that the drivers must determine the route, read MAPSCO, and choose alternate routes. The majority opinion further noted that these skills require the workers to use industry and efficiency indicative of independence and nonemployee status. 5) Relative investment of the worker and alleged employer: The court found that the necessity of owning a vehicle, paying insurance, and buying a dolly, tarp, a two-way radio, pager, and a medical delivery bag constituted a substantial investment.

36. Wisconsin was the first state to pass a comprehensive workers' compensation law (1911), and Mississippi was the last state (1948) Guyton (1999).

37. See Federal Employers' Liability Act (FELA); 45 U.S.C. Section 5(1), *et seq.* (airline and railroad employees); Longshoreman's and Harbor Worker's Compensation Act, 33 U.S.C. Section 901 *et seq.*, and the Federal Employees' Compensation Act, 5 U.S.C. Section 8101 *et seq.* Unemployment compensation benefits also are offered under state laws to complement workers' compensation. However, the basic features of these state programs must comply with federal laws to be eligible for revenues and funding from the federal unemployment tax (FUTA).

38. Other state jurisdictions have reached a similar conclusion in analogous cases. For example, a Florida court reached a similar conclusion. In *Maxson Construction Co. v. Welch* (1998), an injured leased employee brought a tort action against the client company of his leasing company employer. The Florida Court of Appeals held that immunity would apply to the client employer even though Florida's leasing statute made the leasing company responsible for paying workers' compensation premiums. As in the Rhode Island decision, the court justified its decision pointing out that the client company indirectly paid workers' compensation premiums. Also see cases in California, Iowa, Michigan, Minnesota, New Hampshire, Texas, South Dakota, and Wisconsin (*Wedeck v. Unocal Corp.* (1997); *Jones v. Sheller-Globe Corp.* (1992); *Danek v. Meldrum Mfg. and Eng'g Co., Inc.* (1977); *Farrell v. Dearborn Mfg. Co.* (1982); *LaVallie v. Wire and Cable Co.* (1992); *Regalado v. H.E. Butt Grocery Co.* (1993); *Gansch v. Nekoosa Papers, Inc.* (1990)).

39. For example, an injured employee in North Dakota who was covered by the workers' compensation policy of the leasing company that hired him brought a tort action against the client company. The North Dakota Supreme Court declined to extend employer status and its accompanying immunity to both the leasing company and the client company. The court explained that the North Dakota workers' compensation law relieves only "contributing employers," even though the client company paid an hourly fee that "probably" covered the cost of workers' compensation premiums. The court noted that allowing such indirect

payment to trigger immunity could extend immunity to most independent contractors who indirectly recoup the costs of benefits from their clients (*Cervantes v. Drayton Foods, L.L.C.* 1998). A similar decision was rendered by the Ohio appellate court, which also held that such indirect payments were insufficient to extend immunity to the client company (*Carr v. Central Printing Co.* 1997).

40. Telephone and personal interviews conducted by Thomas Coens with representatives and members of these associations in several states and Washington, D.C. (March 1999–September 1999).

41. For examples of cases of judgments against client companies in workers' compensation cases, see West Publishing Company (2001, 2003) and *Del Industrial, Inc. v. Texas* (1998).

42. Equal Pay Act: 29 U.S.C. § 206 (1963).

43. The Equal Employment Opportunity Commission (EEOC) is responsible for the enforcement of Title VII, the ADA, ADEA, and EPA (EEOC 1997).

44. The 16 factors are 1) the firm or the client has the right to control when, where, and how the worker performs the job; 2) the work does not require a high level of skill or expertise; 3) the firm or the client rather than the worker furnishes the tools, materials, and equipment; 4) the work is performed on the premises of the firm or the client; 5) there is a continuing relationship between the worker and the firm or the client; 6) the firm or the client has the right to assign additional projects to the worker; 7) the firm or the client sets the hours of work and the duration of the job; 8) the worker is paid by the hour, week, or month rather than for the agreed costs of performing a particular job; 9) the worker has no role in hiring and paying assistants; 10) the work performed by the worker is part of the regular business of the firm or the client; 11) the firm or the client is itself in business; 12) the worker is not engaged in his or her own distinct occupation or business; 13) the firm or the client provides the worker with benefits such as insurance, leave, or workers' compensation; 14) the worker is considered an employee of the firm or the client for tax purposes, i.e., the entity withholds federal, state, and Social Security taxes; 15) the firm or the client can discharge the worker; and 16) the worker and the firm or client believe that they are creating an employer-employee relationship (U.S. EEOC 1997).

45. For example, see the following cases: *Deal v. State Farm County Mut. Ins. Co. of Tex.* (1993); *Jones v. Seko Messenger, Inc.* (1997); and *Lane v. David P. Jacobson & Co., LTD.* (1995).

46. The EEOC's position stems, in part, from an earlier case, *Amarnare v. Merrill Lynch* (1984). In this case an employee of a temporary agency sued for race and gender discrimination under Title VII when she was discharged from her temporary assignment and the client company refused to offer her a regular position. The client company contended that there was no employer-employee relationship. The court found, however, that the client company was the employer because it controlled the plaintiff's hours, workplace, and assignments; it supervised and trained her; and ultimately it "discharged" her.

47. The threshold for liability for the client firm is 15 employees for Title VII and ADA and 20 employees for the ADEA.

References

Abraham v. Exxon Corp. 1996. 85 F3d 1126.

Age Discrimination in Employment Act. 2003. U.S. Code Annotated. Vol. 29, secs. 621 *et seq.*

Amarnare v. Merrill Lynch. 1984. 611 F. Supp 344 (S.D. N.Y. 1984), *aff'd,* 770 F.2d 157 (2d Cir.).

Americans with Disabilities Act. U.S. Code Annotated. Vol. 42, sec.12111(4).

Assessments. 2003. *U. S. Code Annotated.* Vol. 26, Sec. 6205.

Barran, P.A. 2005. "Commentary: Not So Fast—That Temp May Be Your Employee." *Kansas City Daily Record,* October 31. Available at http://www .findarticles.com/p/articles/mi_qn4181/is_20051031/ai_n15823980   (accessed April 26, 2006).

Baystate Alternative Staffing, Inc. v. Herman. 1998. 163 F.3d 668 (D. Mass.).

Bonney Motor Express Inc. v. United States. 1962. 206 F. Supp. 22 (E.D. Va.).

BPI Communications. 1999. "Employee Leasing Laws Abstracts." BPI Communications. August/September: 1.

Brock v. Superior Care, Inc. 1988. 840 F.2d 1054 (2nd. Cir.), (*motion for clarification*), 840 F.2d 1064 (2nd. Cir.).

Bronk v. Mountain States Telephone and Telegraph, Inc. 1996. 943 F. Supp. 1317 (D. Colo. 1996), *rev'd,* 140 F.3d 1335 (10th. Cir.).

Butts v. Comm'r. 1993. 66 T.C.M. (CCH) 1041 (1993), *aff'd* 49 F.3d 713 (11th Cir.).

Carr v. Central Printing Co. 1997. CA Case No. 16091, 1997 Ohio App LEXIS 2525, at *1 (Ohio Ct. App. June 13, 1997).

Cervantes v. Drayton Foods, L.L.C. 1998. N.D. 138, 582 N.W.2d 2.

Civil Rights Act. 2003. *U.S. Code Annotated.* Vol. 42, sec. 2000(e) *et seq.*

Clark v. E.I. DuPont De Nemours and Co., Inc, No. 98-2845, 1997 U.S. App. LEXIS 321, at *1 (4th Cir. Jan. 9, 1997).

Cole, P. 2005. "Firm Engages in Sweeping Violations of Overtime Pay." *California Employment Law Letter* 15(October): 16.

Consolidated Flooring Services v. United States. 1997. 38 Fed. Cl. 450.

*Danek v. Meldrum Mfg. and Eng'g Co., Inc.*1977. 312 Minn. 404, 252 N.W.2d 255.

Deal v. State Farm County Mut. Ins. Co. of Tex. 1993. 5 F.3d 117 (5th Cir.).

Del Industrial, Inc. v. Texas. 1998. 1998 Tex. App. LEXIS 4331, 973 S.W.2d 743.

Dunn and Berkery. 2005. "Employee Leasing: The Risks for Lessees." *Michigan Bar Journal* 84(August): 22.

Employee Retirement Income Security Act. 2003. *U.S. Code Annotated.* Vol. 29, sec. 1002(6).

Fair Labor Standards Act. 2003. *U.S. Code Annotated.* Vol. 29, secs. 201, 203(e)(1), 206, 213(a)(3).

Family and Medical Leave Act. 2003. *U.S. Code Annotated.* Vol. 29, secs. 2611 *et seq.*

Farrell v Dearborn Mfg. Co. 1982. 416 Mich. 267, 330 N.W.2d 397.

Federal Insurance Contribution Act. 2003. *U.S. Code Annotated.* Vol. 42, sec. 410(e).

Federal Unemployment Tax Act. 2003. *U.S. Code Annotated.* Vol. 26, sec. 3306(a).

Gansch v. Nekoosa Papers, Inc. 1990. 158 Wisc. 2d 743, 463 N.W.2d 682.

General Motors Corp. v. United States. 1990. No. 98-CV-73046-DT, 1990 US Dist. LEXIS 17986, at *1 (E.D. Mich. Dec. 20, 1990).

Guyton, G.P. 1999. "A Brief History of Workers' Compensation." *The Iowa Orthopaedic Journal* 19: 106–110.

Hensley v. Northwest Permanete P.C. 2001. 258 F.3d 986 (9th Cir.), *cert. denied,* 534 U.S. 1082 (2002).

Herman v. Express Sixty-Minutes Delivery Service, Inc. 1998. 6 F.3d 299 (5th Cir.).

Herman v. Time Warner Inc. 1999. 56 F. Supp. 2d 411 (S.D.N.Y.).

Hipple, S. 1998. "Contingent Work: Results from the Second Survey." *Monthly Labor Review* 121(November): 22–35.

Hodgson v. Griffin and Brand, Inc. 1973. 471 F.2d 235 (5th. Cir.), *reh'g denied,* 472 F.2d 1405 (5th. Cir.), *cert. denied,* 414 U.S. 819 (1973).

"Idaho Supreme Court Reviews Test for Independent Contractor Status." 2005. *Idaho Employment Law Letter* 10(August): 5.

Illinois Tri-Seal Products Inc. v. United States. 1965. 353 F.2d 216 (Ct. Cl.).

In re Rasbury, 130 B.R. 990 (Bankr. N.D. Ala. 1991), *aff=d on other grounds,* 141 B.R. 752 (Bankr. N.D. Ala. 1992).

In re Vizcaino, 173 F.3d 713 (9th Cir. 1999).

Jones v. Seko Messenger, Inc. 1997. 955 F. Supp. 931 (N.D. IlL.).

Jones v. Sheller-Globe Corp. 1992. 1992 Iowa App. LEXIS 54, 487 N.W.2d 88.

Lane v. David P. Jacobson & Co., LTD. 1995. 880 F Supp 1091 (ED Va).

Langone v. USCO Distribution Services, Inc. 2005. U.S. Dist. LEXIS 20410 (D. Mass., 2005).

LaVallie v. Wire and Cable Co. 1992. 135 N.H. 692, 609 A2d 1216.

Maxson Construction Co. v. Welch. 1998. 23 Fla. L. Weekly D. 2324, 72 So.2d 588.

McKissic v. Bodine. 1972. 42 Mich. App. 203, 201 N.W.2d, 333.

Michigan. 2002. *Michigan Compiled Laws Annotated.* St. Paul, MN: West Group.

Moldover, J.A. 2005. "Outsourcing: Who's the Boss?" *New York Law Journal,* April 4.

Muhl, Charles J. 2002. "What Is an Employee? The Answer Depends on the Federal Law." *Monthly Labor Review* 125(1): 3–11.

National Labor Relations Act. 2003. *U.S. Code Annotated.* Vol. 29, sec. 152(3).

Nationwide Mutual Insurance Co. v. Darden. 1992. 503 U.S. 318.

Nicholas, A. 2005. "FedEx Independent Contractors Sue for Employee Benefits." *Corporate Legal Times* (June): 68.

Occupational Safety and Health Act. 2003. *U.S. Code Annotated.* Vol. 29, sec. 652(6).

Regalado v. H.E. Butt Grocery Co. 1993. Tex. App. LEXIS 2729, 863 S.W.2d 107.

Rutherford Food Corp. v. McComb. 1947a. 331 U.S. 722.

Rutherford Food Corp. v. McComb. 1947b. 331 U.S. 728.

Society for Human Resource Management. 2005. "SHRM Predicts the Human Capital Metrics of the Future." *HRFOCUS,* August, 7.

Sorenson v. Colibri Corp. 1994. 650 A.2d 125 (R.I.).

U.S. Department of Labor (DOL). 1969. W & H Op. Ltr. No. 960 (March 6).

———. 1975. W & H Op. Ltr. No. 1403 (July 31).

———. 2003. "Wage-Hour Division." *Field Operations Handbook.* Rev. 596, October 20.

———. 2004. *Report and Recommendations: Executive Summary: Commission on the Future of Worker Management Relations.* Washington, DC: U.S. Department of Labor, p. 13.

U.S. Department of the Treasury. Internal Revenue Service. Notice 98-21, 1998-15 I.R.B. 14.

———. Rev. Proc. 2003-44, 2003 - C.B.

———. Rev. Rul. 55-248, 1955-1 C.B. 117.

———. Rev. Rul. 55-370, 1955-1 C.B. 122.

———. Rev. Rul. 57-155, 1957-1 C.B. 333.

———. Rev. Rul. 65-262, 1965-2 C.B. 391.

———. Rev. Rul. 71-273, 1971-1 C.B. 286.

———. Rev. Rul. 71-274, 1971-1 C.B. 287.

———. Rev. Rul. 87-41, 1987-1 C.B. 296.

U.S. Equal Employment Opportunity Commission (EEOC). 1997a. EEOC Notice No. 915.002. "Enforcement Guidance: Application of EEO Laws to Contingent Workers Placed by Temporary-Employment Agencies and Other Staffing Firms."

Vizcaino v. Microsoft Corp. 1996. 97 F.3d 1187 (9th Cir.).

Vizcaino v. Microsoft Corp. 1997. 120 F.3d 1006 (9th Cir.) (en banc).

Wedeck v. Unocal Corp. 1997. 59th Cal. App. 4th 848, 69 Cal. Rptr. 2d 501.

West Publishing Company. 2001. "Rates and Rating Organizations, Rate and Rate Making." In *West's Oregon Revised Statutes.* St. Paul, MN: Thomson/ West.

———. 2002 "Labour and Workers' Compensation." In *West's Louisiana Revised Statutes Annotated.* St. Paul, MN: West Group.

———. *West's Florida Statutes Annotated.* St. Paul, MN: West Group.

6
Public Policy and Contingent Workers

Jeffrey B. Wenger
University of Georgia

The growth of contingent employment from 1970 to the present has been met with a resounding silence about possible federal and state-level public policy responses. This lack of response is not surprising since systematic public policy responses to changes in the labor force are difficult to enact in the United States due to the absence of a true national labor policy. There exists instead a fragmented system: federal legislation is implemented by the states, but the rules are interpreted by the courts. Policy responses therefore are limited by both U.S. federalism and the autonomy of the states. (For one example see the detailed discussion of the constitutional issues surrounding the Social Security Act of 1935 in Haber and Murray [1966]). This cumbersome system often fails to keep pace with the needs of workers as labor market conditions change. Current public policies governing contingent employment have arisen from the haphazard application of existing policies rather than the development of new policies designed to address the specific circumstances of contingent workers.

The policy difficulties inherent in the system stem from the single-minded aim of policymakers when the existing labor market policies were being developed: to provide protections for the benefit of regular full-time workers. This focus was a historical accident because the workforce was primarily full time and male when the key U.S. labor policies such as unemployment insurance and the minimum wage were enacted in the 1930s. Policies that have an impact on nonstandard and contingent workers do so only because contingent workers are caught in the penumbrae of policies developed for full-time workers, not because policies have been developed specifically for the benefit of contingent workers.

Eligibility requirements are the key to understanding the impact of labor market policies on contingent workers. These requirements establish the rules by which an individual qualifies for benefits. By specifying eligibility criteria, policymakers determine whom they want covered by the policy. Often the unintended consequence of these eligibility requirements is to limit access to social insurance by minorities and women, who are disproportionately represented in the contingent workforce (as discussed in Chapter 2).

There are essentially three ways in which a contingent worker may be deemed ineligible for coverage. Most commonly, the contingent worker fails to meet the work-based requirements for eligibility. These requirements stipulate rules governing the hours worked, amount earned, or the distribution of earnings during the year. Those with full-time jobs and those who earn more qualify for benefits, while those with part-time jobs or limited hours of work are deemed ineligible. A second factor determining ineligibility is employment in an industry or with a firm that is exempted from the legislation. There are numerous examples of farm workers and employees of small firms that are not covered by labor legislation. Finally, there are the gray areas of labor legislation where the courts have not yet decided whether the laws apply to certain types of workers. These gray areas have emerged in issues concerning the Occupational Safety and Health Act (OSHA) discussed on p. 192 and employer-provided benefits such as pensions and stock options, as in *Vizcaino v. Microsoft Corporation* (May 12, 1999).

When evaluating the impact of labor market policies, analysts use four criteria: 1) economic efficiency, 2) equity, 3) security, and 4) liberty. (For a complete discussion of these criteria, see Stone [1988]). Economic efficiency is determined by evaluating the relationship between the increased coverage and its marginal cost. In this sense we can consider a policy efficient if the most people are covered for the least cost. Equity means treating people in similar situations in the same way. Security is defined as providing benefits to those most at risk. However, economic efficiency and security often will be at odds with one another. For example, providing health insurance to the most ill may improve security, but the extra cost is likely to be disproportionately high. Finally, liberty examines when a policy intervention is justified: when should a government impress a collective outcome on an individual? This is generally interpreted to mean that government should intervene during those times when an individual's actions adversely affect other people. One example is when an individual does not take into consideration the effects of auto emissions on others. In this case there is an opportunity for government action to correct this outcome.

For each of the public policies discussed in this chapter, eligibility rules are used as a starting point to examine the efficiency and equity of the program. Eligibility rules determine whether contingent or nonstandard workers are likely to be eligible and therefore covered (equity), and whether coverage can be expanded to include contingent workers with only modest increases in cost (efficiency). The likelihood that nonstandard workers will need the program (security) and the rationale for altering the eligibility criteria and coverage of these public policies (liberty) also are examined.

The discussion is focused on those policies that affect individual workers directly: employer-provided benefits of health insurance and pensions, unemployment insurance, family and medical leave, minimum wages, and occupational safety and health. Clearly this is not an exhaustive list of public policies affecting workers; however, these policies are representative of those that are likely to directly impact contingent and nonstandard employment relationships.

EMPLOYER-PROVIDED BENEFITS

Employer-provided benefits have recently been the subject of considerable litigation and debate in the courts and state and federal legislatures. The Ninth Circuit Court of Appeals found in the widely publicized case *Vizcaino v. Microsoft* that temporary employees were in fact "common law" employees of the Microsoft Corporation. Consequently, the court found that Microsoft had wrongly denied benefits worth millions of dollars to employees because they had been misclassified as independent contractors or freelancers.

Legal challenges to the classification of contingent workers have a long history. Part of the challenge of properly classifying employees results from the ambiguity of the tax status of these workers. The Internal Revenue Service (IRS) has filed a number of lawsuits in an effort to determine who is responsible for an employee's payroll taxes. (For a discussion of the legal relationship between temporary help employers and workers, see Parker [1994)]; Gonos [1997]; duRivage, Carré, and Tilley [1998]). The court also has made considerable headway in determining who is an "employee" and under what criteria the employer is responsible for enforcing a number of federal statutes. Carnevale, Jennings, and Eisenmann (1998) have outlined many of the requirements necessary to be considered an employee (as opposed to a contractor or temporary worker). As discussed in Chapter 5, there are a number of multifactor legal tests for distinguishing between an employee and an independent contractor. One of the most important factors has been determining "the extent of the employer's control and supervision over the worker, including directions on scheduling and performance of work" (p. 288).

Health Insurance

Legislative changes extending employer-provided benefits to employees have been considerably more modest than legal rulings. Most changes have been concerned with maintaining worker access to health insurance benefits. The Consolidated Omnibus Budget Reconciliation Act of 1985 (COBRA) allows employees (under certain circumstances[1]) to continue their employers' group health care plan by paying for the policy themselves. COBRA provides insurance at group rates rather than individual health insurance rates for up to 18 months after coverage would have otherwise ended. More recently, the Health Insurance Portability and Accountability Act (HIPAA) of 1996 protects workers when they seek to buy, keep, or switch their health insurance, even when workers have serious preexisting medical conditions.

From the perspective of contingent workers, these workplace policies have two highly problematic eligibility criteria. To be eligible, your employer must have insurance that covers 20 or more employees. Also, the worker must have been laid off or had her working hours reduced. A worker fired for gross misconduct is ineligible. One of the most serious limitations of the policy is that it provides no subsidy for those who cannot afford the coverage. HIPAA protects only those who can demonstrate health insurance coverage for 18 months without a significant interruption, where significant interruption is defined as an interruption that exceeds 63 days.

However, these policies are of little help to contingent workers since very few have health insurance coverage provided by their employer. We can see in Table 6.1 that most contingent workers and most nonstandard workers do not receive health insurance from their employers.

The low rates of employer-provided health insurance among nearly all types of nonstandard employment demonstrates the narrow cast of HIPAA. Few workers are helped by a policy providing health insurance portability if they do not have health insurance initially. Looking at the insurance rates overall, a better picture emerges: workers in nonstandard employment are approximately 12.6 percent less likely to have health insurance coverage than regular full-time workers (75.6 percent and 88.2 percent, respectively). It is also likely that some of those with insurance will fail to meet the continuous coverage requirements of HIPAA that ensure portability. The biggest differences are among part-time and full-time workers. For example, only 18.5 percent of regular part-time workers receive health insurance from their employers, while 69.0 percent of regular full-time workers receive employer-provided health insurance.[2]

While Table 6.1 indicates that the majority of workers in nonstandard employment do not receive health insurance benefits from their employers, the majority of nonstandard workers do have some insurance, most likely through a family member or the government. While the lack of coverage is not dire for nonstandard workers, spousal coverage is costly since employers typically pay only their employees' portion of the premium. This means greater out-of-pocket expenditures for health coverage for workers in nonstandard employment relative to regular full-time jobs.

Pensions

Much like health insurance, pension coverage for nonstandard workers is very limited. Table 6.2 shows that workers in full-time employment are about 3.5 times more likely to receive a pension from their employer than are workers in nonstandard jobs (52.8 percent and 16.0 percent, respectively). The biggest differences in pension coverage are based on hours of work. Part-time workers are considerably less likely to have pension coverage. This finding is consistent with some literature

Table 6.1 Percentage of Workers with Health Insurance Coverage, by Work Arrangement and Sex, 2001

	All		Women		Men	
	Any coverage	Through own employer	Any coverage	Through own employer	Any coverage	Through own employer
All	84.8	54.3	86.0	50.7	83.8	57.4
All nonstandard arrangements	75.6	13.7	77.7	14.8	73.0	12.4
Full-time						
Temporary help agency	46.9	12.8	49.9	11.0	43.0	15.2
On-call/day laborer	69.1	49.0	76.4	39.8	66.3	52.5
Self-employed	82.2	n/a	80.1	n/a	83.0	n/a
Independent contractor, WS[a]	66.8	23.2	65.4	17.6	67.5	25.8
Independent contractor, SE[b]	73.2	n/a	75.2	n/a	72.5	n/a
Contract company	84.7	58.2	88.8	54.9	83.3	59.4
Regular full-time	88.2	69.0	89.6	66.8	87.0	70.8
Part-time						
Temporary help agency	58.3	0.6	70.0	0.9	36.9	0.0
On-call/day laborer	67.0	11.0	69.9	10.6	60.8	12.0
Self-employed	85.6	n/a	88.0	n/a	78.5	n/a
Independent contractor, WS[a]	72.8	10.1	77.8	4.7	64.5	19.0
Independent contractor, SE[b]	75.1	n/a	81.5	n/a	61.4	n/a
Contract company	81.0	14.9	80.5	12.7	82.0	19.0
Regular part-time	76.6	18.5	78.5	19.4	72.0	15.9

[a] Wage and salary.
[b] Self-employed.
SOURCE: U.S. Department of Labor, Bureau of Labor Statistics, The Current Population Survey (CPS) Supplements, Contingent and Alternative Employment Arrangements, February 2001; analysis by author.

Table 6.2 Percentage of Workers with Pension Coverage, by Work Arrangement and Sex, 2001

	All		Women		Men	
	Any coverage	Through own employer	Any coverage	Through own employer	Any coverage	Through own employer
All	60.4	52.8	59.3	52.4	61.5	53.3
All nonstandard arrangements	38.5	16.0	37.7	20.1	39.6	11.1
Full-time						
Temporary help agency	24.1	11.3	24.9	10.2	23.0	12.7
On-call/day laborer	51.9	47.7	48.2	40.4	53.3	50.4
Self-employed	51.7	n/a	38.8	n/a	57.0	n/a
Independent contractor, WS[a]	37.2	17.8	36.7	15.8	37.5	18.7
Independent contractor, SE[b]	44.5	n/a	44.4	n/a	44.5	n/a
Contract company	64.7	56.1	68.7	64.0	63.3	53.2
Regular full-time	68.3	66.2	68.9	66.5	67.9	66.0
Part-time						
Temporary help agency	7.7	2.2	11.5	3.3	0.0	0.0
On-call/day laborer	30.9	17.3	33.6	18.7	25.5	14.4
Self-employed	43.9	n/a	42.7	n/a	47.2	n/a
Independent contractor, WS[a]	32.7	8.8	28.0	4.3	40.1	15.9
Independent contractor, SE[b]	41.5	n/a	44.9	n/a	34.0	n/a
Contract company	27.5	14.5	28.3	17.1	26.1	9.6
Regular part-time	32.0	25.2	36.1	28.0	21.4	17.1

[a] Wage and salary.
[b] Self-employed.
SOURCE: U.S. Department of Labor, Bureau of Labor Statistics, The Current Population Survey (CPS) Supplements, Contingent and Alternative Employment Arrangements, February 2001; analysis by author.

that shows that firms use nonstandard work arrangements to offset the high benefits costs of regular full-time employees (Abraham 1988).

Policy Evaluation

While these findings for health insurance and pension coverage are not surprising given the design of the public policies, there is little evidence that public policy is moving to remedy the lack of coverage for workers in nonstandard employment. Temporary employment agencies have been sensitive to the criticism that workers are unable to receive health insurance; many of these agencies have begun to make it available to their workers. Despite the increased availability, few workers take advantage of the insurance, most likely due to the high costs relative to their earnings.

The health care and pension systems demonstrate the difficulty public policy has in adequately addressing incomplete markets, that is, those markets where there are only limited products available at a wide range of prices. From an economic efficiency standpoint (as defined above), it is unlikely that the market is efficient; many uninsured workers with health statuses similar to workers with insurance do not get health insurance as a result of where they work. Thus, many workers who have relatively low insurance costs go without insurance. From a social standpoint health insurance markets are very flawed. Many workers who initially have low-cost insurance go without medical care. Some of them get treatment too late, raising overall medical costs and potentially decreasing their health outcomes. Since employers who do not provide insurance bear only a fraction of the cost of uninsured workers, there is little economic incentive to provide insurance. From an equity standpoint these markets are very inequitable: workers in ostensibly the same work situation receive different compensation.

Perhaps the most important aspect of this policy is security. The analysis in Table 6.3 from the matched February/March 2001 Current Population Surveys indicates that workers in nonstandard employment are much more likely to report "fair" to "poor" health. Involuntary part-time workers (part-time workers who would prefer full-time work) are 4.5 times as likely to report diminished health status as regular full-time workers. This may be due to a variety of factors, not the least of which is employee self-selection: fewer healthy workers may choose

Table 6.3 Percentage of Workers Reporting Health Status as "Fair" or "Poor," 2001

Employment type	Fair to Poor
Regular full-time	2.2
Contract worker	6.3
Independent contractor	6.5
On-call	7.5
Temporary help	10.3
Involuntary part-time	10.0

SOURCE: U.S. Department of Labor, Bureau of Labor Statistics, The Current Population Survey (CPS) Supplements, Contingent and Alternative Employment Arrangements, February 2001 and March Annual Demographic file 2001; analysis by author of matched February/March CPS data.

these forms of employment based on employment flexibility. However, this reduced health status does point to the need for health insurance coverage.

The rationale for government intervention is very strong in this case. Socially, the benefits of insuring this large group of workers are likely to be quite high, and the market has been unable to achieve these improvements on it own. However, it is unlikely that we will see government mandate that businesses cover these workers. Their lower health statuses imply that they would be increasingly costly to insure. Under these circumstances government intervention is warranted and necessary.

SOCIAL INSURANCE: UNEMPLOYMENT INSURANCE

The provision of employer-provided health insurance or pensions fails to provide systematic coverage since only workers whose employers provide benefits and who earn enough to afford the benefits actually receive the coverage. In contrast, social insurance is provided for all people who meet certain eligibility requirements. These requirements often have a differential impact on workers in nonstandard employment arrangements. The most important form of social insurance that directly affects employees is unemployment insurance (UI).

Overview of Unemployment Insurance

The UI system in the United States began with the Social Security Act of 1935, which provides the primary line of defense against earnings losses when workers become unemployed. For those eligible for unemployment insurance benefits, the typical state program provides 26 weeks of benefits at approximately 50 percent of the worker's normal wage. Although federal and state statutes have been revised periodically to increase the level of benefits, the basic system created by the act has remained the same. The most significant change is that the program now covers nearly all employees; therefore, nearly all employees or their employers pay unemployment insurance taxes. However, coverage does not mean eligibility. Unfortunately, this first line of defense is so porous that it leaves many full- and part-time workers uninsured.

The overall picture of unemployment insurance is one of a declining share of the full-time workers who lose their jobs receiving UI benefits (Blank and Card 1991; Vroman 1991; Wenger 2001). In this situation, workers may have to choose some form of contingent work as an earnings substitute for UI benefits. While this may be a good strategy in a robust economy, during periods of economic malaise even these nonstandard jobs will be hard to find. During the current recession, the temporary employment sector lost more than 900,000 jobs. Under these conditions temporary employment is not likely to provide income security to those who have lost jobs in other sectors.

The situation for workers in nonstandard arrangements is even bleaker. Eligibility requirements for hours of work and earnings are particularly onerous for contingent workers. Clearly, both these criteria are related: as hours decrease we see a commensurate reduction in earnings. Due to the sporadic nature of contingent work, hours and earnings are unpredictable, making eligibility difficult to establish.

Determining Eligibility for UI

From the perspective of nonstandard workers, unemployment insurance has five major problems related to the determination of eligibility for UI. First, the system is biased toward regular full-time work. Workers with low wages and those with fewer than full-time hours may have difficulty qualifying for benefits.

Second, the system is confusing. A wide array of initial and continuing eligibility requirements create uncertainty about eligibility. Complex payment and benefit duration formulae confuse workers about the potential value of benefits. Limited labor market experience only compounds the confusion since contingent workers do not have stable employment relationships that allow them to share information about eligibility and benefit amounts.

Third, waiting periods prior to eligibility have a disproportionate negative impact on low-wage workers, especially those with limited resources. Many states have waiting periods for eligibility of one to two weeks. Families with limited resources may find a two-week waiting period financially unmanageable, choosing instead to return to contingent employment if they can find a job in that sector.

Fourth, the most difficult eligibility rules for a nonstandard worker to satisfy may be the rules that deny benefits if the worker refuses to accept a job offer. Part of the ongoing eligibility requirements in UI are the job search requirements. To collect unemployment benefits the unemployed must continue to search for work. In most states a worker who turns down any job offer is no longer eligible to receive benefits. Federal law does provide some worker protections by prohibiting states from denying benefits under the following conditions:

1)   if the job vacancy was the result of a labor dispute;

2)   if the wages, hours, or other conditions of the work offered fail to meet prevailing standards;

3)   if joining a company union or being required *not* to join a bona fide union is a condition of employment.

Thirty-one states and the District of Columbia stipulate that the worker must be available for any type of work to maintain eligibility. Ten states require the worker to accept "suitable work," although this has a broad definition and changes as the duration of unemployment increases. Finally, nine states require the worker to accept work in his usual occupation or in jobs for which he is reasonably matched due to prior training or experience. The penalties for turning down a job offer vary from a reduction in benefits to benefits being postponed for the duration of the unemployment (U.S. Department of Labor 1996).

However, the nonstandard labor market is so volatile that part-time job offers for work in nonstandard jobs may be a regular facet of this type of employment. For workers who seek to leave contingent employment and use their unemployment insurance benefits to subsidize their search for a full-time job, requiring contingent workers to accept any position may amount to placing them in a UI eligibility trap from which escape to better employment is difficult. Thus, this type of eligibility requirement may be particularly difficult for a contingent worker to satisfy. Turning down a job offer in hopes of landing a better job may result in ineligibility.

Finally, a number of states explicitly exclude from eligibility workers who search for part-time work exclusively. These workers are considered "not available" for full-time work and consequently are not eligible to receive benefits (Wenger, McHugh, and Segal 2002). In essence these workers' unavailability is evidenced by their substantial restrictions on the conditions of their employment. Consequently, for nonstandard employees, especially part-time workers, eligibility requirements may all but eliminate them from collecting UI benefits in some states.

Empirical evidence suggests that the eligibility restrictions take a much higher toll on contingent and nonstandard employees. Table 6.4

Table 6.4 Percentage of Workers Satisfying Monetary Eligibility Requirements for Unemployment Insurance, 2001

Type of employment	Status: Ineligible
Temporary help	15.9
Contract	6.8
On-call/day laborer	20.7
Independent contractor, WS[a]	63.1
Involuntary part-time	25.7
Voluntary part-time	30.0
Contingent worker type 1	26.3
Contingent worker type 2	30.5
Contingent worker type 3	11.6
Regular full-time	6.1

NOTE: Self-employed and independent contractors not paid by wage or salary are omitted since these workers are not covered by the UI system.

[a] Paid by wage or salary so covered by UI.

SOURCE: U.S. Department of Labor, Bureau of Labor Statistics, The Current Population Survey (CPS) Supplements, Contingent and Alternative Employment Arrangements, February 2001 and March Annual Demographic file 2001; analysis by author of matched February/March CPS data.

**Table 6.5 Maximum Weekly Benefits, Lowest and Highest Paying
States, 2000 ($)**

Alabama	190	Massachusetts	477
Mississippi	190	Washington	441
Arizona	205	Pennsylvania	430
South Dakota	224	New Jersey	429
California	230	New York	405

SOURCE: U.S. Department of Labor (2001).

compares the monetary eligibility of contingent, nonstandard, and regular full-time workers.[3] Regular full-time workers are more likely than any other group to satisfy the earnings requirements for unemployment insurance. The workers least likely to be eligible are the independent contractors who are paid a wage or salary.

Previous earnings determine both who is eligible and the amount of benefits the unemployed receive. Those workers who have lower earnings and fewer hours of work receive smaller benefit amounts, and are likely to receive benefits for a shorter period of time. These differences in benefit calculations are not trivial; the maximum weekly benefit in different states varies by hundreds of dollars. Table 6.5 compares the maximum weekly benefits for the five highest and lowest paying states in the United States.

The difference in maximum weekly benefits between Massachusetts and Alabama is striking. From a policy perspective we can see both sides of the UI debate reflected in these two states. Lower-threshold earnings requirements increase the likelihood of being eligible but often result in low benefit levels. Conversely, higher benefit allowances usually require higher earnings and/or hours. These higher threshold levels may exclude low-wage workers from benefits.

One initially surprising empirical finding is that contingent and nonstandard workers receive higher benefit levels than their regular full-time counterparts. Considering only those who received UI benefits in 1994, nonstandard workers received on average $2,781 (N = 417) while regular full-time workers only received $2,349 (N = 2435). This is likely due to self-selection: only those contingent workers who expect higher benefit payments are likely to apply. Typically these are workers with higher incomes and steadier employment such as contract workers who are independent contractors in the least volatile employment arrangements and paid a wage or salary (see also Kunda, Barley, and Evans [2002]).

Consequently, it appears that there are two groups of contingent employees who view UI options quite differently: those who are reasonably certain of a high benefit amount are likely to choose to apply for UI. However, given the confusing array of eligibility rules and complex benefit formulae, we can speculate that a second group—probably the majority of contingent workers—find it easier to seek other contingent work rather than apply for benefits. Employees in this second group find that reentering the contingent labor market is a way of avoiding the waiting periods, uncertain benefit amounts, administrative hassles, and the potential social stigma arising from being an unemployed worker.

Policy Evaluation

The nature of UI usage is changing. The new labor market actors, contingent and nonstandard workers, are not using UI in the same way that regular full-time workers use the system. Yet despite the reduction in use and inapplicability to new work forms, systematic change is unlikely. States compete among themselves to create favorable business conditions to attract employers. They are unlikely to yield to pressure from labor groups to systematically extend benefits to contingent workers that will increase the cost of labor for employers. When jobs are relatively plentiful, this lack of concern for the public policy reform may not be problematic. Rather than suffer from the social stigma that may occur from UI use, workers will remain productively employed in the labor force, even if in less than full-time positions. However, as the economic climate shifts toward recession, job availability diminishes and contingent employment becomes less of an option. The opportunity to use contingent work as a substitute for UI will be reduced for many of these workers. We therefore would expect UI rolls to increase because they will be more willing to tolerate the waiting period requirements, administrative hassles, and social stigma.

From a policy perspective, unemployment insurance includes many complicated components to analyze. Economic efficiency, as measured by the cost of adding workers in nonstandard arrangements to unemployment insurance, is not likely to be very costly. Wenger (2000) shows that the effects of unemployment insurance on the likelihood of workers becoming unemployed are about the same for regular full-time workers and workers in nonstandard arrangements. It would appear that the cost per person of extending unemployment insurance benefits to workers in nonstandard arrangements is similar to the current per person costs of regular full-time employees.

Unemployment insurance suffers from considerable inequities. Particularly vexing is the inequity across states. Identical workers employed in different states will likely receive different benefit amounts, may have different eligibility outcomes, and may have different weeks of eligibility. This inequity is especially problematic to address since each state makes its own policy within loose federal guidelines. Creating a national policy from such a system would be nearly impossible since states control almost all of the important aspects of eligibility and benefits.

There can be little doubt that workers in nonstandard employment arrangements need UI. They are more likely to become unemployed and less likely to be eligible for benefits. The least stable of these arrangements, such as temporary employment, has both intermittent employment and low wages. This means that UI eligibility will be more difficult to attain due to low wages, but spells of unemployment are more likely due to sporadic employment. Overall, the current UI system is relatively inefficient, highly inequitable, and fails to provide security for a class of workers with considerable need. The justifications for government intervention are myriad. Government clearly has a role in easing the destructive forces that the market rains on the unemployed. Additionally, from a broader economic perspective, UI has a stabilizing effect on the economy as a whole (Chimerine, Black, and Coffey 1999). However, the real shortcoming of the current unemployment insurance program is its lack of modernization to adapt it to the new labor market realities in the United States.

SOCIAL INSURANCE: FAMILY AND MEDICAL LEAVE ACT (FMLA)

One of the most recent additions to the U.S. social insurance system is the Family and Medical Leave Act (FMLA), enacted in 1993. The act was established to "allow employees to balance their work and family lives by taking reasonable unpaid leave for certain family and medical reasons." The act also seeks to promote the "economic security of families" and "national interests in preserving family integrity." The FMLA accomplishes this by providing eligible employees with up to 12 weeks of *unpaid*, job-protected leave each year. Additionally, the act requires employers to continue to provide health benefits during the leave.

Unfortunately, for workers in nonstandard employment the FMLA provides at best a marginal benefit to those contingent workers who already have the option to sporadically leave the labor force for periods of time and receive no pay.[4] While the job protections and especially the preservation of health insurance may be of some benefit for contingent workers and those in in nonstandard arrangements, eligibility rules and low levels of employer-provided insurance provide nearly nonexistent benefits.

Factors That Determine Contingent Workers' Use of FMLA

The FMLA eligibility requirements are much less complex than those for the UI system. However, they are far more likely to classify contingent and nonstandard workers as ineligible. There are three main criteria for FMLA eligibility: the employer must have more than 50 employees, and the employee must have worked for the employer for 12 months or more and worked a minimum of 1,250 hours in the previous 12 months (approximately 31 weeks of work at 40 hours per week). These criteria eliminate the majority of contingent workers from eligibility. Part-time workers (those who work year round fewer than 24 hours per week) or workers who move from job site to job site or who have multiple contracts are unlikely to satisfy the eligibility criteria.

The ability to use the FMLA leave option is determined by the work schedules of contingent workers. Not all workers in nonstandard employment have flexible schedules. For example, part-time workers may have little control over their work schedules. Contract workers may only be able to take time away from work between contracts. The self-employed must schedule time off during the ebb of customer demand. Consequently, for workers like these, the FMLA policies could provide flexibility while affording them some job security. However, contingent workers typically cannot afford the cost of taking the time off even if they would benefit from the protections prescribed in the FMLA. Only long-term contractors and "perma-temps" are likely to benefit from the act. The primary benefit to these two groups is the continued availability of employer-provided health insurance during a leave of absence. However, because contingent workers are unlikely to receive employer-provided health insurance, this benefit will cover few workers, as shown previously in Table 6.1.

Thus, the FMLA is unlikely to be an important policy for contingent workers since very few will be able to satisfy the eligibility criteria. However, the FMLA has created an increased dependence on workers in nonstandard jobs since contingent workers are likely to be hired to replace regular full-time employees when they use the provisions of the act. As of 2000, 98.2 percent of all firms reported assigning work to other employees, while 41.3 percent reported hiring outside temporary-replacement workers. The use of temporary workers declined from 1995 to 2000, but their role in making FMLA successful remains important.

Policy Evaluation

The FMLA does not perform well in terms of our four policy criteria of economic efficiency, equity, security, and liberty. It is clear that the policy was essentially formulated for workers in standard jobs where leaves of absence normally would require an employee to quit a job. Therefore, from an equity perspective, the FMLA program treats inequitably workers in nonstandard jobs who are excluded from this leave option. From the business perspective it would appear that there is little additional cost if all employees are allowed to take leave, regardless of how many hours of service a worker had rendered in the previous 12 months. However, it may be harder for employers to manage the loss of a full-time employee than a half-time employee.

Evaluating the FMLA on the criteria of security poses an interesting problem. Many nonstandard arrangements offer little flexibility. Consequently, workers in part-time and contract jobs may have a considerable need for the policy. In many cases, workers in these arrangements are more likely to meet the hours requirements for eligibility. For the other types of work arrangements such as temporary help agency workers, independent contractors, and the self-employed, these work forms may offer enough flexibility to be able to accommodate an unpaid leave.

After more than 12 years of experience with the FMLA, we have not managed to expand coverage, nor have we found a way to provide paid leave for those who need to take care of children or sick relatives. With an aging U.S. population the demand for this leave option is likely to increase. However, without a mechanism for paying for leave, much of that demand will go unsatisfied. Consequently, the federal government is likely to experience increased pressure to intervene.

Many of the U.S. labor market policies started by providing modest coverage, and over time that coverage has been expanded. This was true for UI, the minimum wage, and disability insurance. It remains to be seen whether the FMLA follows this path as well.

MINIMUM WAGES

In contrast to the public policies discussed above, federal minimum wage legislation instituted with the Fair Labor Standards Act (FLSA) in 1938 provides nearly universal coverage. The FLSA establishes standards for minimum wages, overtime pay, and child labor. States may choose to set minimum wages above the federal level. As of January 2003, 11 states had minimum wage laws that exceeded the federal minimum wage.[5]

While the FLSA provides nearly universal coverage, there are two notable exceptions: the self-employed and independent contractors. As a consequence, nearly one-third of all workers in nonstandard employment arrangements are not covered by minimum wage laws. For those who are likely to be covered, such as workers at temporary help firms, on-call workers, wage and salary independent contractors, and part-time workers, they are more likely to earn low wages.[6] Table 6.6 shows mean wages by work arrangement and gender. Average hourly wages are lowest for workers in part-time jobs and those who work for temporary help agencies. Regression analysis that controls for human capital characteristics also shows that regression-adjusted wages are lower for part-time and temporary workers relative to full-time workers.

The low levels of the minimum wage, the decline of its real purchasing power, and tight labor markets throughout most of the 1990s have eroded the efficacy of the minimum wage.[7] Analysis of the Feb-

187

Table 6.6 Average Hourly Wages (1999) and Percent Change in Wage Since 1997, by Work Arrangement and Sex

	All		Women		Men	
	1999 Wage ($)	% Change	1999 Wage ($)	% Change	1999 Wage ($)	% Change
Regular part-time	11.86	12.2	11.81	11.4	12.00	14.7
Temporary help agency	10.84	−2.9	10.00	−1.9	12.01	−2.0
On-call/day laborer	13.19	8.0	12.89	12.8	13.47	4.0
Self-employed	17.68	2.8	14.21	8.3	19.57	0.5
Independent contractor, WS[a]	17.42	15.6	15.76	22.5	19.10	10.0
Independent contractor, SE[b]	19.60	−0.8	17.66	−3.6	20.50	0.4
Contract company	19.09	13.7	16.86	15.4	20.15	13.7
Regular full-time	15.83	3.7	13.78	0.7	17.43	5.8
All	15.56	4.3	13.51	2.9	17.37	5.6

[a] Wage and salary.
[b] Self-employed.
SOURCE: U.S. Department of Labor, Bureau of Labor Statistics, The Current Population Survey (CPS) Supplements, Contingent and Alternative Employment Arrangements, February 1997 and 1999; analysis by author.

ruary Current Population Survey Contingent Work Supplement from 1999 indicates that, overall, approximately 10 percent of the labor force in 1999 earned less than the federal minimum wage of $5.50 per hour, as shown in Table 6.7. However, there were more low-earning workers in nonstandard arrangements than in regular full-time jobs. The only nonstandard group where the percentage of low earners was below the national average was contract workers. These findings may be somewhat misleading since many contract workers are self-employed and earn the difference between their revenue and expenditures, regardless of the number of hours worked. Consequently many of these workers have very low hourly wages. By contrast, workers in nonstandard arrangements who are employed by others are also much more likely to be low earners.

Since some state-set minimum wages are considerably higher than the federal minimum wage, they may provide more income security to contingent workers. In these states minimum wages ranged between $6.15 per hour in Rhode Island and $7.15 in Alaska. This means that considerably more workers in contingent employment will be covered by the minimum wage legislation in these states. In general, while all

Table 6.7 Percentage of Workers in Nonstandard Arrangements Earning Less Than $5.50 Per Hour, 1999

Regular part-time	22.5
Temporary help agency	5.6
On-call/day laborer	17.1
Self-employed	18.6
Independent contractor, WS[a]	9.5
Independent contractor, SE[b]	12.1
Contract company	4.2
Regular full-time	4.5
All Nonstandard	15.1
All	9.9

[a] Wage and salary.
[b] Self-employed.
SOURCE: U.S. Department of Labor, Bureau of Labor Statistics, The Current Population Survey (CPS) Supplements, Contingent and Alternative Employment Arrangements, February 1999; analysis by author.

states are required to follow federal minimum requirements for the FLSA, many have chosen to raise the minimum requirements. This occurs more frequently when the federal government fails to maintain the real value of the minimum wage as in the 1980s.

Policy Evaluation

The heterogeneity of workers across nonstandard employment arrangements means that earnings will vary. The lack of coverage for the self-employed and independent contractors means that the minimum wage is not a policy with a high score on equity. The economic efficiency considerations for the minimum wage have been written about extensively. In general, researchers argue that increases in the minimum wage result in a reallocation of labor that is not efficient. The standard claim is that increases in the minimum wage increase unemployment, thereby displacing lower-skilled workers. However, research conducted using quasi-experimental analyses of state minimum wage increases has called into question much of the earlier results.[8] There is little reason to believe that workers in nonstandard arrangements present a unique case in terms of efficiency. Empirical evidence suggests that the minimum wage does not cause meaningful reductions in efficiency within a relatively narrow range of values.

As with many of the other policies discussed in this chapter, the largest failing of the minimum wage is on the criterion of security. The people with the most exposure to the vicissitudes of the market are receiving neither enough coverage nor the same coverage. Simply stated, an increase in minimum wages will have a disproportionate impact on part-time workers and temporary help workers.

Perhaps the most controversial aspect of minimum wage policy from an economic point of view is determining whether the government has a legitimate role to play in setting a wage floor (liberty). Many economic analysts believe that markets are better suited to determining wages and that government intervention is unwarranted. This neoclassical or libertarian viewpoint overlooks some of the inequities between the parties negotiating a wage. Employers are in a much better bargaining position; they have more resources, more information, and more bargaining power. Workers in contingent employment arrangements are often at a disadvantage. They have limited bargaining power, largely as a result of many people vying for the same job, and often have limited information about the job requirements and hence an appropriate wage. In these cases it would seem appropriate to impose a collective outcome on the lowest wage earners and employers.

OTHER EMPLOYMENT POLICIES: SAFETY AT THE WORK SITE

The discussion in this chapter has shown that many of the employment policies in the United States were enacted before the large shifts to contingent and nonstandard employment occurred. The fundamental problem with these policies is that their institutional development took place at a time when the contingent workforce was minuscule. As the nature of work and U.S. labor markets have changed, public policy has increasingly relied on the judicial interpretations of the statutes rather than redesigning the policies to keep pace with the changing patterns of employment. Many of the statutes that seek to provide other protections for workers, such as the reduction of discrimination, protection from workplace hazards, and the protection of workers' rights to fair wages and work conditions, also suffer from these same drawbacks.

Although the Occupational Safety and Health Act of 1970 (OSHA) is used here to illustrate the problems inherent in much workplace law, these lessons are applicable across a broad range of workplace policies. Included among these are the National Labor Relations Act (1935) that governs collective bargaining activities, the Fair Labor Standards Act—Equal Pay Amendment (1963), the Civil Rights Acts of 1964 and 1981, the Age Discrimination in Employment Act (1967), the Americans with Disabilities Act (1990), as well as a host of federal and state labor and employment statutes (Maltby and Yamada 1997).

The mandate of OSHA is to provide, inasmuch as is possible, a safe and healthful work environment for every working man and woman in the United States. The continuing problem for OSHA has been determining who is responsible for providing this safe and healthful workplace as these new employment relations and forms of work have been developing. OSHA places this burden squarely on the employer. The *employer* has the responsibility of providing "a place of employment which is free from recognized hazards that are causing or likely to cause death or serious physical harm to his employees" (OSHA 1970). However, identifying the employer is not always easy. One illustrative example is the case of workers employed through a temporary help agency who have dual employment relationships: they have one administrative employer (the employer of record) such as a temporary help agency, and a host employer where the work is actually performed. Considerable litigation has resulted around this coemployment issue (see Chapter 5 for more details).

Thus the determination of who employs the worker is the first step in determining the party responsible for carrying out the mandates of OSHA. The issues can be thorny. The administrative employer such as the temporary employment agency has little control over the risk associated with working at the host employer's work site, and may have only limited knowledge of the potential employment hazards. As a consequence, an information asymmetry is established. This may result in workers being unfamiliar with the risks associated with the work. Worse yet, the information asymmetry may be exploited by host employers who use temporary workers to perform tasks or work under conditions that their regular full-time employees would find objectionable.

The problem that has created much concern is employers classifying their workers to evade the requirements of various federal labor and employment laws. The legal issues center on the legal definitions of "an employee" (Carnevale, Jennings, and Eisenmann 1998). While numerous criteria have been used, the policy consensus reached by the Commission on the Future of Worker Management Relations recommends that a single definition of employer be developed based on the "economic realities" test employed by the courts (Dunlop Commission 1995). The commission recommends "adopting a single definition of employer for all workplace laws based on the economic realities of the employment relationship." The commission also advises the National Labor Relations Board to develop policies governing joint employment relationships to prevent employers from using "contract arrangements . . . as a subterfuge for avoiding collective bargaining or evading other responsibilities under labor law" (p. 4).

Policy Evaluation

Perhaps the largest single factor relating to the inadequacy of our public policies and the concomitant gaps in coverage for contingent workers is multiple employer relationships for these workers. Enforcement of antidiscriminatory or sexual harassment laws is difficult under these circumstances. The differences in coverage for contingent workers and noncontingent workers is a considerable source of inequity. A worker employed by a temporary agency has the same rights as the permanent worker, but the mechanism for enforcement is not available. In this sense the contingent worker may be treated in a highly inequitable manner.

From an economic efficiency standpoint, there is no reason to believe that enforcing the health, discrimination, and equal pay rules for contingent workers would be more costly than enforcing them for regular full-time workers. However, from a security standpoint, contingent workers are more likely to need the protections since there are opportunities for employers to take advantage of the information asymmetries described earlier. If contingent workers are hired for the purpose of "protecting" core employees this would result in an increased role for government to ensure security for these workers.

CONCLUSIONS AND DIRECTIONS FOR FUTURE RESEARCH

Labor market policies in the United States rarely work for contingent and nonstandard workers. The problem is twofold: U.S. employment policies were not designed to protect contingent and nonstandard employees, nor have they kept pace with evolving trends in employment. The fault lies with the development and evolution of labor market policies rather than with the employers and employees.

Public policies that fail to meet their objectives represent an opportunity for change. While any revisions will be complex matters of law, they should be based on consistent criteria.

1) **Economic efficiency.** Policies should be efficient in that they should not be so onerous as to cause undue hardship to employ-

ers or eliminate the practice of contingent work. Since there is some evidence that both employers and employees benefit from certain types of contingent and nonstandard employment, eliminating or curtailing the practice may do more harm than good.

2) **Equity.** Policies should be fairly and justly applied to all workers regardless of their employment relationship. To the extent possible, coverage should be extended to all employees regardless of occupation, industry, or firm size.

3) **Security.** Policies should be targeted to protect the most vulnerable workers from the volatility of the market. There is considerable evidence that workers in nonstandard arrangements are exposed to more market volatility than other types of workers. If this is truly the case, then protecting these workers through social insurance and public policy is important.

4) **Liberty.** To the extent that governmental intervention is unnecessary, markets and private parties should be allowed to operate. However, private markets for the provision of disability and unemployment insurance have not been forthcoming. Markets are not likely to provide many protections to these types of workers due to their limited bargaining power relative to employers.

Analysts should avoid understanding liberty as the freedom from government intervention. Liberty is a much broader concept, and individual preferences may be such that freedom from fear and want outweigh freedom from intervention. On occasion, liberty may justify governmental intervention in the market rather than thwart it.

Making employment policy more economically efficient, equitable, and just means that both employers and employees understand their rights and responsibilities. Furthermore, these rights and responsibilities are universal: they do not depend on the class or kind of employment. To that end reform should promote economic efficiency, equity, and security for both employers and employees. Therefore, reforms should do the following:

- Simplify the eligibility rules for workplace policies such as unemployment insurance and family and medical leave. Additionally, reforms should extend these benefits to cover all workers regardless of the industry or size of employer.

- Extend unemployment insurance so that it provides health insurance during the period of unemployment. This could be done by paying the COBRA copayment to the previous employer.

- Strengthen the public pension system. Since so few workers in nonstandard employment receive a pension from their employers, many more nonstandard workers will have to rely on the public pension, Social Security. Nearly all workers are covered by Social Security, and 40 quarters of work are enough to qualify a worker for benefits, but the system must be made fiscally viable in the future to guarantee benefits for the next generation.

- Increase the portability of benefits. For example, once eligible for family medical leave, a worker would remain eligible so long as they continued to work—even after they change jobs.[9] Additionally, increased pension portability would expand coverage for workers who move from employer to employer.

- Provide incentives to business to allay some of the costs associated with increased coverage and portability.

- Adopt the Dunlop Commission's recommendation calling for "a single definition of employer for all workplace laws."

If enacted, these policy recommendations would provide increased coverage for contingent and nonstandard workers by making them equivalent, at least in the eyes of the government, to regular full-time workers.

All responsible policy recommendations walk a fine line between job creation and employee protection. Those concerned with the rights of workers believe too little is being done to protect them from the hazards and vicissitudes of the labor market and workplace. Others believe that saddling business with the burden of workplace protections reduces employment and leads to a more insidious harm, strangling innovation and job creation.

It can be argued that the development of contingent and nonstandard employment forms was, and continues to be, a direct response to the increasing burden placed on firms in the form of new legislation. In particular, Autor (2001) has found that limitations on the employment-at-will doctrine have resulted in an increased use of temporary help by firms. (Employment-at-will basically guarantees the employer the right to fire or lay off an employee without cause. In many states the courts have curtailed the rights of employers to dismiss workers.) In programs such as UI and disability insurance, employer costs are experience-rated; that is, employers are required to pay premiums based on their employees' claims. More claims result in higher payments. Experience-rated programs create incentives for firms to hire contingent workers so that when a worker is laid off or injured, the claim is made against the temporary firm. If policymakers believe that legislation protecting workers from discrimination, unemployment, and workplace hazards is important, they must work to close the loopholes that currently exist and make the system flexible enough so that responding to changes in employment relations is readily accomplished.

Given the increasing role of nonstandard employment both domestically and internationally, the need for policy changes is likely to become more pressing. The U.S. labor force is becoming older and the society is experiencing more inequality. As a result, nonstandard employment will likely increase over time as workers demand flexible work schedules and employer demand for nonstandard employment services increases.

Directions for Future Research

Scholarship on nonstandard employment to date has focused primarily on identifying nonstandard workers by their characteristics and motives for engaging in this type of employment arrangement and why this type of employment has grown. Recent research has begun to outline the deficiencies of current public policies in achieving the goal of protecting these workers by providing them with the same safety net available to regular full-time employees. The next phase of research will have to answer the question "What can be done?" Much of the challenge of this research is that it must transcend traditional disciplines and employ an interdisciplinary approach. Four topics worthy of further research are discussed below.

First, the excellent economy of the latter 1990s masked considerable inequalities in the U.S. labor force. With the onset of recession in 2001, health insurance coverage and pension coverage have emerged as areas of concern. As health insurance costs continue to climb, coverage for workers in nonstandard employment will become more difficult to secure. Shoring up the existing Social Security program will become more important as the labor force ages. In both these cases research should be done that specifically focuses on older workers in contingent or nonstandard work arrangements. In particular, to what extent was reemployment in contingent work necessary for the older retirees who lost considerable sums in the equities markets? How will the lack of health insurance coverage impact the health of older workers in these types of employment?

Second, recessionary periods always refocus attention on the social safety—in particular, the unemployment insurance system. The UI system is rife with inequality and fails to provide the security that many workers need. Policy research about the design of a system that better serves a more dynamic and mobile labor force than the one the current system was created to serve is much needed.

Third, casual empiricism indicates that few contingent workers are eligible for FMLA benefits. However, to understand the factors determining need, the Commission on Family and Medical Leave (1996) recommends "additional research should be done to assess the impact of family leave policies (both those required by the FMLA and those voluntarily provided) on temporary, part-time and contract workers."

Finally, as this chapter has repeatedly noted, eligibility criteria determine who is covered under a specific law. Since the Fair Labor Standards Act does not cover the self-employed, there is an increasingly large group of workers who are not protected by this act and its provision for overtime pay. Other workers are not covered by minimum wage laws for similar reasons. One promising area of research is to investigate how well the Fair Labor Standards Act is operating. Are workers being misclassified as independent contractors to avoid payroll taxes? Have workers used nonstandard employment to lower their experience ratings on social insurance?

Workers in the United States have come to expect certain characteristics in a "good" job: reasonable wages, health and pension coverage, and government policies that protect them from the volatility of the market (Kalleberg, Reskin, and Hudson 2000). Unfortunately, many workers in nonstandard employment cannot expect any of these. Wages are typically below those of their full-time counterparts, pension and health insurance coverage are limited, and government policies have not kept pace with these changes in the workforce.

The four main criteria used in this analysis—economic efficiency, equity, security, and liberty—demonstrate very clearly the inadequacy of much of our safety net for contingent workers. The irony is that many of the policies that are inequitable (those that deny coverage to many contingent workers while covering the full-time labor force) are also those that would provide much-needed security to the contingent workforce. In essence, the workers who most need protection from the vicissitudes of the market are denied coverage. Extending coverage to contingent workers will likely cost more, but not disproportionately, so that making most of these extensions in coverage is relatively efficient.

It is the issue of liberty around which much of the debate centers. The legitimate role of government to intervene is hotly contested and will be the battleground for this issue for years to come. Future research on expanding the safety net for those in need will help determine how the characteristics of "good jobs" can be extended to nonstandard employment. But research alone will not make political decisions to extend the legitimate role of government. A deeper understanding of government's role coupled with political pressure remains the catalyst for that type of change.

Notes

1. Typically, an employer must have at least 20 employees and offer a health insurance plan. COBRA allows continued coverage only for those who would be losing coverage for certain reasons such as the loss of a job, the reduction in hours of work, the death or divorce of a parent or spouse, or the change in status as dependent.
2. For a more general discussion of the role of professional part-time employees, see Lawrence and Corwin (2003).
3. Monetary eligibility is determined by state requirements. It is a measure of whether a worker earned enough to qualify for the state's minimum benefit.
4. While the FMLA is not likely to provide much benefit to workers in contingent and nonstandard employment arrangements, this should not be considered a wholesale criticism of the policy. There is considerable evidence that the policy provides real benefits to those 50 percent of full-time workers covered by the policy in small firms and the 95 percent of full-time workers covered by the policy in large firms (Waldfogel 1999). However, the use of the FMLA leave has been fairly modest. About 1.2 percent of all employees took leave under

the provisions of the FMLA between its enactment and 1999 (see Cantor et al. 2001). Those who needed leave but did not take leave represent 3.4 percent of the sample. When asked, employees consistently remark that this low level of usage is brought about by the lack of paid leave. Of those who needed leave for a birth or illness in the family, fully 63.9 percent of respondents claimed they "cannot afford the accompanying loss of wages" (Cantor et al. 2001).

5. Alaska ($7.15); California ($6.75); Connecticut ($7.10); Delaware ($6.15); Hawaii ($6.25); Maine ($6.25); Massachusetts ($6.75); Oregon ($6.90); Rhode Island ($6.15); Vermont ($6.25); Washington ($7.01).

6. Wage and salary independent contractors are paid on a regular basis with a wage or salary instead of by the task.

7. From 1981 until 1990, the nominal value of the minimum wage remained constant at $3.35, while its real value shrank due to inflation. Phased increases in the minimum wage from 1995 through 1997 have done little to restore it to its pre-1980 levels.

8. There is considerable evidence that the employment disincentives have been overstated by previous research (see, for example, Card and Kreuger 1995).

9. The only way to reform these types of policies is to generalize and make portable a fund for both UI and FMLA. In this way workers make contributions to the UI and FMLA funds. Once sufficient payments have been made, a worker may draw them down. This eliminates eligibility requirements and long-term employment relationships necessary for eligibility without eliminating the work requirement of the policy.

References

Abraham, K. 1988. "Flexible Staffing Arrangements and Employers' Short-Term Adjustment Strategies." In *Employment, Unemployment and Labor Utilization*, R.A. Hart, ed. Winchester, MA: Unwin Hyman, pp. 288–311.

Autor, D. 2001. "Outsourcing at Will: Unjust Dismissal Doctrine and the Growth of Temporary Help Employment." JCPR working paper 153. Chicago: Northwestern University/University of Chicago Joint Center for Poverty Research.

Blank, R., and D. Card. 1991. "Recent Trends in Insured and Uninsured Unemployment: Is There an Explanation?" *Quarterly Journal of Economics* 106(4): 1157–1189.

Cantor, D., J. Waldfogel, J. Kerwin, M. Wright, K. Levin, J. Rauch, T. Hagerty, and M. Kudela. 2001. *Balancing the Needs of Families and Employers: Family and Medical Leave Surveys, 2000 Update.* Rockville, MD: Westat.

Card, D., and A. Kreuger. 1995. *Myth and Measurement: The New Economics of the Minimum Wage.* Princeton, NJ: Princeton University Press.

Carnevale, A., L. Jennings, and J. Eisenmann. 1998. "Contingent Workers and

Employment Law." In *Contingent Work*, K. Barker and K. Christensen, eds. Ithaca, NY: ILR Press, pp. 281–305.

Chimerine, L., T. Black, and L. Coffey. 1999. "Unemployment Insurance as an Automatic Stabilizer: Evidence of Effectiveness over Three Decades." Unemployment insurance occasional paper 99-8. Washington, DC: U.S. Department of Labor.

Commission on Family and Medical Leave. 1996. *A Workable Balance: Report to Congress on Family Medical Leave Policies*. Washington, DC: U.S. Department of Labor, Women's Bureau.

Dunlop Commission. 1995. *Fact Finding Report: Commission on the Future of Worker-Management Relations*. Washington, DC: U.S. Government Printing Office.

duRivage, V., F. Carré, and C. Tilley. 1998. "Making Labor Law Work for Part-Time and Contingent Workers." In *Contingent Work: American Employment Relations in Transition*, K. Barker and K. Christensen, eds. Ithaca, NY: ILR Press, pp. 263–280.

Gonos, G. 1997. "The Contest over 'Employer' Status in the Postwar United States: The Case of Temporary Help Firms." *Law and Society Review* 31(1): 81–110.

Haber, W., and M. Murray. 1966. *Unemployment Insurance in the American Economy: An Historical Review and Analysis.* Homewood, IL: Richard D. Irwin.

Kalleberg, Arne L., Barbara F. Reskin, and Ken Hudson. 2000. "Bad Jobs in America: Standard and Nonstandard Employment Relations and Job Quality in the United States." *American Sociological Review* 65(2): 256–278.

Kunda, G., S. Barley, and J. Evans. 2002. "Why Do Contractors Contract? The Experience of Highly Skilled Technical Professionals in a Contingent Labor Market." *Industrial and Labor Relations Review* 55(2): 234–261.

Lawrence, T., and V. Corwin. 2003. "Being There: The Acceptance and Marginalization of Part-Time Professional Employees." *Journal of Organizational Behavior* 24(1): 1–21.

Maltby, L., and D. Yamada. 1997. "Beyond 'Economic Realities': The Case for Amending Federal Employment Discrimination Laws to Include Independent Contractors." *Boston College Law Review* 38(2): 239–274.

Occupational Safety and Health Act, 29 U.S.C. § 654(a) (1970).

Parker, R. 1994. *Flesh Peddlers and Warm Bodies: The Temporary Help Industry and Its Workers*. New Brunswick, NJ: Rutgers University Press.

Stone, D. 1988. *Policy Paradox and Political Reason*. New York: Harper Collins.

U.S. Department of Labor. Employment and Training Administration. 1996. "Comparison of State Unemployment Insurance Laws." Washington, DC:

200 Wenger

- U.S. Department of Labor, Unemployment Insurance Division, January 7.
————. 2001. "Comparison of State Unemployment Insurance Laws." Washington, DC: U.S. Department of Labor, Unemployment Insurance Division, January 7.
Vizcaino v. Microsoft Corporation, 97 F.3d 1187 (Ninth Cir. 1995).
Vroman, W. 1991. "The Decline in Unemployment Insurance Claims Activity in the 1980s." Unemployment insurance occasional paper 91-2. Washington, DC: U.S. Department of Labor, Employment and Training Administration.
Waldfogel, J. 1999. "Family and Medical Leave: Evidence from the 2000 Surveys." *Monthly Labor Review* 124(9): 17–23.
Wenger, J. 2000. "Falling through the Cracks: Unemployment Insurance in an Era of Contingent Work." PhD dissertation, University of North Carolina.
————. 2001. "Divided We Fall." Briefing paper no. 110. Washington, DC: Economic Policy Institute.
Wenger, J., R. McHugh, and N. Segal. 2002. "Part-Time Work, Inadequate Unemployment Benefits." *Indicators—The Journal of Social Health* 1(4): 99–112.

Part 4

Perspectives on the Shadow Workforce from Japan and Europe

7
Japan's Growing
Shadow Workforce

Cynthia Ozeki
California State University, Dominguez Hills

Akira Wakisaka
Gakushuin University

Temporary clerical workers. Computer programmers on short-term contracts. Manual laborers hired by the day, part-time store clerks, middle managers on loan from related firms. The work they do is different, but all have something important in common: they are *hiseishain*, or nonregular workers, and by label at least they are non-core employees, handicapped in their ability to take advantage of Japan's strong internal labor markets. They are less likely than co-workers with the status of regular employees to have access to the career ladders and relative employment security that are often referred to as Japan's "lifetime employment system."[1]

According to a Japanese government survey, in July 2005 the country had an estimated 16.5 million nonregular workers in a workforce that includes about 50 million employees nationwide (Japanese Statistics Bureau 2005). Nonregular workers thus represent nearly one-third of the nation's employees. Their ranks have been rapidly growing over the past few years, while the number of regular employees has declined. Figure 7.1 illustrates how the percentage of Japanese employees with nonregular status has climbed as companies have turned to nontraditional employment arrangements in their struggle to deal with years of economic malaise.[2] Since the early 1990s, a sustainable recovery has seemed elusive. Throughout 2005 there were several positive signs, including the first rise in real estate prices in 15 years, an impressive stock market index rise of around 40 percent, and indications of an impending end to years of continued deflation. Many analysts are

Figure 7.1 Changes in the Number and Ratio of Regular and Nonregular Employees

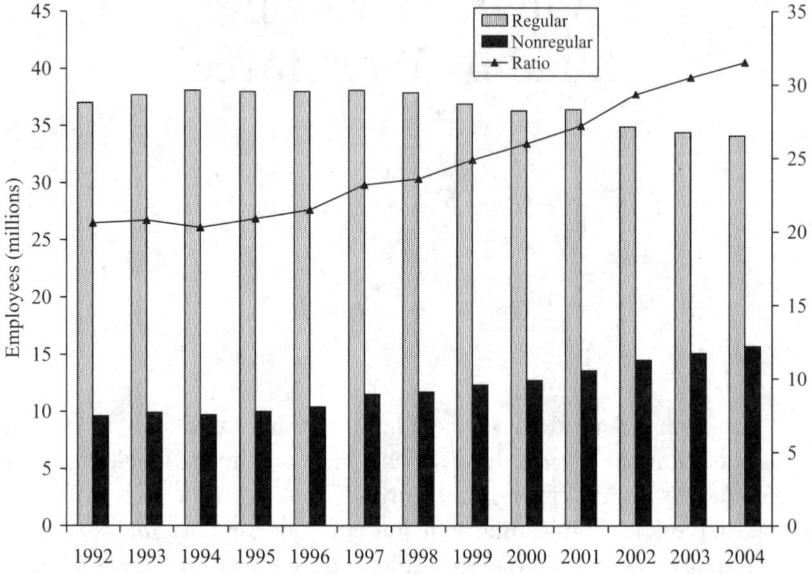

SOURCE: Japanese Ministry of Health, Labour and Welfare (2004).

optimistic that this time an end to years of misery is in sight, especially since there has been considerable restructuring in many areas (Fackler 2006; Reuters, Bloomberg News 2005). Because of the economy, many companies have been forced to merge, restructure, and reduce the number of employees through attrition, early retirement programs, or layoffs. Affected companies have also limited the number of new regular employees hired, and many workers, both young and midcareer, found themselves joining the ranks of the shadow workforce.

Who are these people? In this chapter we look at contingent work in Japan and discuss the various types of workers that make up the nonregular category of employees. Government statistics on nonregular workers provide a good starting point for exploring this issue. Although the terms nonregular employee and contingent worker are far from synonymous, these statistics are particularly helpful in understanding the situation because employers themselves classify the workers as regular or nonregular.[3] We use demographic and industry data to identify the kinds of people employed in nonregular positions, the kind of work they do, and where they work.

In the second section, we focus on the largest group of contingent workers—part-time workers—and the group of workers expected to grow the most rapidly—workers dispatched by temporary employment agencies. From a policymaking perspective, the growth of contingent employment raises an important issue: whether becoming a contingent worker is a voluntary or involuntary decision. Are workers choosing these jobs because they find them appealing for some reason, or do they fall into them because they have few other options? To what extent are organizational needs and worker desires behind the growth in nonregular employment? To evaluate this, we review the results of government surveys of employers and employees. An important part of this issue is the effect of nonregular employment on workers, and we look briefly at some of the implications of such arrangements. We conclude with a discussion of recent social and regulatory trends that may affect growth in contingent work arrangements in the future and provide suggestions for future research.

CORE AND CONTINGENT WORKERS: CATEGORIES AND DEMOGRAPHICS

To understand the position of core and contingent workers, it is useful to first discuss the terminology. In Japan, the majority of workers are hired as *seishain*, which is frequently translated as "regular employees" or "lifetime employees." This group of full-time employees works with the understanding that, barring serious misconduct or severe organizational problems, they will have jobs until retirement; in this chapter we refer to them as regular or core employees. Those outside this category are called nonregular or noncore employees. In general, regular employees have greater access to training, promotion tracks and associated pay raises, pensions and other forms of social insurance, as well as greater job security. However, it is important to note that these core employees will not all remain in their firms until their mid-sixties, and many nonregular workers form long-term ties to the organizations where they work. Consequently, these categories are not as mutually exclusive as they may appear.

To investigate where the changes in nonregular employment are the most pronounced, we use the results of the Japanese Ministry of Health, Labour and Welfare's (MHLW's) Comprehensive Survey on Diversification Employment Forms.[4] This survey provides information on employment status based on industry, place of employment, gender, and firm size in 1999 and 2003; these are summarized in Tables 7.1 and 7.2. Because of changes in classification, comparison with earlier editions of the study are difficult; only data for 2003 are presented in Table 7.2.

As shown in the Table 7.1, in 2003 the vast majority of Japanese (65.4 percent) were classified as regular employees. In this chapter we focus on the remaining 34.6 percent who are nonregular employees. They have been divided into seven major categories: transferred workers, reemployed seniors, workers dispatched by temporary employment agencies, part-timers, temporary and day workers, contract workers, and other nonregular workers, an ad hoc category that is not discussed in detail here.

Transferred Workers

The first group of nonregular employees provides some insight into Japanese personnel systems: *shukko shain*, or "transferred workers" who are on loan from another organization, usually one with close ties, like a parent firm, main bank, or sister subsidiary. While there are various reasons why a worker might be transferred, one increasingly common personnel practice is to transfer older workers who have reached a career plateau to smaller, related firms (Sato 1997). Initially, these workers remain part of their original firms and are paid at their current salary rates, and their pay is often subsidized or provided by their original organizations. However, after two to five years they may be asked to officially join the new firm. If they do, they are no longer classified as transferred employees but rather would be considered regular employees of the new firm. Salaries at the new organization are often lower, but one advantage for individuals is that they may be able to work longer. This practice also can provide value for the new firm if it lacks experienced managerial personnel and is able to acquire them in this way. Transferred workers generally work full time. Although they

Table 7.1 Regular and Nonregular Employment Forms, by Sex and Establishment Size (%)

	Total regular		Nonregular employees													
			Total		Transfer		Temporary		Contract		Dispatched		Part-time		Other	
	1999	2003	1999	2003	1999	2003	1999	2003	1999	2003	1999	2003	1999	2003	1999	2003
Sex																
Total	72.5	65.4	27.5	34.6	1.3	1.5	1.8	0.8	2.3	2.3	1.1	2.0	14.5	23.0	6.5	4.8
Male	85.1	80.0	14.9	20.0	1.8	2.2	1.8	0.9	2.1	1.9	0.6	1.0	5.2	9.6	3.4	4.4
Female	53.0	44.4	47.0	55.6	0.4	0.6	2.0	0.8	2.6	2.9	1.8	3.4	28.9	42.5	11.3	5.5
Establishment size																
1,000 +	74.9	81.0	25.1	19.0	1.0	1.8	0.4	0.2	2.7	2.4	2.0	3.7	14.1	7.4	4.9	3.4
500–999	75.7	73.8	24.3	26.2	2.0	2.9	0.9	0.4	1.7	3.4	1.1	3.9	12.3	11.1	6.4	4.5
300–499	69.1	69.1	30.9	30.9	2.5	1.9	6.7	0.2	3.3	2.8	1.1	2.6	12.1	18.1	5.2	5.4
100–299	73.4	68.6	26.6	31.4	1.9	1.5	0.7	0.3	2.8	3.1	0.9	2.3	13.8	18.5	6.5	5.6
50–29	69.8	63.9	30.2	36.1	1.5	2.0	2.2	0.6	1.7	2.5	0.7	2.6	14.9	23.6	9.3	4.7
30–49	74.6	63.4	25.4	36.6	0.7	1.4	1.8	0.7	2.2	2.2	0.5	1.5	13.4	26.1	6.9	4.8
5–29	70.2	62.1	29.8	37.9	0.5	1.2	2.6	1.3	1.8	1.9	0.4	1.2	17.3	27.5	7.2	4.8

NOTE: In 2003, the part-time worker category does not include pseudo-part-timers (those who are on part-time career paths but work over 35 hours a week). In 1999, such workers accounted for 5.8 percent.
SOURCE: MHLW Comprehensive Survey on Diversification of Employment Forms, 1999, 2003.

Table 7.2 Regular and Nonregular Workers, by Industry and Workplace (percent of employed workers), 2003

	Regular	Nonregular	Transferred	Reemployed seniors	Dispatched	Contract	Temporary & day	Part-time	Other
Industry									
Construction	85.6	14.4	1.8	1.6	1.0	1.9	0.8	2.5	4.8
Manufacturing	76.7	23.3	1.7	1.5	2.0	1.4	0.3	12.7	3.8
Utilities	91.2	8.8	1.1	2.0	0.8	2.2	0.0	1.6	1.1
Transportation	77.3	22.7	1.5	2.2	1.6	3.2	0.7	10.8	2.7
Wholesale/retail	54.7	45.3	0.8	0.8	1.4	1.4	0.7	37.3	3.0
Finance/insurance	78.3	21.7	1.4	1.6	8.7	2.2	0.0	6.2	1.6
Real estate	64.1	35.9	5.0	5.2	2.0	4.8	0.5	15.5	3.0
Restaurant/hotel	29.1	70.9	0.4	0.6	0.5	2.0	0.5	62.8	4.1
Medical/welfare	70.2	29.8	1.5	1.3	0.8	2.8	0.2	20.7	2.4
Education	60.8	39.2	0.4	1.7	2.0	10.3	0.3	21.7	2.8
Complex service	79.8	20.2	0.6	1.0	0.7	1.9	1.1	7.9	7.0
Service	58.7	41.3	2.6	2.3	2.2	3.5	2.8	23.6	4.4
Workplace									
Office	74.7	25.3	2.3	1.9	2.9	2.8	1.4	10.7	3.3
Factory	73.8	26.2	1.6	1.4	1.9	1.1	0.4	15.9	3.9
R&D lab	82.9	17.1	3.4	0.7	5.7	3.0	0.2	3.7	0.4
Branch	73.1	26.9	1.7	1.6	2.2	3.8	0.3	14.7	2.7
Sale outlet	35.2	64.8	0.3	0.4	0.7	1.1	0.8	57.8	3.7
Other	66.7	33.3	1.3	1.5	1.3	4.1	0.8	20.7	3.5

SOURCE: MHLW Comprehensive Survey on Diversification of Employment Forms, 1999, 2003.

are not labeled as regular staff during this period, they are clearly still participants in the lifetime employment system and tend to be covered by social insurance and pension policies.

While this system has been gaining in legitimacy, the number of workers on loan at any given time is fairly low. As shown in Tables 7.1 and 7.2, transferred workers are more likely to be older males, and they are most strongly represented in the real estate industry. However, growth in this type of employment has been limited in recent years. Transferred workers made up only 1.5 percent of employees in 2003, similar to the percentage reported in 1999 and previous years. Such workers made up only 2.9 percent of employees in midsize firms with 300–500 employees, where they were most strongly represented. It is important to recognize, however, that workers no longer fall into this category if they have officially become regular employees of their new firms, so this measure includes only those currently "on loan."

Reemployed seniors

The second group of nonregular employees is older workers nearing the end of their careers. *Shokutaku*, reemployed seniors, is a group of older workers who generally have either resigned or retired from positions as regular employees. Most Japanese companies have mandatory retirement, usually at age 60 or 65.[5] However, many companies find that they can still use senior citizens' knowledge and skills. Employees, too, may wish to work longer for personal fulfillment or financial reasons. As a result, many companies are rehiring retired senior citizens as nonregular employees, often with different work responsibilities, conditions, and compensation packages. This approach, while likely to grow in importance as the workforce ages, is relatively new, so data were not collected on this group as part of the Survey on Diversification of Employment Forms until 2003. As Table 7.2 indicates, these workers are most concentrated in real estate, where they represent already 5.2 percent of industry workers. They also represent 2.2 percent of employees in the transportation industry and around 1.5 percent of employees in the construction, manufacturing, finance, medical, and education fields. Reemployed seniors are most likely to be found working in offices, where they make up about 2 percent of workers, or factories and branches, where they make up about 1.5 percent. Few work in sales or research and development.

Because of the falling birthrate, the number of young people entering the workforce has been declining over the years. Reemploying seniors is one way to deal with the challenges of an aging workforce, so this category of nonregular employees should be closely watched.

Temporary and Day Workers

While the number of reemployed seniors seems poised to grow, the situation for the next category of nonregular workers is unclear—the numbers of temporary and day workers have been shrinking, but they may grow if the economy does. Approximately 2.8 percent of workers in service industries and 0.8 percent of those in the construction industry are classified by their employers as temporary or day workers (Table 7.2). Temporary workers are those with work agreements extending between one month and one year; day workers have been hired for a period of less than one month. Many, however, are regularly "rehired" under such agreements and may enjoy more employment security than this implies, particularly when the economy is strong. The current percentages, particularly in the construction industry, are much lower than in previous, more prosperous times.

In fact, employees in this category made up just 0.8 percent of the country's total workforce in 2003, as shown in Table 7.2. This is a drop from the 1.8 percent estimated for 1999, which again is lower than in previous surveys. While currently small, the number of workers in this category, particularly in construction, may rise if economic recovery continues strong.

Contract Workers

Contract workers, whose employment agreements have specific rather than open-ended time limits, made up 2.3 percent of all employees in both 1999 and 2003, as shown in Table 7.1. Both genders are represented: 1.9 percent of Japanese male workers and 2.9 percent of female workers were employed on a contract basis in 2003. Foreign workers and computer specialists are among those often hired on a renewable contract basis. Of all the categories of employment in Japan, this one most closely resembles the short-term consulting or project-based hiring that has become a regular practice in some U.S. businesses as firms have sought to downsize, only to discover that they still occasionally need the skills of their former employees. However, contract workers in Japan are not necessarily former employees. The similarity is due to the fact that they are hired for their skills for limited periods which may be extended if the need continues.

Contract workers are most likely to be found in the education field, where they made up 10.3 percent of all employees, or in real estate or services, where around 5 percent of employees were hired under such contracts. They are most often found working in branches, labs, or offices (Table 7.2). Another group of workers that are hired under time-limited contracts are those who are dispatched by agencies.

Workers Dispatched by Temporary Employment Agencies

Although there were some firms that specialized in locating contract employees, temporary employment agencies were officially prohibited until 1985. This prohibition was at least partially because of Japan's history of limiting the activities of temporary agencies to encourage long-term employment relationships between employers and employees. Even when legalized, temporary employment agencies were limited to providing staff for a few types of white-collar positions, such as computer programming or secretarial work.

Workers dispatched by temporary employment agencies represented a mere 2.0 percent of all employees in Japan in 2003, as shown in Table 7.1, but this is up from just 0.07 percent in 1994 and 1.1 percent in 1999. This category has strong potential for continued growth due to regulatory changes. In 1985 the Japanese government instituted new regulations that opened the way for the expanded use of temporary employment agencies and gradually increased the number of occupations for which agencies were allowed to provide workers to 26 by 1996. In 1999, the government further expanded the industries and occupations that could be staffed by temporary workers to include all except port transportation (longshoremen), construction, security services, and others so designated by the government. More regulatory changes came into effect in 2004, when the length of time dispatched employees could be used for a position was increased from one year to three.[6] The new policy direction was chosen in the hopes of opening up new options for skilled women and older men seeking employment.[7]

Dispatched workers are most concentrated in the finance sector. Table 7.2 shows that they made up 8.7 percent of workers in that industry in 2003, a jump from the 3.6 percent reported in a similar survey done in 1994. With the use of dispatched workers recently made legal in most jobs, continued growth can be expected and additional study is needed. The attention that dispatched workers have already received from researchers and policymakers is rivaled only by employees in one other nonregular category, part-time workers.

Part-Time Workers

By far the largest group of nonregular workers is composed of part-time workers. As shown in Table 7.1, 23.0 percent of all Japanese employees were hired as part-timers in 2003, up from 14.5 percent in 1999. While nearly 10 percent of male employees were part-timers in 2003, 42.5 percent of female workers fell into this category, nearly equaling the 44.4 percent of women who were hired as regular employees. As shown in Table 7.2, 62.8 percent of employees in the restaurant and hotel industry were part-timers in 2003, as were 37.3 percent of employees in the wholesale and retail field, and just over 20 percent of workers in the medical and education areas. Even in factories, nearly 16 percent of workers are part-timers.

Although the data are somewhat older, one of the best sources of information on this group of workers is the 2001 MHLW Survey on Part-Time Workers. That study found that there were approximately 11.2 million part-time workers, representing 26.1 percent of all employees and about three-quarters of all nonregular workers. The difference in percentages reflects a difference in the definition of part-timers. While the Comprehensive Survey on Diversification of Employment Forms includes only workers who work shorter hours, the MHLW study includes *giji-paato*, or what we refer to in this paper as "pseudo-part-timers," workers who are officially hired by their companies as nonregular workers and classified as "part-timers" but who actually work over 35 hours a week. The study found that approximately 14.9 percent of the country's part-time workers are "other part-timers," a broad classification that comprises pseudo-part-timers and several different types of nonregular employees, such as seasonal workers at auto factories.

In Japan, then, there are two different types of part-time workers—those who work shorter hours, and those who have been labeled part-timers as a way of showing that they are not regular "lifetime" employees. In the United States, the determination of part-time employment is based solely on hours of work. In Japan, on the other hand, the identification of an employee as part-time is a description of a career path and the human resource (HR) practices that accompany it. The part-time label in Japan is similar to the American idea of a "mommy track" career option for women. In the United States, the idea of a "mommy track" first gained popularity in prestigious law firms where female lawyers wished to reduce their weekly work hours from the 70-plus often required at junior levels to a more reasonable 35 to 45 hours, giving them more time for their families. While a 40-hour week is not part-time, it involves working fewer hours than more career-focused colleagues at such firms. In Japan, the situation involving part-time workers is often similar.

Many Japanese organizations have developed "part-time" positions largely as a way to hire women in their thirties and older who wish to combine work with caring for their families. These nonregular workers vary in the degree to which their positions are truly contingent. Some have low-skill, short-term, dead-end jobs, but others may do skilled work for the same organization for years. They often perform the same tasks as regular employees and work alongside them. While some organizations are experimenting with career paths specifically for part-timers or allowing workers to switch from part-time to regular employee status, one problem for motivated "part-time" workers is that they are less likely to have access to the same career options as regular workers. They also tend to have lower hourly wages, something we will discuss in greater detail later in the chapter.

Differences in education also provide some insights into wage differentials. Table 7.3 indicates that 59.8 percent of workers with only a junior high education are in contingent work arrangements, while only 17.1 percent of university graduates are in such arrangements. Just under 40 percent of workers with a high school or technical school education are in contingent work, along with just over 30 percent of junior college graduates.[8]

Table 7.3 Employed Workers with Regular and Alternative Work Arrangements, by Educational Attainment (percentage of graduates), 2003

	Junior high	High school	Technical school	Junior college	University
Regular employees	40.2	61.2	62.0	68.2	82.9
Nonregular employees	59.8	38.8	38.0	31.8	17.1
Transferred	1.4	1.5	1.1	0.8	2.5
Reemployed seniors	6.9	1.7	1.0	0.5	1.0
Temporary	2.3	1.0	0.3	0.2	0.4
Contract	3.4	2.0	4.3	2.5	2.6
Dispatched	1.5	1.6	2.9	3.7	1.9
Part-time	34.2	27.6	23.8	21.2	7.1
Other	10.1	3.9	4.4	2.9	1.6

NOTE: Figures indicate percentage of workers at each level of schooling whose jobs fall into the employee category.
SOURCE: MHLW (2005).

Dramatic growth in the percentage of employees with part-time status can be seen in nearly every industry and type of workplace. Because they represent the fastest-growing category as well as the majority of nonregular workers, we will explore the conditions and motivations of workers classified as part-timers in greater detail.

Nonregular Employment: A Summary

While nonregular employment may not be strictly viewed as contingent, workers in this category in general enjoy less job security and are less likely to be considered for training and promotion opportunities. As nonregular employees, they would rarely be considered for middle- or upper-level management positions in larger organizations. Although there are slight differences in the findings of various government surveys, it is clear that the number of nonregular workers is increasing in Japan. This trend is important since more than one-third of the country's workforce already falls into the nonregular category.

We have discussed all of the categories generally included in nonregular employment. We will now turn our focus to the largest group, part-time workers, and the group most likely to show strong growth in the future: employees dispatched by temporary employment agencies. Because these two groups have been studied more extensively than other nonregular workers, there are more data available about them.

WHY CONTINGENT EMPLOYMENT ARRANGEMENTS?

The two groups on which we have chosen to focus have one important thing in common: they both are predominantly female. According to the Japanese Ministry of Public Management, Home Affairs, Posts and Telecommunications (MPHPT) Labour Force Survey, in 2001 7.1 million of Japan's 7.7 million part-timers were female (92 percent), and women make up the majority of dispatched employees as well (MPHPT 2003). Currently, well over half of all working women fit into one of these two categories, a marked contrast to 1960, when just 5.9 percent of working women were classified as part-timers and worker dispatching was not permitted. Over subsequent years the percentage of female employees who are classified as part-timers has gradually risen, passing the 20 percent mark in the early 1980s, the 30 percent mark in the early 1990s, and the 50 percent mark early in the new century (Bureau of Labor Statistics 2002, 2005). During that time, the percentage of self-employed women and those working in the fields or family enterprises also has declined. As women have moved into the corporate world, part-time employment and dispatching agencies have emerged as routes to jobs for those who have quit regular employment to focus on family. In this next section we will look at why employers and workers are choosing nonregular employment arrangements and some of the broader implications.

Nonregular Employment: The Employer Perspective

Firms in the United States have found that the potential benefits of using contingent workers include reducing wage and benefit costs, saving money on training by employing already trained employees, and flexibility in adjusting the size of the workforce to changing economic conditions. A common strategy is to keep core competencies in the hands of more permanent core employees, with temporary workers doing more simple and/or peripheral work and serving as buffers against changing circumstances and needs.[9] Japanese employers apparently have found similar benefits in hiring nonregular employees.

As part of the General Survey on Part-Time Workers, the MHLW surveyed both employers and employees on their reasons for choosing this employment arrangement, analyzing the responses separately for part-timers working less than 35 hours a week and for those hired on part-time or other nonregular career tracks (pseudo/other part-timers) but working essentially full-time hours. The results are summarized in Tables 7.4 and 7.5.

Employers were allowed to choose all applicable reasons for hiring part-time workers. As might be expected, the leading reason given for hiring part-timers in all cases was reducing personnel expenses, chosen by 65.3 percent of employers in 2001 (see Table 7.4). While this was also the leading response in 1995, at that time it was selected by only 38.3 percent of employers as a reason for hiring part-timers, and 29.3 percent as a reason for hiring pseudo-part-timers. Also among the top four reasons for hiring part-time workers in 2001 were coping with peak demand periods on an annual (39.2 percent) and daily (27.3 percent) basis, and the fact that work tasks were easy (31.4 percent). While increased work volume was also a popular response in 1995, only 17.1 percent of employers cited it as a reason for hiring part-timers in 2001, about the same number who said that it was easy to hire such workers, and that such arrangements lead to easier employment adjustments when work volume declines.

The 1995 survey asked employers to consider separately their reasons for hiring "true" and "other" part-timers. Overall they were similar, but some differences did emerge. Respondents were much more likely to say that they had hired pseudo- and other part-timers because they wanted workers with skills, knowledge, and experience, and because this was viewed as a useful mechanism for rehiring women who had previously left the organization, presumably to care for their families. They were much less likely to say that such workers were easy to hire, that their tasks were easy, or that they were hired to help cope with annual peaks in demand.

Perhaps almost as interesting as looking at the reasons employers gave for hiring workers as part-timers are the reasons they did not. In

Table 7.4 Employer Perspective: Reasons for Hiring Nonregular Employees (percentage of employers who agreed)

	Part-timers		Pseudo/other part-timers[a]
	1995	2001	1995
Increased work volume	29.8	17.1	26.8
Difficult to hire new graduates as regular employees	10.7	5.8	9.1
Easy to hire such workers	19.9	17.8	9.8
Cope with peak demand periods each day	9.3	27.3	10.7
Cope with peak demand periods on an annual basis	37.3	39.2	9.2
To hire workers with experience, skills, and knowledge	13.2	12.2	21.1
The tasks involved are easy	35.7	31.4	19.0
To reduce personnel expenses	38.3	65.3	29.3
Easier to make employment adjustments when work volume declines	12.4	16.4	12.8
Way of rehiring or extending the work years of older workers	4.4	7.3	3.6
Useful to rehire women who have previously left the organization	5.8	5.1	20.9
Other	9.0	6.5	16.8

NOTE: Figures given indicate the percentage of responding employers who checked each reason given for hiring such workers. Figures are totals for all industries; multiple responses were permitted.

[a] Pseudo-part-timers are those who are classified as part-time workers by their employers but who actually work over 35 hours per week. Other part-timers are those who have been included in this category because they are not regular employees but generally do not work shorter than normal hours (e.g., seasonal factory workers).

SOURCE: MHLW (2002).

2001 a mere 7.3 percent mentioned using this as a means to extend the employment of older workers, and only 5.8 percent said that they had hired part-timers because it was difficult to hire fresh graduates as regular employees.

In summary, employers preferred to hire workers under a part-time arrangement because it reduced costs and provided labor force flexibil-

Table 7.5 Employee Perspective: Reasons Women Work as Nonregular Employees (percentage of workers who agreed)

	Part-timers		Pseudo/other part-timers[a]	
	1995	2001	1995	2001
The hours are a convenient fit with my daily schedule	55.8	50.9	23.0	21.0
Shorter hours	27.9	34.2	10.5	12.2
Good pay and conditions	7.7	7.4	11.2	12.7
Interesting work	18.0	21.7	23.6	25.0
Easy to quit	7.8	5.6	6.1	3.7
Could not find a full-time position	14.3	20.8	33.0	37.6
Cannot work full time due to household responsibilities	19.8	18.3	8.9	9.0
Cannot work full time due to elder/invalid care responsibilities	2.0	2.2	2.0	1.3
Cannot work full time due to personal health problems	5.9	4.7	5.9	2.9
Because my friends and acquaintances are part-timers	6.8	5.5	6.8	2.8
Other	8.3	9.2	8.3	20.1

NOTE: Figures given indicate the percentage of responding female employees who checked each reason given for taking a "part-time" position. Figures are totals for all industries and demographic groups; multiple responses were permitted.

[a] Pseudo-part-timers are those who are classified as part-time workers by their employers, but who actually work over 35 hours per week. Other part-timers are those who have been included in this category because they are not regular employees, but generally do not work shorter than normal hours (e.g., seasonal factory workers).

SOURCE: MHLW (2002).

ity. In the case of pseudo- and other part-timers, the firms hired these workers in part because of their skills and knowledge, often obtained through previous regular employment. Employers did not indicate they were hiring part-timers because they were unable to recruit regular employees; instead, they appreciated the benefits of hiring workers under nonregular agreements.

Why Nonregular Work? The Employee Perspective

If economic benefits are the primary reason for employers to hire nonregular employees, what is the appeal for the workers themselves? The same study sheds some light on the issue. As shown in Table 7.5, in 2001 only 7.4 percent of true female part-time workers cited good pay and conditions as a reason they chose to take on their jobs. Only 5.6 percent of the surveyed women cited ease of quitting. The most popular responses were that the hours were convenient given their daily routine (50.9 percent) and the shorter working hours (34.2 percent). About one-fifth cited interesting work and the need to handle household responsibilities as reasons for taking a part-time position. Almost 21 percent in 2001 said they did so because they could not find a full-time position; 14.3 percent gave that response in 1995.

As might be expected, there were differences between the reasons given by true part-timers and those who are merely labeled as such. The leading reason pseudo- and other part-timers were in such a position: they could not find a full-time job as a regular employee. A lack of regular employment options was cited by 37.6 percent of such part-timers in 2001, up from 33.0 percent in 1995. On a more positive note, 25 percent gave interesting work as a reason for choosing their position, while about one-fifth noted that their work hours were convenient. Pseudo- and other part-timers were slightly more enthusiastic about the economic benefits of their jobs than their truly part-time colleagues: 12.7 percent noted that the pay and conditions were good. As might be expected, given that these employees worked over 35 hours a week, the inability to work full-time was not a major factor; however, 12.2 percent cited shorter hours as a reason for taking such a position.

A separate survey conducted in 2003 provides information on the motivation of part-time and dispatched employees of both sexes (MHLW 2005). The responses of male part-timers were similar to their female counterparts, as shown in Table 7.6. The leading reason for taking a part-time position, mentioned by almost 50 percent, was convenient hours. About one-fourth gave shorter hours and the need to supplement family income as reasons for taking their part-time jobs, and about one-fifth cited convenient fit with family or personal activities and a shorter commute. Over one-fourth of the part-time men could not find a position as a regular full-time employee. The main differences between the

Table 7.6 Reasons for Choosing Nonregular Jobs, 2003 (percentage of employees choosing each option, multiple responses allowed)

	Part-timers		Dispatched workers	
	Male	Female	Male	Female
Utilize qualification or skill	11.9	9.0	35.4	17.8
More money	6.8	7.0	20.4	14.6
Could not find work as a regular employee	26.8	20.5	42.0	39.6
Dislike restrictions by firms	11.5	6.7	16.4	24.6
Shorter hours	23.3	29.9	4.9	17.0
Convenient hours	45.4	37.6	8.6	16.7
To qualify for income-related tax or social insurance benefits	4.3	13.9	1.6	5.7
Easy tasks and less responsibility	11.9	10.6	6.1	6.3
Supplement household income	23.4	46.0	5.9	17.7
Compatible with family or other activity	17.9	27.3	10.2	26.6
Shorter commute	18.5	36.0	12.1	15.7
Health	2.5	6.2	2.1	2.9
Earn personal spending money	30.7	27.4	10.8	18.1
Other	0.5	1.9	6.7	3.8

SOURCE: MHLW (2005).

responses of male and female part-timers in this survey is that women were slightly more enthusiastic about work schedules that would allow them to balance their work and family lives, as well as somewhat less likely to have been unable to find a job as a regular employee.

The inability to secure a position as a regular employee was one of the leading reasons both men and women chose to become dispatched workers, cited by 39.6 percent of women and 42 percent of men. Nearly one-fifth of female dispatched workers also cited family needs or the ability to use special qualifications or skills as a reason for taking a nonregular position or reported disliking restrictions at regular jobs. Financially, too, some dispatched workers feel they have an advantage over employees in "regular" positions: more money was given as a reason by 20.4 percent of men and 14.6 percent of women. While some men also referred to a dislike for company restrictions on regular workers (16.4

percent), male dispatched workers were much less likely than women to have such feelings or to be motivated by shorter, more convenient hours, shorter commutes, or the notion that a nonregular position was compatible with family or other activities.

To summarize, convenient hours that mesh well with personal schedules are one of the main reasons many nonregular employees, particularly women, have taken such positions. Shorter, convenient hours appear to provide a strong attraction for women in truly part-time positions, and even a fair number of dispatched workers appreciate this aspect of their work. On the other hand, high proportions of both men and women working as dispatched employees or pseudo/other part-timers reported that they had tried and failed to find positions as regular employees. For men, good pay or the ability to use skills often were reasons for choosing their work.

INSTITUTIONAL INFLUENCES

Several institutional characteristics influence the labor market choices made by Japanese women and the staffing decisions made by Japanese employers.

Factors Affecting Women's Choices

Some workers seek shorter hours because they need to combine employment with household responsibilities. Their decision is reinforced by the expectations placed on employees in the lifetime employment system and the income tax system.

The benefits of being a regular employee are many in Japan: beyond a high degree of job security, career-track employees have traditionally gained through predictable salaries designed to match life-cycle needs. As regular employees' skills (and often family responsibilities) grow, so does their income. On the downside, however, Japanese companies require regular employees to work long hours, socialize with co-workers and customers in the evenings, attend company sporting events on the weekends, and relocate whenever and wherever requested. The dedication required can make it difficult for regular employees to contribute to the household in other respects since many will be away from home from 7 in the morning until 8 or 10 at night, leaving little time to wash the dishes or help children with homework. Thus, while the relatively stable economic contribution of a regular employee is valuable, it is difficult for a family to handle daily tasks if both parents work. Having one partner who stays at home or has a less time-consuming job makes sense for families with children or elders who require care.

Japanese personnel systems have traditionally tended to promote men and track women into lower-paying, dead-end positions with the often-fulfilled expectation that they will leave when they marry or have children.[10] Generally it is the wife who adjusts her employment and handles the bulk of family responsibilities. A Japan Institute of Labour study on occupations and family life found that most wives working part time handled about 85 percent of household duties. Full-time work appears to be made possible with assistance from grandparents or other relatives, who reduce the wife's share to 65 percent; 16 husbands contributed very little.[11] Thus, demands that regular employees work long hours and relocate when requested, combined with the need for someone to handle household tasks, is one source of institutional pressure encouraging some women to select a nonregular employment option.

There are also direct financial inducements for married women to choose less-lucrative employment options. The government does not assess income taxes on the wages of a household's second earner if that person's annual earnings fall below a certain threshold, currently set at ¥1.03 million (about $8,650), although due to tax deductions the actual level at which taxes are paid is generally higher.[12] In addition, as long as earnings remain below ¥1.3 million (roughly $11,000), the second earner does not have to pay national health and pension insurance premiums, while retaining access to such benefits through the primary earner.[13] For families this means that when the second earner's income falls into the range just above ¥1.3 million, there is a drop in real earnings. Many companies also pay family allowances to male employees with wives whose earnings fall below a specified level, most commonly ¥1.3 million or ¥1.03 million (about $8,650), with the amounts varying by firm.[14] Thus, Japanese wives have several incentives to keep their earnings at a level equal to approximately $700 to $900 per month. In fact, the 2001 MHLW General Survey on Part-Time Workers' Conditions found that 29.1 percent of female part-timers earned between ¥.8

and ¥.1.0 million, and that 26.7 percent adjusted their hours so that their earnings would fall below these thresholds, with 19.4 percent of female part-timers seeking to keep their wages below ¥1.03 million (MHLW 2002).

Incentives for Employers

Companies also have financial incentives and the need for flexible staffing that make alternative forms of employment attractive, even if the wages paid regular and nonregular employees are the same. Employers bear one-half of the burden of supporting social insurance plans, but do not have to make contributions to unemployment insurance, pensions, or health insurance, and do not have to handle payroll taxes for many part-time or temporary workers. They do not make unemployment insurance contributions for part-time employees who work less than 20 hours per week, and get a reduction on rates for those who work between 20 and 30 hours per week. Although they must make contributions to social insurance schemes for those labeled as part-timers who work full-time hours, they do not pay pension or health insurance taxes for part-timers who work less than three-quarters of the weekly hours of regular workers.[15] In the case of temporary workers, many of these costs are paid by the agencies that dispatch them (Houseman and Osawa 1995). Many firms also do not provide optional benefits, such as corporate insurance, company retirement allowances, or semiannual bonuses, to nonregular workers.

Table 7.7 shows the proportion of employers who pay social insurance premiums for all, some, or none of their part-time employees, as well as the proportion providing retirement allowances, or bonuses. While most provide these benefits to all regular employees, few provide them for all part-time workers, and the difference may or may not be reflected in the wages paid to nonregular employees. The cost savings can be significant. Most regular Japanese employees receive bonus payments twice annually, in July and in December. Bonuses give Japanese companies some flexibility in personnel costs; they are adjusted to reflect firm performance and are therefore lower when the company is not doing well. In 2005, the average semiannual bonus for summer was ¥470,00 ($3,917) (MHLW 2005).

Table 7.7 Percentage of Employers Providing Benefits for Regular and Part-Time Employees, 2003

	Regular	Part-time
Employer survey		
Unemployment insurance	100.0	53.2
Health insurance	100.0	36.0
Pension insurance	100.0	33.1
Corporate insurance	23.0	3.1
Retirement allowance	66.1	7.3
Bonus	79.3	37.4
Employee survey		
Unemployment insurance	99.4	56.4
Health insurance	99.6	36.3
Pension insurance	99.3	34.7
Corporate insurance	34.0	4.3
Retirement allowance	74.7	6.0
Bonus	82.4	29.2

NOTE: Provision of unemployment, health, and pension insurance for regular workers is compulsory.
SOURCE: MHLW (2005).

Another reason that nonregular employment arrangements appeal to employers is their need for flexibility. Under the Japanese traditional lifetime employment system, employees joined the firm when young, worked hard for many years, and enjoyed gradual improvements in salary and position as they aged. As an organization grew, it was able to hire ever-larger numbers of young people who were relatively inexpensive and managed by the more experienced workers. Without growth, there was an oversupply of more expensive middle-aged workers for the limited number of management posts available.

For much of the period following World War II, the Japanese economy grew rapidly, allowing the lifetime employment model to develop and flourish. However, in recent years Japanese firms have found that constant growth is not possible. Furthermore, due to the rapid aging of Japan's population, the average age of the Japanese workforce has increased. The high level of uncertainty that characterized the 1990s when even leading financial firms failed and many businesses undertook restructuring efforts, combined with the population demographic trends, made more flexible employment arrangements attractive. Consequently, more temporary and part-time workers have been hired, without the implicit understanding that they will be trained, promoted, and given life-cycle wages.

EFFECTS OF CONTINGENT EMPLOYMENT ON EMPLOYEES

How does being hired as a noncore worker affect the economic welfare of these employees? In this section, we look briefly at the differences in compensation, social insurance coverage, career options, and legal protections. The question of whether employees voluntarily or involuntarily choose nonregular employment is discussed. Factors that may affect the future growth of nonregular employment are reviewed.

Compensation

The best data on wage disparities deal with part-time workers. There is a significant difference between the average hourly wage for full- and part-time employees. In 2004, the average hourly wage for part-time female employees was ¥833 (roughly $7.00), less than two-thirds of the pay received by women in full-time positions (see Figure 7.2). Part-time male employees earned more money, on average, but took home just over half of the average pay of their full-time counterparts (see Figure 7.3). Part-time workers of both genders earned, on average, considerably more than the Japanese minimum wage.[16]

Figures 7.2 and 7.3 show how the difference between part- and full-time wages has changed. In 1990, part-time women earned about 72 percent of the wages full-time women did; this declined to about 65 percent in 2004. Partly because full-time men tend to earn more than their female counterparts, the decline of about 7 percent has been less dramatic for part-time males.

Due to the weak economy and continued deflation, wage growth for all types of workers in Japan has been limited. However, in general, part-time workers who stay with their employers do see their wages rise.

**Figure 7.2 Wage Disparity between Part- and Full-Time Workers
(Women)**

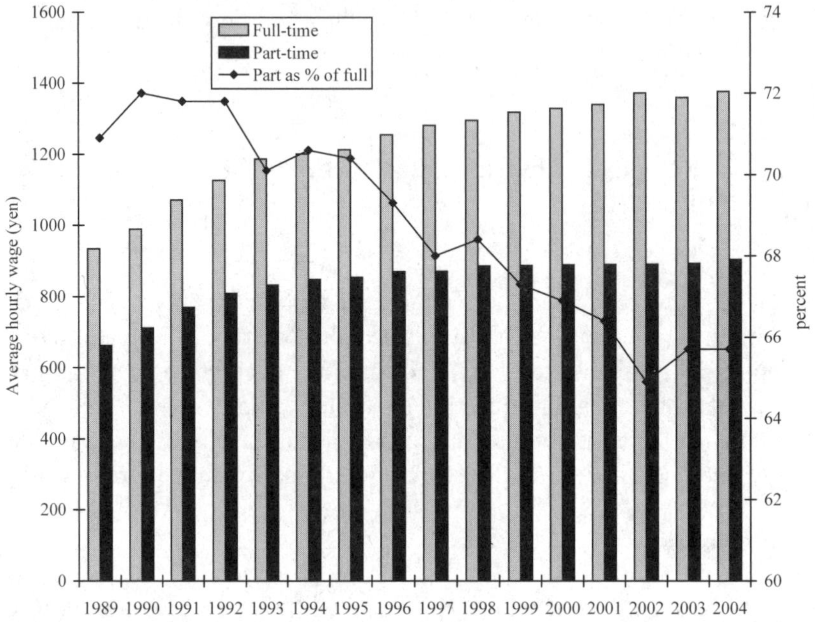

SOURCE: MHLW Basic Statistical Survey on Wage Structure, various years.

Some 29 percent of companies who participated in the MHLW study on
part-time work reported that they had implemented periodic wage increases for their part-time workers; 31 percent offered pay raises based
on seniority and 56 percent offered semiannual bonuses to workers in
this category (MHLW 2005). Several researchers have concluded that
there is little difference in the pay raises offered to regular full-time and
part-time female employees when wage data is adjusted for tenure with
the employer and women who reduced their hours to remain under the
¥1.3 million tax benefit threshold are eliminated from consideration.[17]

The courts have prevented firms from taking unfair advantage of
workers by simply labeling them nonregular workers. For example, in
1996 an auto parts manufacturer was required to pay compensation to
28 female pseudo-part-time workers who were doing essentially the

Figure 7.3 Wage Disparity between Part- and Full-Time Workers (Men)

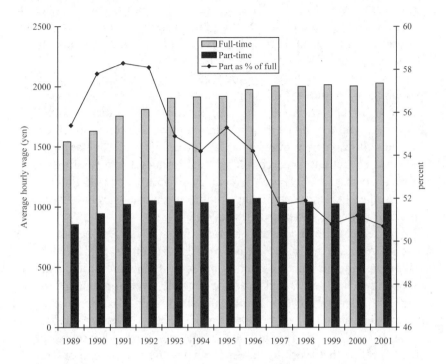

SOURCE: MHLW Basic Statistical Survey on Wage Structure, various years.

same work as full-time workers but were paid less. The court concluded that the guiding principle should be "same job, same pay" and that
paying part-time workers less than 80 percent of the wages earned by
full-time female employees in the same position with equal seniority is
illegal (Japan Institute of Labour 1996).

Compensation, however, involves more than pay, and there are
concerns that contingent workers may not receive important benefits.
Health insurance coverage, a major issue in the United States, is not a
problem for Japan's nonregular employees due to the country's national
health insurance system, which covers everyone. Occupational safety
and health coverage also is universal for all workers. However, the level
of coverage for unemployment insurance, almost universal among regular employees, stands at only 53.2 percent for part-timers (Japan Insti-

tute of Labour 1997). Similarly, just 33.1 percent of part-time workers are covered by the government's mandatory pension scheme, similar to Social Security in the United States. However, married workers whose spouses are enrolled in these programs qualify for benefits through their working spouses (Houseman and Osawa 1995).

Nonregular employees also may suffer from not being allowed to participate in employer bonus or retirement allowance programs established for regular workers. Table 7.7 shows three-quarters of surveyed employers said that all of their regular employees were involved in retirement allowance programs and 82.4 percent gave all regular employees bonuses, but only 6 percent reported offering retirement allowances to part-timers and only 29.2 percent gave bonuses to part-timers. As discussed earlier, those semiannual bonuses represent a relatively large amount of money: about $8,000 for 2005.

Retirement allowances are one-time lump sum severance payments given to workers when they leave an organization. In firms that have such plans, the amount received is based on company policy, usually reflecting salary, level, and years of service. Even for young female workers the amounts can be significant, and for older workers they represent a considerable retirement resource. The average retirement allowance paid to a 60-year-old male college graduate who retires after spending his entire working career at a single firm in clerical or technical positions and was promoted at an average rate was ¥24.35 million (approximately $202,000) in 2005.[18] Nonregular workers who do not benefit from bonus and retirement allowance plans may be at a financial disadvantage compared with regular workers.

To summarize, benefit coverage is not as complete for many nonregular workers as for regular workers, although the lack of medical insurance is not a problem. Wages, on average, are lower, but those who remain in their positions see their earnings rise at about the same pace as regular employees with similar tenure.

Career Paths

Many part-time workers remain with the same firm for many years. Over 40 percent have tenure of 5 years or more, and 18.1 percent have been with their employers 10 years or more, with the average being 5.8 years. This compares to an average of 4.8 years in 1995, when only 30 percent of part-timers had tenure of 5 years or longer. As these figures show, average tenure is growing as part-time workers remain with the same organization (MHLW 2002). Those who stay longer may become quite valuable to their employers. Several researchers have made a distinction between "core" part-timers, who may handle important tasks, including managing other part-time workers, and "supplementary" part-timers whose work tends to involve more simple, repetitive tasks and who have little opportunity for advancement or pay increases. There are no data that provide a good estimate of how many part-time workers fall into the two categories. However, it is clear that some of these workers do have opportunities for skill development and advancement, although they do not have access to the same management-training programs available to regular career-track employees. In the case of dispatched workers, the main opportunities lie in improving skills to justify better assignments and pay. In addition to development through work assignments, some dispatching firms offer training programs. While some dispatched workers are eventually hired by the firms to which they are sent, there currently is not a strong trend toward using temporary assignments as a way to screen prospective employees, as has become popular with some firms in the United States. However, the idea that such a strategy may work appears to lie behind the recent changes in the Worker Dispatching Law, and many larger companies do report having systems for switching workers to regular employee status.

Legal Protection

Nonregular workers have the same protections that regular workers do and may not be discriminated against because of their nationality, age, or gender. Since so many nonregular workers are women, the Equal Employment Opportunity Law passed in 1986 and strengthened in 1999 is particularly relevant. While the first version of the law encouraged employers to "endeavor" not to discriminate against women, the current (1999) version flatly forbids unequal treatment of male and female workers in terms of hiring, pay, promotion, and training, in addition to requiring employers to help prevent sexual harassment in the workplace. Part-time workers also have some legal protection under the admittedly weak Part-Time Work Law, which states that employers should "endeavor" to effectively utilize part-timers' abilities and maintain balance with regular workers in terms of working conditions, training, improving employee welfare, and improving employment management. The law also says that part-time workers employed continuously for one year or more should be given advance notice when the employment contract is to be terminated (Kezuka 2000).

Employment security is one major respect in which contingent workers are often viewed as being at a disadvantage. Japanese non-regular workers can, however, obtain employment security through continual renewal of contracts and long tenure. In general, Japanese employers are prohibited from abusing their right to dismiss employees, and without being able to show significant cause, it is more difficult to justify the termination of workers who have worked at a firm for a long period of time, whether as a regular employee or through regular renewal of employment agreements.[19] However, employers are more strictly bound in terms of their ability to dismiss regular workers with indefinite-term contracts than they are nonregular workers with fixed-term contracts. When economic conditions within a firm necessitate layoffs, employers have been allowed to dismiss part-time and other such nonregular workers first, depending on the circumstances (Kezuka 2000). Recently, however, employers seem to be choosing to add nonregular workers rather than cut them. It is interesting to note that, despite the economic struggles that have forced many firms to lay off employees as part of restructuring efforts, the number of nonregular workers continues to grow. Fewer than one in five employers gave the ease of conducting employment adjustment as a reason for hiring nonregular employees in the survey summarized in Table 7.4. Employers apparently are not simply seeking workers they can quickly eliminate. They are in large part motivated by the other benefits associated with hiring nonregular workers.

Voluntary or Involuntary Decision?

Have nonregular workers taken such jobs by choice or because they did not have other employment options? The answers are complex. Workers in the two major groups of nonregular employees do not have the same benefits as core workers in terms of compensation or career options, but it does not appear that all of these workers have low-paying, dead-end jobs. In the surveys reported earlier we noted that many enjoyed the shorter hours, flexibility, and in the case of male dispatched workers, good pay. On the other hand, the less-permanent nature of such employment agreements is bound to bother some. Indeed, in a 1999 survey 22 percent of temporary and 20 percent of other nonregular employees and dispatched workers wished to change jobs. Some 30 percent of the unhappy part-time and temporary workers cited the casual nature of their employment as a major reason, as did 26 percent of other nonregular workers and dispatched workers (Japan Institute of Labour 1999b).

As several writers have noted, the relatively high job-opening-to-applicant ratio for part-timers seems to indicate that employer desires are driving the growth in nonregular employment (Osawa and Kingston 1996; Wakisaka 1997). The same could be said of the rapid growth in dispatched employment, which has occurred during an economic slump that has made it more difficult for female workers, particularly, to find positions as regular employees. However, the issue is complex. As we have shown, there are many reasons why women with families may find more flexible working conditions and shorter hours attractive, particularly if they are offered some opportunities for advancement and pay increases. For some workers, nonregular employment may in fact be a voluntary choice to support their preferred lifestyle. Others, however, are dissatisfied with these employment arrangements and have taken nonregular positions only because they were unable to find other work. While this may be partly due to the poor economy, it is somewhat of a concern that the majority of the affected workers are women. Not all women in Japan enjoy the financial support of an employed spouse. Divorced and widowed women and others who must earn money to support their families need access to regular employment opportunities that will provide them with good incomes and opportunities.

Trends That May Affect Nonregular Employment

There are a number of trends in Japan that may have an impact on the growth in nonregular employment. The first is the rapid aging of the country's workforce. Birthrates have been falling for years and are now at a record low, meaning there will be fewer young, inexpensive recent graduates for Japanese firms to hire in the future. The fertility rate in 2004 showed that the average Japanese woman is having just 1.3

children in her lifetime. Given the decline in fertility, a labor shortage is a strong possibility in the next 20 years. However, shortages have not yet occurred due to a decade of economic malaise and Japan's "second baby boom generation." The corporate restructuring and bankruptcies related to the weak economy, however, have left many former regular employees seeking jobs in an unwelcoming job market. Opportunities for older workers, particularly, are limited.

The government has introduced a number of policies in response to these trends, and some of them have implications for nonregular employment in the future. First, the government has announced the goal of working toward a "gender-equal" society (Japan Institute of Labour 1999c). Concrete measures include the introduction of a mandatory child care leave to care for infants up to 18 months old. The law was recently expanded so that both male and female workers qualify for leave. While government targets call for 80 percent of mothers and 10 percent of fathers to use the program, current rates are 73.1 percent for women and a mere 0.44 percent for men. The government has recently set up a new grant program to encourage small and midsize firms to develop leave programs by partially subsidizing them. Workers also receive financial support for leaves. Through the social security system mothers and fathers of new infants on leave receive 30 percent of their salaries, and upon return to work 10 percent of their salaries are temporarily subsidized. This leave program makes it possible for new mothers to keep their jobs as regular employees (Japanese Institute for Labour Policy and Training 2005b). Inexpensive, high-quality, government-supported day care has long been available to Japanese women who are working, studying, or caring for invalids, although the centers are not necessarily open as late as many regular employees are expected to work.

Officials are also encouraging firms to hire all regular employees —male and female—under the same system, rather than having both a "career track" for men and exceptionally promising women and a "support staff track" for other women, as has been common in the past. Although heavy work expectations still pose a barrier for those with families, such measures may open the way for more women to start in and keep the same sort of regular, career-track positions as their male colleagues rather than starting out as support staff, quitting, and then returning as nonregular employees.

For those who find themselves working in nonregular positions, laws on part-time employment and worker dispatching have been created to ensure more fair treatment; a special panel convened to study these issues. These measures are discussed in greater detail in Chapter 8. The recent amendments to the Worker Dispatching Law, of course, hold great potential impact. In allowing nearly all types of jobs to be filled by dispatched workers, and permitting dispatched workers to be used for longer periods, the government has sought to introduce greater flexibility in the external labor market and create new ways for workers to find firms that need their skills.[20] The downside is the possibility that these policies could open the way for workers to fall into "permanently temporary" slots. This is one area that certainly bears close watching.

CONCLUSIONS AND DIRECTIONS FOR FUTURE RESEARCH

Nonregular employment has grown dramatically over the past few years, with about one-third of Japan's workforce and over 40 percent of working women falling into this "contingent" category. Workers in part-time employment, the largest nonregular sector, are attractive to employers because of lower costs and flexibility. Many female employees choose part-time work because of shorter hours that fit with their schedules. Growth also appears poised to take off in the dispatched employee category due to regulatory changes that allow expanded use of temporary workers and a large pool of potential workers who have had fewer regular employment options in the sluggish economy, although this may be changing. However, the future of nonregular employment also will depend on changes in the way that companies are managed, social trends concerning women, and changing demographics. The effects of new regulations will need to be carefully researched in order to make any accurate projections.

There are several important topics to be addressed in future research. One important area for analysis is worker dispatching by temporary employment agencies. Researchers need to closely follow the effects of deregulation to uncover where and how such workers are used, as well as the characteristics of dispatched workers and the effects of nonregular employment on them and their families. Particularly important from the standpoint of policy development is to determine whether a permanently less-advantaged class of workers is developing. Successful temporary-to-permanent hiring programs should be identified and any important lessons shared.

Additionally, it is important to track the effects of government efforts to create a more gender-equal society. Until now, nonregular employment has been very much a gender issue with most affected workers being female. If the new policies are effective, the percentage of nonregular employees who are women should fall. If it does not, future research should look at why the government's approach is not working and what else can be done.

Another important topic for future research is how the nonregular workers are being used in industries where growth in this type of employment is most noticeable, including transportation, wholesale/retail trade, and restaurants. Because of the prevalence of nonregular workers in the retail industry, this is one area where new ways of treating such workers has emerged. For example, one large supermarket chain has announced a policy allowing workers to switch between different employment tracks as their family situations change. Part-timers willing to switch to regular full-time status and accept transfers to other locations may be able to earn promotions; regular full-timers may choose to become part-timers assigned to just one area (Japan Institute of Labour 2002). Approaches like this one provide greater flexibility to make changes in employment status, work hours, and location throughout the very different stages of a worker's family life cycle and career, with strong potential benefits for both workers and employers. Such innovative programs need to be studied so that they can be improved and "best practices" spread throughout the country.

Nonregular employment holds advantages for both workers and employers. However, both researchers and policymakers must closely monitor this growing phenomenon to ensure that nonregular workers are not permanently enshadowed by clearly inferior conditions without obtaining some benefits.

Notes

1. Japan's so-called lifetime employment system represents an overall approach to human resource management. However, it does not necessarily mean a guaranteed job for life for all workers. This system involves a strong reliance on internal labor markets: firms focus their recruitment and hiring efforts on new graduates who are trained by the organization and promoted as their skills and experience increase. Students at high schools, technical schools, and universities are recruited for organizational career tracks designed to fit their presumed ability levels and interests. When faced with financial difficulties, firms try other approaches to boosting firm performance, including reassigning staff to new areas or related companies, before laying off regular employees in any career track.

2. Slow economic growth has been a problem for Japan for over a decade, as companies have struggled to deal with the after effects of an investment "bubble" that developed in the late 1980s and burst as the Bank of Japan moved to raise interest rates and tighten the money supply at the end of the decade. Recovery has been complicated by the need to switch to a more service-oriented, advanced economy. Since the early 1990s, the Japanese economy has struggled with falling stock and real estate prices, which skyrocketed during the bubble period and have gradually fallen to the levels of a much earlier era. According to the most recent *Japan Statistical Yearbook* (Japanese Ministry of Public Management, Home Affairs, Posts and Telecommunications 2003, 2005), by 2002 real estate values in the country's urban areas stood at just 65 percent of what they were at their peak in 1990, and in the country's six largest cities average land prices were just 30 percent of 1990 levels, having fallen to where they stood in the early 1980s. A similar pattern can be seen in stock prices. Despite an impressive rise during 2005, at year's end the Nikkei average was still less than half where it stood in 1990.

3. Many writers have pointed out that workers at smaller subcontracting firms also have "contingent" employment as the work they do for larger companies may be handled internally during slow periods, leading to bankruptcy or layoffs among subcontractors. However, since regular employees at even small firms enjoy the full benefits of employment as long as their firms are operating, we have chosen to focus on workers in organizations of all sizes whose employment agreements are more flexible. For a lengthier discussion of how employment at subcontracting firms may be viewed as somewhat contingent, see Clark (1988) and Abegglen and Stalk (1990).

4. Japan's Ministry of Health, Welfare, and Labour (MHWL) performs many of the same functions as the U.S. Department of Labor. It is responsible for drafting and enforcing labor regulations, as well as gathering, synthesizing, and providing information on labor-related topics. The former Ministry of Labour was recently combined with the Ministry of Health and Welfare, creating a larger organization with a wider set of responsibilities.

5. Due to changing demographics in Japan, the workforce is growing older and the government has been working to gradually raise the age at which workers can benefit from the national pension system—just as the U.S. has been raising the age at which people can collect Social Security benefits. See Fujimura (2001) for a discussion of mandatory retirement as well as pensions. The article also describes a reemployment program for retirees at Matsushita.

6. See Morishima and Shimanuki (2005) for a discussion of dispatching, and for legal changes see Mizushima (2004).

7. For further information on the purpose and content of the legislation see Araki (1999). Also see Chapter 8 for a more detailed discussion of the changes.

8. A breakdown of these data by age or gender is not available; however, historical trends in education are reflected here. In the 1960s only 15 percent of the population attended college and 50 percent completed high school, while today these numbers are 50 percent and 95 percent, respectively. Returns to education have traditionally been lower for women, and men have historically been more likely to have a higher level of schooling. Therefore, many of those with low education levels are older workers, and quite a few of them are women.

9. For a discussion of reasons temporary employment can benefit firms in the U.S. context see Greenberger, Heneman, and Skoglind (1997), pp. 93–104. Also see Chapters 2 and 3.

10. For an analysis of reasons companies have treated women differently, see Wakisaka (1997).

11. A lengthier discussion and data are found in Imada (1997).

12. Yen figures have been converted at an exchange rate of ¥120 = US$1, which has been a common level over the past few years.

13. Women whose earnings fall above the threshold and thus must pay social insurance premiums do not necessarily receive higher benefits, so married women working part-time are not disadvantaged in terms of health care or pensions.

14. For further discussion of the allowances see Houseman and Osawa (1995).

15. While the United States has had a standard 40-hour work week in all industries for many years, Japan has phased out a six-day work week more recently, so three-quarters of the hours of a regular worker was used as a cutoff rather than 30 hours.

16. Minimum wage levels in Japan vary by region and industry. They are revised annually by the government. In October 2005 the highest general hourly minimum wage in Japan was applied in Tokyo, at ¥714 per hour.

17. For detailed analyses of the effects of financial and tax incentives on women's work hours, see Ichino (1985, 1989). Also helpful are Kantani (1994) and Wakisaka (1997). For an excellent discussion on how the ¥1.03 million tax/earnings threshold and minimum wage rates may affect part-time wages, see Abe (2002) and Nagase (2002).

18. For more information see the September 2004 survey of companies belonging to Nippon Keidanren and the Tokyo Employers' Association, as reported in Japanese Institute for Labour Policy and Training (2005a).

19. Unlike U.S. companies who regularly initiate layoffs as a way of improving an

already-strong financial performance, legally Japanese firms must show that they are seriously suffering financially and have tried all other reasonable means before cutting staff.
20. For a discussion of the background of these changes, see Araki (1999).

References

Abe, Y. 2002. "Does the ¥1.3 Million Tax Exempt Limit Depress the Hourly Wage of Part-Time Workers?" *Japan Labour Bulletin* 41(9): 6–7.

Abegglen, J.C., and G. Stalk. 1990. *Kaisha—The Japanese Corporation.* Tokyo: Charles E. Tuttle.

Araki, T. 1999. "1999 Revisions of Employment Security Law and Worker Dispatching Law: Drastic Reforms of Japanese Labor Market Regulations." *Japan Labour Bulletin* 38(9): 5–12.

Bureau of Labor Statistics. 2002. "Special Labour Force Survey, 2002." Washington, DC: Bureau of Labor Statistics.

———. 2005. "Labour Force Survey Quarterly Summary, 2005." Washington, DC: Bureau of Labor Statistics.

Clark, R.1988. *The Japanese Company.* Tokyo: Charles E. Tuttle.

Fackler, M. 2006. "Getting Reacquainted with Good Times." *New York Times*, January 14, C:4.

Fujimura, H. 2001. "Revision of Pension System and Workers in Their Early 60s." *Japan Labour Bulletin* 40(7): 5–13.

Greenberger, D.B., L.R. Heneman, and J.D. Skoglind. 1997. "Temporary Employment: Can Organizations and Employees Both Win?" *The Academy of Management Executive* 11(1): 93–104.

Houseman, S., and M. Osawa. 1995. "Part-Time and Temporary Employment in Japan." *Monthly Labor Review* 118(10): 10–18.

Ichino, S. 1985. *Joshi Paato Rodoshano Koyo Chingin Kozo* (Employment and Wage Structure of Women Part-Timers). *Monthly Labour Statistics and Research Bulletin* 37(January): 16–30.

———. 1989. *Paatotaimu Rodoshano Henbo Katei* (Transformation Process of Part-Time Workers). *Japan Labour Bulletin* 31(4): 16–30.

Imada, S. 1997. "Work and Family Life." *Japan Labour Bulletin* 36(8): 4–8.

Japan Institute of Labour. 1996. "Wage Gap between Full-Time and Part-Time Workers Doing the Same Job Illegal." 1996. *Japan Labour Bulletin* 35(6): 4.

———. 1997. "General Survey on the Real State of Personnel Management for Part-Time Workers." 1997. *Japan Labour Bulletin* 36(1): 2.

———. 1998a. "First Fall in Retirement Allowance: the Preliminary Results of the 1997 Survey on Wages." 1998. *Japan Labour Bulletin* 37(4): 2–3.

————. 1998b. "Labor Dispatchers Continue to Expand." 1998. *Japan Labour Bulletin* 37(6): 3–4.

————. 1999a. "Preliminary Report on Job Applicant Survey: Twelve Percent of Employed Want to Change Jobs." 1999. *Japan Labour Bulletin* 38(4): 2.

————. 1999b. "Fewer Regular Employees, Longer Periods of Unemployment." 1999. *Japan Labour Bulletin* 38(8): 1.

————. 1999c. "Fundamental Law for a Gender-Equal Society." 1999. *Japan Labour Bulletin* 38(9): 4–5.

————. 2001. "Men and Women Indifferent to Men's Child-Care Leave." *Japan Labour Bulletin* 40(7): 4–5.

————. 2002. "Major Supermarkets Institute Similar Conditions for Part-time and Regular Employees." 2002. *Japan Labour Bulletin* 41(7): 2–3.

Japanese Institute for Labour Policy and Training. 2005a. "College Graduate Employees Receive 24.35 Million Yen as Retirement Allowance." *Japan Labor Flash* 36(April 15): 2.

————. 2005b. "The Ministry of Health, Labour and Welfare to Grant Subsidy to SMEs with Employees on Child Care Leave." 2005. *Japan Labor Flash* 39(June 1): 3.

Japanese Ministry of Health, Labour and Welfare (MHLW). Annual. Basic Statistical Survey on Wage Structure (Chingin Kouzou Kihon Toukei Chousa). Tokyo: Ministry of Health, Labour and Welfare.

————. 2002. "General Survey on Part-Time Workers' Conditions, 2001." Tokyo: Ministry of Health, Labour and Welfare.

————. 2005. "Comprehensive Survey on Diversifying Employment Forms, 2003." Tokyo: Ministry of Health, Labour and Welfare.

Japanese Ministry of Public Management, Home Affairs, Posts and Telecommunications (MPHPT). 1997. 1996 Basic Survey of Social Life. Tokyo: Ministry of Public Management, Home Affairs, Posts and Telecommunications.

————. 2003. *Japan Statistical Yearbook*. Tokyo: Ministry of Public Management, Home Affairs, Posts and Telecommunications.

————. 2005. *Japan Statistical Yearbook.* Tokyo: Ministry of Public Management, Home Affairs, Posts and Telecommunications.

Japanese Statistics Bureau. 2005. "Labour Force Survey Detailed Tabulation, July–September 2005." Tokyo: Ministry of Internal Affairs and Communication.

Kantani, T. 1994. *Joshi Jikankyu Paatotaimu Rodoshano Nenkan-chingin* (Yearly Earnings of Female Part-Timers under Hourly Wage Contracts: Changes and Factors Across the Tenure). *Japanese Journal of Labour Studies* 36(415): 13–32.

Kezuka, K. 2000. "Legal Problems Concerning Part-Time Work in Japan."

Japan Labour Bulletin 39(9): 5–10.

Mizushima, I. 2004. "Recent Trends in Labour Market Regulations." *Japan Labor Review* 1(4): 6–26.

Morishima, M., and T. Shimanuki. 2005. "Managing Temporary Workers in Japan." *Japan Labor Review* 2(2): 78–89.

Nagase, N. 2002. "Wife Allowance and Tax Exemption Behind Low Wages of Part-Time Workers." *Japan Labour Bulletin* 41(9): 8–10.

Osawa, M., and J. Kingston. 1996. "Flexibility and Inspiration: Restructuring and the Japanese Labor Market." *Japan Labor Bulletin* 35(1): 4–8.

Reuters, Bloomberg News. 2005. "Outlook is Positive for Japan's Economy." *International Herald Tribune.* Dec. 14, p. 13.

Sato, H. 1997. "Human Resource Management Systems in Large Firms." In *Japanese Labour and Management in Transition*, M. Sako and H. Sato, eds. New York: Routledge, pp. 104–130.

Wakisaka, A. 1997. "Women at Work." In *Japanese Labour and Management in Transition*, M. Sako and H. Sato, eds. New York: Routledge, pp. 131–149.

8

Employment Policies and Labor Union Activities for Part-Time Workers and Dispatched Workers in Japan

Kazunari Honda
Kokugakuin University

This chapter discusses part-time workers and workers dispatched to client companies by temporary employment agencies from the viewpoint of government employment policies and labor union activities in Japan. Although there are several types of nonregular employment in Japan, part-time and dispatched workers hired through temporary employment agencies are, respectively, the largest and most rapidly growing groups. Government and unions concentrate their policies, employment services, and activities on these two groups in the labor force.[1]

This chapter also provides an overview of the governmental institutional framework for the employment policies of the Japanese Ministry of Health, Labor and Welfare (MHLW, formerly the Ministry of Labour, MOL) for part-time and dispatched workers. It discusses the content of the Part-Time Work Law (PWL) designed to protect the economic welfare of part-time employees and employer efforts to implement the law, and reviews the main features and recent reforms of the Worker Dispatching Law (WDL) that legalized temporary employment agencies in Japan. In addition, the chapter describes the public employment services provided to these two groups of workers.

Another objective of this chapter is to review labor union activities focused on part-time and dispatched workers, in particular the role of unions in the development of the PWL and WDL and union organizing activities targeted at part-time workers. The chapter concludes by discussing implications for future government and union activities and identifying issues for future research.

EMPLOYMENT POLICIES: THE INSTITUTIONAL FRAMEWORK

According to Article 4 of the Employment Measures Law of 1966, the Japanese government is required to develop periodic employment plans to support the goal of full employment.[2] The Ninth Basic Plan for Employment (covering 1999 through 2009) encourages several actions to improve employment conditions for part-time workers and workers dispatched by temporary employment agencies. These recommendations were developed in response to recent changes on both the supply and demand sides of the labor market. Some of the changes in the current and future supply of labor include the reduced rate of child bearing by Japanese women, an increasing population of older workers, and interest in enhancing female labor force participation. The changing industrial and occupational composition of the Japanese labor force in response to the growth of the technology and service sectors has resulted in a greater interest from Japanese employers in hiring workers who are not part of the lifetime employment system. These changes in the labor market have increased the need for part-time and temporary workers.

The Japanese government considers part-time and dispatched workers to be economically vulnerable; they need better job information and employment assistance to improve their working conditions. Also, they need protection from employers who have poor management practices; for example, cancelling a dispatched worker's contract without notice prior to its expiration date.

New protections through improvements in Japanese labor laws are recommended by the Ninth Basic Plan (for further details see Sugeno and Suwa [1997]). The plan recommends that the Japanese government help part-time workers find jobs by expanding the public employment offices and services and seeking appropriate treatment by employers for part-time workers based on the PWL discussed in the following section. For dispatched workers, the plan recommends streamlining the labor market adjustment function by having the government monitor the dispatching worker business in industries and occupations where the use of dispatched workers is already popular. Particular concerns are conditions of employment, training opportunities, and the provision of social security coverage. The plan also recommends further discussion about dispatched work and the collection of data to document and analyze the workplace and labor market conditions that these workers face. The plan thus holds out the promise of a redesign of the range of the industries and occupations which can be served by temporary employment agencies and improvements in the working conditions of dispatched workers.

EMPLOYMENT POLICIES FOR PART-TIME WORKERS

Japanese employment policies covering part-time workers include two major components: the PWL of 1993 and a national system of job placement assistance. However, since the PWL is not legally binding to employers, relatively few have fully implemented its requirements.

Part-Time Work Law

The PWL and the public policies that preceded it were a response to the many problems encountered by this group of workers. For example, although employers were required by the Labour Standards Law to hire part-time workers based on a written contract, contracts often were not provided.

The PWL was based on two earlier public policies: a 1984 government memorandum on part-time work and part-time work guidelines developed in 1989.[3] The PWL defines part-time workers as those whose working hours in a week are shorter than full-time regular workers (normally 40 hours a week) in the same business unit. This means that part-time workers who actually work full time are not covered by the PWL. For example, see the critical discussion of Mizumachi (1997). The law's primary purpose is to improve the treatment of these workers through three objectives: 1) secure appropriate employment conditions, 2) provide education and training to support improvements in management practices, and 3) improve the social security system for part-time workers.

The critical section of the PWL is Article 6, which requires employers to provide both written employment contracts to part-time workers and advance written notice of the termination of a contract to a part-time worker who has been continuously employed for more than one year (Kezuka 2000). The MHLW has advised employers to issue written employment documents, called employment notices, which describe major working conditions. In addition, subsidies are provided by the Japanese government to help employers improve their systems for managing part-time workers, such as providing management training and hiring personnel who specialize in managing part-time workers.

Unfortunately, the employer responsibilities defined by the PWL are not legally binding. As a result, many of the problems the PWL sought to remedy still exist. The current policy debate focuses on whether or not the law should shift to a compulsory basis to ensure equal treatment of part-time workers and full-time regular workers. Japanese labor lawyers are divided over the creation of a new law with strict enforcement mechanisms (Mizumachi 1997).

Employer Implementation of the PWL

Despite publicity about the PWL, many employers are unaware of it. According to the Tokyo Metropolitan Government (1998), which surveyed employers in Tokyo to determine their awareness of the law, only 29 percent of the respondents indicated the law was "known" to them. At the other extreme, 15.2 percent indicated they had "never known" about the PWL. The largest respondent category was 52 percent of employers who answered "knows the law, but does not know the condition," that is, they did not know what the law required of them.

However, according to three MHLW reports on part-time workers, more employers have begun to use written rather than oral employment contracts with part-time workers (MHLW 2002; MOL 1991a, 1997). Table 8.1 indicates the methods used to explain the expected employment conditions to part-time workers during the hiring process. Three primary methods are identified: 1) reliance on oral contracts, 2) issuing written contracts specifying the conditions of employment, and 3) applying existing work practice rules.

The total indicating the use of "any methods to clarify the working conditions of part-time workers" did not change appreciably in 1990,

Table 8.1 Employer's Clarification of Part-Time Working Conditions in Hiring (%)

| All industries number of employees | Grand total | Total | | | Clarifying the working conditions by any methods | | | | | | | | | | | | Not clarifying | | |
| | | | | | Mainly unwritten oral contracts | | | Mainly issuing the contract stating the working conditions | | | Mainly applying the existing workplace rules | | | Others | | | | | |
		1990	1995	2000	1990	1995	2001	1990	1995	2001	1990	1995	2001	1990	1995	2001	1990	1995	2001
All industries	100.0	98.1	98.2	98.4	66.5	59.6	45.9	15.8	24.6	40.2	13.9	14.4	12.7	1.9	1.4	1.1	1.9	1.8	1.6
1,000+	100.0	99.8	100.0	99.9	32.1	18.8	13.5	21.9	31.8	61.0	44.7	47.8	24.9	1.1	1.5	0.5	0.2	0.0	0.1
500–999	100.0	100.0	99.9	100.0	24.0	23.3	13.4	40.2	38.9	68.1	27.4	31.8	18.4	8.3	6.1	0.0	0.0	0.1	—
300–499	100.0	99.1	100.0	100.0	27.1	30.7	23.6	39.5	46.5	62.7	26.2	22.5	13.6	6.3	0.3	0.1	0.9	0.0	—
100–299	100.0	97.7	99.8	99.7	49.7	42.1	44.3	20.9	37.7	44.3	26.3	18.8	11.2	0.9	1.4	0.2	2.3	0.2	0.3
30–99	100.0	98.3	97.7	99.6	64.3	62.3	45.9	21.7	26.3	41.2	9.1	10.9	12.5	3.2	0.5	0.4	1.7	2.3	0.4
5–29	100.0	97.5	97.2	96.7	81.7	81.2	66.6	9.2	12.4	23.5	5.5	5.5	8.5	1.1	0.8	1.5	2.5	2.8	3.3

SOURCE: MHLW 2002; MOL (1991a, 1997).

246 Honda

1995, and 2001, but some response categories changed. For example, the use of "unwritten oral contracts" decreased from 66.5 percent to 45.9 percent between 1990 and 2001. Also "mainly applying the existing work practice rules" declined slightly, from 13.0 percent to 12.7 percent. However, during the same period, the use of written contracts "mainly issuing the contract stating the working conditions" increased from 15.8 percent of employers to 40.2 percent. Clearly a trend toward switching from verbal agreements to written contractual agreements when hiring part-time workers is evident, particularly in large companies with 1,000 or more employees.

Table 8.2 illustrates the same trend toward formalizing employment arrangements for part-time workers. Respondents replying "no part-time working rules" decreased from 38.8 percent of employers in 1990 to 15.2 percent in 2001. A marked decline occurred for all employers except those employing 500–999 employees.

Other evidence of the positive effects of the PWL on management practices is an increase in the percentage of employers who contract employment for a specified period and clearly indicate the termination date of the contract. As Table 8.3 shows, employers who have contracts with part-time workers for work for specified periods of time increased from 30.4 percent in 1990 to 52.9 percent in 2001. Employers who inform part-time workers of their end dates of employment 30 days beforehand increased from 15.8 percent in 1990 to 69.0 percent in 2001. These survey results are consistent with the results in Table 8.1 and Table 8.2 and for companies of all sizes.

Table 8.2 Companies without Rules for Part-Time Workers (%)

	1990	1995	2001
Total	38.8	19.9	15.2
Number of employees			
1,000 +	11.4	5.6	2.4
500–999	1.8	10.9	1.8
300–499	20.5	7.2	3.1
100–299	24.3	19.0	5.8
30–99	28.8	23.6	6.5
5–29	53.1	25.4	27.7

SOURCE: MHLW 2002; MOL (1991a, 1997).

Table 8.3 Situations of Determining Employment Periods and Giving Previous Information Regarding the Termination of Employment (%)

	Total			Determining employment period												
				Subtotal			Previous information										
							Inform 30 days before			Do not inform 30 days before			Several cases			Not determined		
				1990	1995	2001	1990	1995	2001	1990	1995	2001	1990	1995	2001	1990	1995	2001
All industries number of employees	100.0			30.4	40.6	52.9	15.8	66.5	69.0	4.5	4.5	5.3	10.2	29.0	25.8	69.6	59.4	47.1
1,000+	100.0			71.6	80.4	92.2	49.2	79.1	76.4	7.0	5.0	7.4	15.3	15.9	16.2	28.4	17.8	7.8
500–999	100.0			67.2	82.2	85.1	44.4	66.3	86.1	13.8	10.3	1.0	9.0	23.4	12.9	32.8	26.1	14.9
300–499	100.0			70.2	73.9	66.7	40.3	62.9	80.9	9.7	6.9	8.5	20.1	30.3	10.6	29.8	50.3	33.3
100–299	100.0			41.2	49.7	62.6	22.8	63.2	59.9	7.9	2.7	7.4	10.5	34.2	32.7	58.8	62.8	37.4
30–99	100.0			27.3	37.2	47.4	12.3	60.3	63.8	4.2	3.6	6.2	10.8	36.1	30.0	72.7	80.5	52.6
5–29	100.0			16.8	19.5	30.1	6.6	55.4	61.5	2.8	3.0	2.9	7.5	41.6	25.6	83.2	80.5	69.9

SOURCE: MHLW 2002; MOL (1991a, 1997).

Public Employment Services for Part-Time Workers

The most significant MHLW service for part-time workers is the national system of public employment service offices,[4] called "part-timers banks," and their associated satellite offices. The satellite offices offer the same services as the banks, but are smaller offices placed in more locations to improve access by those workers needing their services. The first 3 banks were created in 1982 and the first 15 satellites were created in 1991, followed by the continual increases in the numbers of both types of offices. As of 1998 there were 80 banks and 85 satellite offices.

Both the part-timers banks and satellite offices were created specifically to help part-time workers find jobs other than public employment positions. The MHLW provides a variety of services to accomplish this objective. These services include the provision of information about employment opportunities, skills training, individual career counseling, training in job search methods, and other forms of job placement assistance. However, while workers are looking for part-time employment, they have to apply to the regular public employment service office to receive unemployment insurance benefits.

Figure 8.1 shows the number of part-time workers who looked for and found jobs by using all public employment offices, including the part-time workers offices. The number of part-time workers using these services rose from about 178,000 in 1980 to 1,046,000 in 2001. Of these, the number of those who worked more than one month and less than four months ranged between 5,000 and 8,000 in each year.

The number of part-time workers who had jobs rose steadily in most of the years from 1980 through 2001. There were about 485,000 workers with jobs in 2001 as compared to about 76,000 in 1980. The ratio of those who sought part-time jobs to those who found part-time jobs was relatively stable in the range of about 35 percent to 47 percent. The number of the workers who sought and found part-time jobs has increased since the 1990s primarily because during the last recession employers shifted to hiring more part-time workers instead of full-time regular employees to reduce their labor costs.

Figure 8.2 shows the number of part-time workers who looked for and found jobs by using only the part-time worker banks and their satellite offices. From 1982 (when these specialized offices were created)

Figure 8.1 Number of Workers Who Sought and Found Part-Time Work by Using All Public Employment Offices

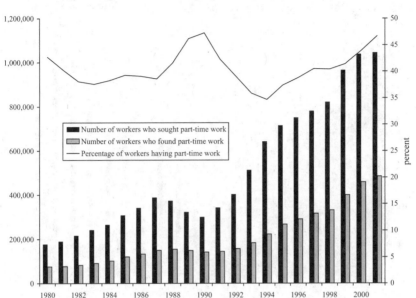

SOURCE: Japanese Ministry of Health, Labour, and Welfare, Annual Reports on Labour Markets.

through 2001, the percentage of part-time workers who found employment with their assistance ranged from approximately 4 percent to 40 percent.

The trend in Figure 8.2 is quite similar to that in Figure 8.1. The number of part-time workers using the services of these offices rose from about 8,500 in 1982 to about 305,000 in 2001. Part-time workers who found jobs also constantly increased from about 2,900 in 1982 to about 114,000 in 2001. The percentage of those being hired was between about 34 percent and 43 percent.

Figure 8.2   Number of Workers Who Sought and Found Part-Time Work by Using Part-Time Worker Banks and Satellite Offices

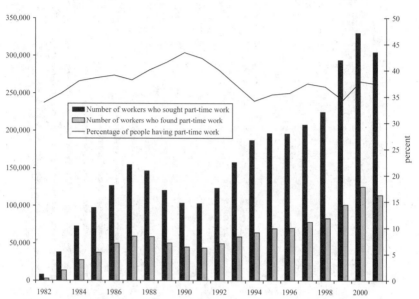

SOURCE: Japanese Ministry of Health, Labour, and Welfare, Annual Reports on Labour Markets.

EMPLOYMENT POLICIES FOR DISPATCHED WORKERS

Worker dispatching businesses, called temporary employment agencies in the United States and Europe, supply workers to clients who employ these workers in their businesses. Although worker dispatching businesses grew in Japan during the 1970s, their growth was restricted by the Employment Security Law, which prohibited them except where employment arrangements were made by written contracts with strict requirements about the content of the contracts. Since many worker dispatching companies disguised their work as contract work in the 1970s, most were probably illegal.

Thus, although the Japanese government did not prohibit these businesses due to strong market demands for temporary workers, they were strictly regulated. However, as the number of temporary employment agencies expanded, some regulation became necessary. Consequently, the Worker Dispatching Law (WDL) was enacted in 1985. It created a legal private sector mechanism to supplement the public employment offices in matching workers and employers, with strict regulation of the methods of operation of temporary employment agencies. In addition, a variety of public services were provided to dispatched workers.

The WDL has four major components. First, the law restricts by occupation the kinds of jobs at which dispatched workers can work.[5] Second, it creates two types of worker dispatching businesses: those that handle workers who are already employed, and those that handle workers seeking jobs. The former is usually called "employment dispatching," and the latter is referred to as "register dispatching."[6] One business unit cannot offer both types of service. Workers can be registered by one or more dispatching businesses. Third, the law aims to improve the working conditions of dispatched workers. For example, the law requires both the dispatching business and the client company hiring the workers to issue a written contract to dispatched workers, thereby regulating the conditions of employment and dismissal.[7] Finally, the WDL stipulates penalties for possible infractions of the law by dispatching companies.

The last revision of the WDL became effective in December 2000.[8] This revision included four significant changes. First, it changed the regulation from listing only the 26 occupations that could be filled by dispatched workers (the "negative list" system) to listing only the narrow set of jobs for which dispatched workers cannot be hired (the "positive list" system). Second, it sets a limit on the employment period of one year for dispatched workers for the same jobs as those filled by full-time employees to encourage employers to move dispatched workers to full-time regular employment.

Third, the law establishes client employers' responsibilities for covering the damages of dispatched workers who were discharged before the end of their contracts. This change is designed to address identified abuses of treatment. For example, a Tokyo Metropolitan Government (1999) survey showed that 13.9 percent of register dispatched workers were asked to leave their jobs or were discharged during the contract period; 57.1 percent of dispatching agents had their contracts broken by the client employer.

Finally, the Japanese government was concerned about protecting the privacy of dispatched workers. The revision of the law outlines the responsibilities of the dispatching company for managing individual information.

Public services for dispatched workers are administrated by the MHLW. The main services are the deployment of advisors to provide assistance to employers on managing their dispatched workers and on procedures for handling grievances. The advisors provide training for the management specialists at both the dispatching and receiving client companies. Also, subsidies are provided to help cover the employers' costs for appropriate employment management services for dispatched workers.

Assistance with the handling of grievances is important because there is a high rate of grievances from dispatched workers against both the dispatching and receiving companies. For example, according to the Tokyo Metropolitan Government survey (1999), 30.6 percent of register dispatched workers filed grievances. Grievances cover such matters as contract concerns, wage levels, and shop floor human relations issues. The MHLW also directly receives grievances from dispatched workers through telephone calls. However, since the system covers just a small portion of those who have grievances, it is unclear how effective the advice and consultation provided by telephone is in the settlement of grievances.

UNION ACTIVITIES: THE CONTEXT

Approximately 20 percent of the Japanese labor force was unionized in 2002 (MHLW 2002). Unions are particularly important in large enterprises with more than 1,000 employees; about 55 percent of workers in these large companies are unionized. What makes the Japanese union structure distinctive is the dominance of unions organized at the enterprise level. These enterprise unions account for more than 90 percent of all union membership.[9]

Until relatively recently, Japanese unions did not actively seek part-time workers and dispatched workers as members. However, as the employment of low-wage part-time and dispatched workers has grown, unions have realized a potential danger: if a gap exists between the wage levels of full-time regular workers and part-time and dispatched workers, employers will seek to replace more expensive full-time regular workers with nonregular workers.

In response to this threat, unions have used two strategies to maintain their bargaining power. First, unions have supported public policies that seek to reduce, and ultimately eliminate, the differences in the employment conditions between full-time regular workers, part-time workers, and dispatched workers. Second, some unions have begun to organize part-time workers as union members to enhance union bargaining power.

UNION ACTIVITIES FOCUSED ON PART-TIME WORKERS

Union Involvement in the Development of the Part-Time Work Law

Labor unions have been heavily involved in the development of Japanese government employment policies, including those aimed at part-time and dispatched workers.[10] The Japanese Private Sector Trade Union Confederation (Private Rengo) strongly supported the PWL and urged the MOL to enact this legislation in 1984.[11] Instead, the Japanese government produced a memorandum on part-time work, which failed to present a clear direction for the growth of part-time work. Subsequently, in 1988 Private Rengo developed its own policies for part-time workers to encourage government commitment to union guidelines.

In response the MOL took two actions in 1989. First, it replaced the 1984 working memorandum with guidelines for employers on part-time work. These guidelines clearly identified part-time workers as a key workforce in industry. They offered guidance to employers on providing appropriate working conditions. Second, the MOL extended the coverage of the Employment Insurance Law, which provides unemployment insurance to qualified part-time workers. However, Rengo criticized the government guidelines because they only offered advice to employers and did not provide a legal enforcement mechanism. Rengo continued to advocate the enactment of the PWL from 1990 until its passage in 1993.

The passage of the PWL still did not satisfy Rengo, however. It argued that the PWL did not provide the level of protection for part-time workers that was needed, particularly due to the absence of legal penalties for the employers who did not follow the law. Consequently, Rengo pursued two strategies simultaneously. It continued to develop draft proposals for revisions of the PWL, which were submitted to the MOL. In addition, Rengo again developed new policies on part-time work. It urged discussion of revisions of the PWL in 1996 in the government councils discussing part-time work. In response to pressure from Rengo, the MOL set up the Part-Time Work Special Committee composed of the government, union, and employer representatives. However, no further essential changes have been made in the PWL since its passage in 1993.

Organizing Part-Time Workers

Like other industrialized nations, Japan has experienced a decline in labor union membership rates. However, one growth area is part-time workers. Although the number of unionized part-time workers remains small, the membership rate for part-time workers has increased slightly from 1.5 percent in 1990 to 3.3 percent in 2005 as shown in Table 8.4.

However, labor unions are not enthusiastic about organizing part-time workers, even though increasing part-time worker membership is predicted to strengthen unions. Table 8.5 shows that in 1990 only 10.7 percent of Japanese unions had organized part-time workers and planned to continue to organize them, while 12.6 percent of unions had not organized part-time workers but planned to organize them in the future. In contrast, 56.0 percent of the unions did not and were not planning to organize part-time workers. The wholesale, retailing, and restaurant sectors were more interested in unionizing part-time workers than the service and manufacturing sectors.

The unions that had organized or were planning to organize part-time workers preferred to target only those workers who meet some specific requirements. As Table 8.6 shows, 39.2 percent of the unions targeted all part-time workers, while 56.4 percent of these unions identified potential members by some criteria such as minimum length of

Table 8.4 The Trends Reflecting Union Membership Rates of Part-Time Workers

	(1) Number of part-time union members	(2) Number of employees	$(3) = (1)/(2) \times 100$ Union membership rate (%)
1990	97,150	6,290,000	1.5
1991	113,380	6,940,000	1.6
1992	131,880	7,540,000	1.7
1993	155,810	7,980,000	2.0
1994	168,120	8,370,000	2.0
1995	184,240	8,640,000	2.1
1996	196,090	8,890,000	2.2
1997	218,030	9,230,000	2.4
1998	239,600	9,570,000	2.5
1999	244,000	9,930,000	2.5
2000	260,000	10,170,000	2.6
2001	280,000	10,420,000	2.7
2002	293,000	10,970,000	2.7
2003	331,000	10,980,000	3.0
2004	363,000	11,070,000	3.3
2005	389,000	11,720,000	3.3

SOURCE: Number of union members from Japanese Ministry of Health, Labour and Welfare, Basic Survey on Labour Unions. Number of employees from Japanese Ministry of Public Management, Home Affairs, Posts and Telecommunications, Monthly Surveys on Labour Force.

service, hours of work, and annual earnings as a cutoff. For the latter group, the most important characteristics were length of service (45.3 percent) and hours of work (37.6 percent).

Table 8.7 shows the two major reasons unions have not sought to organize part-time workers. Unions reported that these workers do not join enthusiastically in the union activities (29.6 percent). Also, 44.7 percent of the unions perceived the differences between the interests of full-time and part-time union members or part-time workers to be too large for accommodation in the same union.

In contrast to the negative attitude of many unions toward organizing part-time workers, some part-time workers view union membership positively. Based on his analysis of a survey of members of Rengo,

Table 8.5 Union Interests in Organizing Part-Time Workers, by Industry in 1990 (%)

	Total of unions where part-time workers are employed	Organized part-time workers or will organize in the future	Did not organize but will organize in the future	Organized part-time workers but will not organize in the future	Did not organize and will not organize	Others	No response
All industries	100.0	10.7	12.6	1.0	56.0	15.5	4.1
Manufacturing	100.0	6.2	9.5	1.6	60.3	18.3	4.2
Wholesale, retailing, and restaurants	100.0	27.4	19.0	0.3	39.1	12.7	1.6
Service	100.0	13.1	14.3	1.0	53.1	13.6	5.0

SOURCE: MOL (1991b).

Table 8.6 Part-Time Workers Targeted by Union Organizing Activities in 1990 (%)

| | Subtotal of unions that do and will organize part-time workers | All part-time workers | Characteristics used to identify potential members | | | | | | | |
			Total	Length of service	Working hours	Kinds of jobs	Annual earnings	Other	No response	No response
All industries	100.0	39.2	56.4 (100.0)	(45.3)	(37.6)	(8.0)	(0.3)	(6.7)	(1.9)	(4.4)
Manufacturing	100.0	33.4	62.8 (100.0)	(47.4)	(36.9)	(3.6)	(0.0)	(7.0)	(5.0)	(3.8)
Wholesale, retailing and restaurants	100.0	23.9	75.4 (100.0)	(49.4)	(35.7)	(4.1)	(0.2)	(10.4)	(0.3)	(0.7)
Service	100.0	61.4	27.5 (100.0)	(28.5)	(40.0)	(29.2)	(2.3)	(0.0)	(0.0)	(11.1)

SOURCE: MOL (1991b).

Boyles (1993) concluded that the attitudes of female part-time workers toward the unions were more positive than those of male and female full-time regular employees. Of the female part-time workers who were already organized in enterprise unions, 30.3 percent preferred the enterprise unions consisting of only part-time members, and 26.0 percent preferred the traditional full-time workers' unions. This contrasted with the 4 percent who preferred other types of union organization, such as regional unions rather than enterprise unions. Thus, more than half of the organized female part-time workers preferred enterprise unions to outside unions.[12] This perspective reflects the popularity of enterprise unions with Japanese workers. These views of part-time workers are consistent with this general attitude toward unions in Japan.

The findings from Furugori (1997) help explain why part-time workers are interested in union membership. She finds that the wage levels of part-time workers in unionized companies are higher than in nonunionized companies. Consequently, joining unions should be advantageous for part-time workers. Boyles (1993) also finds that the union effects on the wage level and job content were relatively higher than expected.

Consequently, it can be concluded that there is a mismatch between the negative attitudes of many unions toward organizing part-time workers and the positive attitudes of part-time workers toward union membership. However, it appears unlikely that the needs and interests of part-time workers will be served by unions in the near future due to the lack of aggressive union organizing activities.

UNION ACTIVITIES FOCUSED ON DISPATCHED WORKERS

Union Involvement in the Development of the Worker Dispatching Law

Unions and employers disagreed on the need for the WDL even before it was enacted in 1985. Unions argued that strong employment protections were needed for dispatched workers because of abuses by client employers. One example was the sudden termination of employment before the expiration of the contract period. Employers who ter-

Table 8.7 Reasons for Not Organizing Part-Time Workers in 1990 (%)

	Total	Did not identify reasons	Part-time workers do not join enthusiastically in the union activities	Interests between part-time workers and full-time regular workers do not match	Other reasons
Total of three industries	100.0	7.5	29.6	44.7	18.2
Manufacturing	100.0	6.1	30.5	48.9	14.5
Wholesale, retailing, and restaurants	100.0	3.5	31.5	44.3	20.7
Services	100.0	9.5	29.2	39.7	21.5

SOURCE: MOL (1991b).

minated workers in this manner did not face any penalties. Employers, on the other hand, proposed complete deregulation for worker dispatching businesses. Rengo proposed changes during the reviews of WDL, which were conducted every three years.

The perspectives of unions and employers remained the same in the 1996 and 1999 WDL reviews. For example, Rengo's official position for the revision in 1996 included limiting the type of jobs in which dispatched workers could be hired and promoting stronger protections for the working conditions of dispatched workers. The proposal submitted by Rengo contained five major points. The confederation

1) opposed an increase in the number of jobs eligible for dispatched work, the expansion of eligible occupations, and an increase in the permissible length of the employment contract;

2) clarified the differences between similar types of employment, such as subcontracted workers, temporary transferred workers, and transferred shop assistants, and secured legal worker dispatching businesses;

3) promoted the protection of the working conditions of dispatched workers and the enhancement of their working conditions at the dispatching companies;

4) promoted the protection of the working conditions of dispatched workers and enhancement of their working conditions at receiving client companies; and

5) supported the strengthening of the inspection system for dispatched working through MHLW.

In contrast to the advice provided by Rengo, the revision of the WDL in 1996 added 12 new occupations for which dispatched workers could be hired, thereby bringing the total to 26 occupations. However, throughout the discussions preceding the 1999 revisions, Rengo continued to argue for expanded use of formal employment contracts in hiring dispatched workers and setting limits on the number of occupations open to dispatched workers. It also continued to document the problems faced by dispatched workers with both dispatching companies and receiving client companies.

The debates preceding the 1999 revisions were intense due to employer efforts to open more occupations to dispatched workers. Rengo expressed three major concerns. First, Rengo argued that the new concept of temporary dispatched worker proposed by employers would result in undesirable expansion of shorter contracted employment at the cost of employment of full-time regular workers. Second, Rengo requested that legal penalties be added to the law so it could be enforced and worker protection from abuses by dispatching companies improved. Finally, Rengo stressed that the law needed a statement of the rights of dispatched workers in the complex triple employment relationship in which they work. However, Rengo's recommendations were not included in the revised law. The 1999 revision expanded both the industries and occupations that could be staffed by temporary workers so significantly that only a few exclusions were retained.

Supporting Dispatched Workers

In contrast to efforts made to organize some of the part-time workforce, Japanese labor unions have not focused on dispatched workers as potential members. Instead of organizing these workers, Rengo has developed telephone services for receiving and handling grievances and troubleshooting for dispatched workers, and providing advice or consultation on issues related to employment and working conditions. These services are similar to the public services that the MHLW provides to dispatched workers.

CONCLUSIONS AND DIRECTIONS FOR FUTURE RESEARCH

Part-time and dispatched workers represent two segments of the nonregular labor force that have grown over the past 20 years in Japan. This chapter reviews the government employment policies and public services provided for part-time workers and dispatched workers in Japan. It also discusses the perspectives of Japanese labor unions on these two groups of workers and union efforts to improve their economic well-being. However, both the Japanese government and labor unions can do more to protect these workers who are relatively vulnerable to abusive management practices and changing economic conditions.

Several government actions are needed. The MHLW should work with employers to increase their awareness of both the Part-Time Work Law and the Worker Dispatching Law, as well as to enforce the already existing provisions of these laws. In addition, public services to assist part-time and dispatched workers should be expanded and improved. Furthermore, future revisions of these laws should strengthen the protections provided to these two groups of workers. However, improving employment protections for dispatched workers is more complicated since it involves both the dispatching and receiving client companies.

Japanese labor unions have sought actively to counterbalance the influence of employers in the development of public policy toward part-time and dispatched workers. However, unions have placed relatively little emphasis on organizing part-time workers as a means of providing protections for them, and have avoided any organizing activities targeted at dispatched workers. These modest organizing efforts will limit the potential for union growth in the future if these two types of nonstandard employment continue to increase.

There are several issues that should be studied to provide the basis for the development of appropriate changes in public policy for part-time and dispatched workers in Japan. Three topics for future research are identified for each employee group.

Research on part-time workers should examine wage equity, work sharing, and union organizing activities. It is well documented that a gap exists between the hourly wage paid to full-time regular and part-time workers in Japan. Discussions have occurred about the need for equitable pay to eliminate the wage gap between these two groups of workers since this may be the ultimate protection for part-time workers. Researchers should identify policy options for the Japanese government and labor union actions that can eliminate the wage gap.

A second research topic is work sharing. There was heated discussion of work sharing as a panacea to increase employment throughout the recession in the 1990s in Japan. For instance, some companies have started to use "part-time regular workers" whose working hours are shorter than the full-time regular workers'. Since these part-time employees are regular workers, they should have better conditions of employment than traditional part-time workers and they should be paid the same hourly pay as full-time regular workers. Research can determine how pervasive the use of part-time regular workers is, the availability of people who want to be part-time regular workers, and how their treatment compares with that of full-time regular and traditional part-time workers. Also, the appropriate responses from the government and labor unions should be determined.

Finally, researchers can assist labor unions in a reexamination of their attitudes toward organizing part-time workers. In 2001, Rengo developed a plan to organize part-time workers through its regional branches rather than through the traditional approach of enterprise unions. This plan raises questions about whether the organizing functions of the national center and enterprise unions can be complementary.

Research on dispatched workers should focus on pay levels, the impact of deregulation, and union activities. During recessions companies experience pressure to reduce labor costs, including the cost of dispatched workers. Dispatched workers therefore are at risk for lower rates of pay and unfavorable longer working hours. Research can measure the extent to which dispatched workers are economically disadvantaged during a recession and determine how the government and labor unions can address these problems.

In addition, research can explore the impact of the further deregulation of temporary employment, in particular the effects of revising the WDL to open more occupations to dispatched workers by including manufacturing and assembly workers and changing the permissible contract period. If the WDL is revised, the costs and benefits of the changes should be studied.

Finally, as discussed previously, enterprise unions have opposed the substitution of dispatched workers for full-time regular workers due to the impact on the employment opportunities of their members. However, since the latest WDL revision, increased numbers of dispatched workers have been converted to the status of full-time regular workers in the same company. This change from temporary to permanent status has occurred after the employee has served a trial period as a dispatched worker. The prevalence of this practice, and the implications for organizing efforts of enterprise unions, should be analyzed.

Notes

1. As discussed in Chapter 7, "regular" or "lifetime" employees are grouped separately from "nonregular" employees who are in nonstandard employment arrangements. This chapter uses the term "nonregular" for consistency with the discussion in the earlier chapter. See Chapter 7 for further discussion of these two groups of nonstandard employees. Also see Wakisaka (1997). In addition to part-time and dispatched workers, the Japanese Ministry of Health, Labour and Welfare (MHLW) regulates employment policies for older nonregular workers, employees who are family members working in a family business, home helpers, and other groups of workers. However, this chapter does not discuss these policies or any tax or social security policies.
2. Employment policies since 1998 have focused on three types of actions to maintain employment: 1) expanding traditional policy approaches such as subsidies for training or to help cover the costs of transferring employees to a related firm, 2) using the traditional public works approach to absorb unemployed workers, and 3) developing new policies, including subsidies designed to support job creation by covering costs in small and medium-sized firms associated with additional human resource needs or wage subsidies for targeted groups such as older workers. For more details see Ohtake (2000).
3. Since the 1984 revision of the Employment Insurance Law which provides unemployment insurance, part-time workers have been able to receive unemployment benefits. Since 1994 part-time workers who work less than 20 hours a week are no longer eligible for unemployment benefits, while those working more than 20 hours but less than 30 hours can participate on a short-term basis. However, they receive smaller benefits than the full-time workers.
4. In addition to the public employment service offices, the MHLW also designates the 21st Century Vocational Foundation, a nongovernmental public agency, as an assistance center for part-time workers. Its main duties are subsidizing the improvement of the management of part-time workers at companies, developing management specialists for part-time workers, and providing consultants to assist employers with the management of part-time workers. According to the MHLW, approximately 18,000 part-time workers have received vocational training every year since 1995 through this organization.
5. The 1994 amendment of the Older Persons Employment Stabilization Law permitted dispatched workers to be over 60 years of age and allowed them to work in any job except those considered "port transport services, construction, guard services, and production services." The 1996 amendment to the Child Care and Family Leave Act revision permitted dispatched workers to fill vacancies occurring due to child or family care leave. See Araki (1997); Morito (1999).
6. Employment dispatching businesses provide continuous employment for dispatched workers. They place workers for indefinite periods of time or more than one year. These businesses only have to register with the Minister of Health, Labour and Welfare. In contrast, the register dispatching businesses register work-

ers and find employment for them. The worker is placed for a specified period of time. Since their services are similar to those of the public employment agencies, these businesses have to be approved by the MHLW to ensure they have the resources to operate properly. See Araki (1994).

7. The contract with the dispatching company describes the content of the work to be performed, the location of the work site, the direct supervisor, the length of the workday, including starting and ending times, when overtime may be paid, the length of the employment contract, health and safety concerns, and the staff responsible for the worker at both the dispatching and client companies. The conditions specified in these contracts are negotiated between the dispatching company and the client company. For more details see Araki (1994).

8. Prior to this revision, dispatched workers were permitted to remain in a job for three years (for more details see Araki [1999]). In 2000 the permissible period of employment was reduced to one year. Employers were encouraged to employ in full-time jobs the dispatched workers who worked for them for one year. Debates about the effects of this revision are increasing, but little is actually known about what is being done by employers. For example, see Yashiro (1999).

9. In an enterprise union in Japan the wages and conditions of work are negotiated by the union and the employer with little involvement from higher-level union organizations. Decisions are influenced heavily by a sense of being part of a community whose members will share in the future of the business (Shinoda 1997). This approach to labor-management relations has supported the "lifetime employment" practices followed by these enterprises (Nitta 1997) and has maintained stability through close ties between employees and management. However, enterprise unions have evolved somewhat differing features in response to the characteristics of the industry and company in which they operate (Price [1997]. Also see Fujimura [1997]). "The three jewels of the employment system—enterprise unions, lifetime employment and seniority based wages—are not about to suddenly fade into oblivion . . ." (Osawa and Kingston 1996, p. 5).

10. For a discussion of the evolution of the role of Rengo in the development of government employment policies and the consultation processes employed, see Shinoda (1997).

11. Shinoda (1997) provides an overview of the history of the growth of national-level unions in Japan following World War II. The Private Rengo was established by 1987 as the new national center for unions in the private sector. In 1989 Private Rengo and the public sector unions combined to create the Japanese Trade Union Confederation (Rengo).

12. There are several ways to organize part-time workers. For instance, Honda analyzed the way a union organized part-time workers in retailing. He reported organizing methods that did not require these workers to join the existing full-time regular workers' union. For example, there is a part-time council whose members are only part-timers. The council is legally independent from the existing union of full-time regular workers, but it receives some advice and assistance for its activities from the union. For more details see Honda (1993, 2005).

References

Araki, T. 1994. "Characteristics of Regulations on Dispatched Work (Temporary Work) in Japan." *Japan Labour Bulletin* 33(8): 5–8.
———. 1997. "Changing Japanese Labour Law in Light of Deregulation Drives: A Comparative Analysis." *Japan Labour Bulletin* 36(5): 5–10.
———. 1999. "1999 Revisions of Employment Security Law and Worker Dispatching Law: Drastic Reforms of Japanese Labor Market Regulations." *Japan Labour Bulletin* 38(9): 5–12.
———. 2002. *Labor and Employment Law in Japan.* Tokyo: Japan Institute of Labour.
Boyles, C.J. 1993. "Female Member Attitudes toward Labour Union of the Female Members and Their Joining." In *Economics of Labour Unions,* T. Tachibanaki and Rengo Research Institute for Advancement of Living Standards, eds. Tokyo: Toyo Keizai Shinpo Sha (in Japanese): pp. 31–53.
Fujimura, H. 1997. "New Unionism: Beyond Enterprise Unionism? In *Japanese Labour and Management in Transition,*" M. Sako and H. Sato, eds. London: Routledge, pp. 296–314.
Furugori, M. 1997. *Economics of Non-Regular Workers.* Tokyo: Toyo Keizai Shinpo Sha (in Japanese).
Honda, K. 1993. "Re-examination of Unions' Organizing Part-Time Workers." *Journal of Ohara Institute for Social Research* 416: 25–40 (in Japanese).
———. 2005. "The Effectiveness of the Labour Unions' Organizing Activities for Part-Time Workers." *Japanese Journal of Labour Studies* 544: 60–73 (in Japanese).
Japanese Ministry of Health, Labour and Welfare (MHLW). 2002. "General Survey of Part-Time Workers' Conditions, 2001." Tokyo: Okurasho Insatsu Kyoku (in Japanese).
———. Annual. "Annual Reports on Public Labour Service." Tokyo: Japan Institute of Labour (in Japanese).
———. Annual. "Annual Reports on Labour Markets." Tokyo: Okurasho Insatsu Kyoku (in Japanese).
———. Annual. "Basic Surveys on Labour Unions." Tokyo: Okurasho Insatsu Kyoku (in Japanese).
Japanese Ministry of Labour (MOL). 1991a. "General Survey on Part-Time Workers 1990." Tokyo: Okurasho Insatsu Kyoku (in Japanese).
———. 1991b. "Survey on Labour Unions Activities 1990." Tokyo: Okurasho Insatsu Kyoku (in Japanese).
———. 1997. "General Survey on Part-Time Workers 1995." Tokyo: Okurasho Insatsu Kyoku (in Japanese).

————. 1999. "Ninth Basic Plan for Employment." Tokyo: Okurasho Insatsu Kyoku (in Japanese).

Japanese Ministry of Public Management, Home Affairs, Posts and Telecommunications. Various years. "Monthly Surveys on Labour Forces." Tokyo: Nihon Tokei Kyokai (in Japanese).

Kamata, K. 2000. "A Reform of the Law Concerning Temporary Work in Japan." *Monthly Journal of the Japan Institute of Labour* 475: 48–58 (in Japanese).

Kezuka, K. 2000. "Legal Problems Concerning Part-Time Work in Japan." *Japan Labour Bulletin* 39(9): 6–12.

Mizumachi, Y. 1997. *Labour Law Policies on Part-Time Work.* Tokyo: Yuhikaku (in Japanese).

Morito, H. 1999. "Deregulation of Labor Law in Japan." In *Deregulation and Labor Law in Search of a Labor Law Concept for the 21st Century.* JIL report no. 8. Tokyo: Japan Institute of Labour, pp. 149–164.

Nitta, M. 1997. "Business Diversification Strategy and Employment Relations: The Case of the Japanese Chemical Textile Industry." In *Japanese Labour and Management in Transition,* M. Sako and H. Sato, eds. London: Routledge, pp. 265–279.

Ohtake, F. 2000. "Special Employment Measures in Japan." *Japan Labour Bulletin* 39(12): 6–15.

Osawa, M., and J. Kingston. 1996. "Flexibility and Inspiration: Restructuring and the Japanese Labor Market." *Japan Labour Bulletin* 35(1): 4–8.

Price, J. 1997. *Japan Works: Power and Paradox in Postwar Industrial Relations.* Ithaca, New York: Cornell University Press.

Shinoda, T. 1997. "Rengo and Policy Participation: Japanese-style Neo-Corporatism?" In *Japanese Labour and Management in Transition*, M. Sako and H. Sato, eds. London: Routledge, pp. 187–214.

Sugeno, K., and Y. Suwa. 1997. "Labour Law Issues in a Changing Labour Market: In Search of a New Support System." In *Japanese Labour and Management in Transition,* M. Sako and H. Sato, eds. London: Routledge, pp. 53–78.

Tokyo Metropolitan Government. 1998. *Survey on Part-Time Workers.* Tokyo: Toei Sha (in Japanese).

————. 1999. *Survey on Dispatched Workers 1998.* Tokyo: Toei Sha (in Japanese).

Wakisaka, A. 1997. "Women at Work." In *Japanese Labour and Management in Transition,* M. Sako and H. Sato, eds. London: Routledge, pp. 131–150.

Yashiro, N. 1999. *Age of Reform of Employment.* Tokyo: Chuo Koron Shin Sha (in Japanese).

9

Temporary Agency Work in Europe

François Michon
Centre National de la Recherche Scientifique

European countries have been experiencing the growth of employment in nonstandard or flexible work arrangements. The basic causal factors have been similar to those experienced in the United States and Japan: global economic forces have required employers to adapt and change more quickly. In response to these economic forces, temporary agency work (TAW), one of a variety of flexible employment arrangements, has expanded over the past 30 years.[1] Although it existed earlier in some European countries, in others TAW has been authorized for only a few years. In some countries TAW is still restricted to a limited number of professions.

A variety of approaches exist to regulate and monitor temporary work agencies (TWAs) and the services they provide. These variations reflect distinctive national approaches to the regulation of labor markets and their institutions. Because of the diversity of these approaches, TAW is one area where the efforts for harmonization of national labor markets within the European Union (EU) have failed in the last few years. As a result, no common standard for the regulation of TAW has been developed in the EU.

The purpose of this chapter is to provide an overview of TAW within the EU and explain the challenges confronted as the EU continues its efforts to harmonize policies regulating TAW across its member nations. The regulations of EU members and the social debates on TAW are reviewed. Much of the discussion is based on data collected in a 1999 survey of the European Industrial Relations Observatory (EIRO) (2000). A 2002 study of the Dublin European Foundation, which focused on the economic analysis of TAW in EU members, and a 2005 study of the European Industrial Relations Observatory, which actualized the 1999 survey in the context of the EU enlargement, were used to provide updates on some major changes in national regulations that occurred after 1999 (Storrie 2002; Arrowsmith 2006).

The chapter first provides an overview of the growth of flexible work in Europe, including a brief discussion of the problems associated with trying to estimate the prevalence of TAW. Variations in the national definitions and regulations of TAW are then reviewed. The perspectives on TAW of employers' organizations and unions are presented, followed by a discussion of the differences in national approaches to the regulation of TAW through the use of laws and collective bargaining. The rules which the firms that use TAW must follow in each country to secure the social protection of employees also are described. Throughout this discussion the extreme heterogeneity of the regulatory frameworks of the EU nations is emphasized. Finally, concluding comments on the very brief history of "Social Europe" and the future of its labor market institutions are provided. Several future directions for research are identified.

FLEXIBLE WORK AND TEMPORARY AGENCY WORK IN EUROPE

The need for greater labor market flexibility has been discussed for almost 20 years in Europe. When compared to the United States, labor market flexibility in European countries often is viewed as inadequate except in a few countries such as the United Kingdom. Labor market rigidities such as those created by government regulations encouraging standard employment arrangements are often discussed as the main reason for the slower economic growth and the high levels of unemployment in Europe. These discussions of the limited labor market flexibility in the EU focus primarily on adjustments of the number of employees. One of several forms of atypical employment that permit numerical adjustments to be made easily by employers is temporary agency work. However, due to poor data, it is difficult to accurately measure the actual prevalence of TAW in the EU as discussed in more detail below.

EMPLOYMENT TRENDS AND FLEXIBLE LABOR MARKETS IN EUROPE

Since the beginning of the 1990s the rate of economic growth in Europe has been lower than that of the United States. The key trends in Europe during the 1990s were an increase in the importance of both unemployment and atypical work.[2] These trends resulted in greater attention to how labor market flexibility is linked to the regulation of employment contracts such as TAW.

For a short period of time in the late 1990s it appeared that the rate of increase in unemployment had slowed due to the positive response of standard employment to the economic recovery and the creation of jobs. The strong job creation that occurred during the late nineties (European Commission 2002) appeared to have been linked

> . . . to jobs of better quality . . . Recovery is now favoring more stable employment. The proportion of workers on fixed-term contracts (temporary work) in all new jobs created was only slightly over a third in 1999, compared with 50 percent in previous years. . . . For the first time since 1990, full-time jobs created—some 63 percent in 1999—exceeded the number of part-time jobs created. (European Commission 2000)

However, the economic climate began to deteriorate in 2001 and worsened in the following year due to the uncertainty of the international political situation. Since then the EU has had great difficulty recovering a fast and solid economic growth, especially in the old core of its member nations: Germany, France, Italy, Belgium, and the Netherlands. In these countries, the downturn had a significant negative impact on job creation for both standard and atypical employment.

Since the late 1990s the EU has tried to promote a European employment strategy (the so-called Lisbon strategy) which focuses on an increase in employment rates and in the quality of jobs. However, as the European Commission (2005) stated,

> [t]he weak labour market performance in Europe over recent years is an important element in explaining the slow progress towards the Lisbon and Stockholm objectives. The overall employment rate remains 7 percentage points below the employment rate target for 2010.

The evidence of limits, or even failures, of the Lisbon strategy has been presented in many reports, comments, and proposals to increase the efficiency of this strategy (see, for example, Kok [2004]). The main point repeated in these commentaries is that welfare and social justice remain largely a member country issue. Furthermore, many members are opposed to removing any national regulations in favor of the EU institutions. Consequently, in the present environment, the European institutions can only propose objectives, observe the situation of country members relative to these objectives, and give their opinions.

Labor market flexibility, or the lack thereof, is often explained in the context of the regulations defining—and thus potentially constraining—employment contracts, with particular attention given to the amount of flexibility gained from atypical employment arrangements. It therefore is commonly associated with fixed-term contracts and TAW, and in some EU members (especially in France, Spain, and Italy) with part-time contracts. However, within Europe part-time employment and fixed-term contracts are better known than TAW because there are more of them. Part-time contracts are different from the standard full-time contracts because they imply in most of European countries a specific employment status. Part-time employees are not necessarily easier to fire, but it is easier to increase or decrease their daily, weekly, or even monthly work times. The increase in part-time employment and fixed-term contracts from 1990 through 2004 is shown for 10 EU countries in Figures 9.1 and 9.2, respectively. For these two types of employment arrangements the European Labor Force Surveys provide good quantitative data for intra-European comparisons.

The use of these employment arrangements varies by country. Figure 9.1 indicates that in 2004 in the Netherlands, part-time employment was over 45 percent of total employment but just under 10 percent in Belgium and Spain. The other seven nations range from about 15 percent to 45 percent. Fixed-term contracts in Figure 9.2 show a different pattern of prevalence. In 2004 in Spain fixed-term contracts represent over 30 percent of total employment, but the other nine countries are in the range of 5 percent to 15 percent.

273

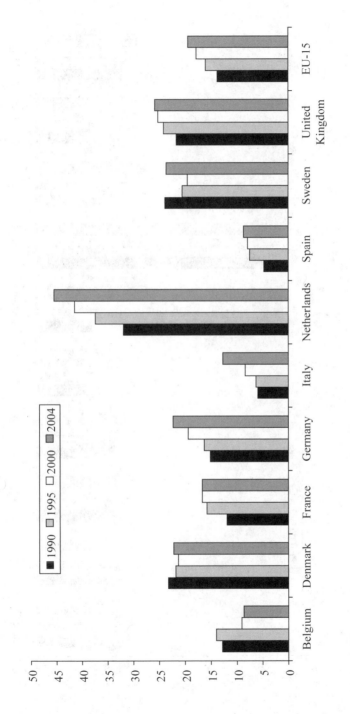

Figure 9.1 Part-Time Employment in Selected EU Countries (% Total Employment)

■ 1990 ■ 1995 □ 2000 ■ 2004

SOURCE: Eurostat.

Figure 9.2 Fixed-Term Contracts in Selected EU Countries (% Total Employment)

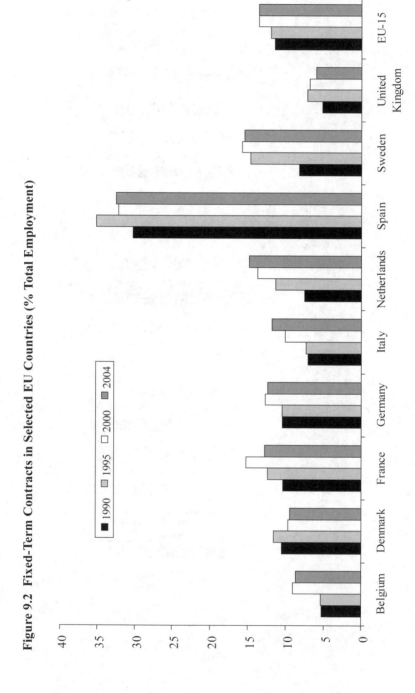

SOURCE: Eurostat.

Prevalence of Temporary Agency Work

TAW was one of the most rapidly growing forms of atypical employment in the 1990s (Storrie 2002). However, this growth is difficult to measure and compare across the EU nations. Unlike the measures of the prevalence of part-time employment and fixed-term contracts, there are no equivalent employment data for TWA. Due to the differences in national regulations, the terms *temporary agency work* or *temporary work agency* refer to very different and noncomparable employment arrangements between the three partners in the relationship: the employee, the TWA, and the client firm. This explains why the available data that compare TAW cross-nationally within the EU nations are unreliable, and there are no data at all for some countries. Due to the lack of common definitions, the Statistical Office of the European Communities (Eurostat) does not try to quantitatively measure the prevalence of TAW.[3] It therefore is difficult to provide a precise and comprehensive picture of the prevalence of TAW in Europe, and estimates of the rate of growth of TWA are even more difficult.[4] Consequently, the estimates provided below of the prevalence of TAW must be used with caution.

In an effort to provide some data, the European Foundation for the Improvement of Living and Working Conditions undertook a study of TAW.[5] The resulting estimates range widely from no TAW in Greece to 4 percent of total employment in the Netherlands, as shown in Table 9.1.

For the 13 nations that reported the use of TAW by sector in the 1999 EIRO survey, 6 reported that TAW was concentrated in the industrial sector, and 7, the tertiary sector (services, public services, and retail). The industrial TAW was dominant in Austria, Belgium, France, Germany, Italy, and Spain; the tertiary TAW was dominant in Denmark, Finland, Italy, Netherlands, Norway, Portugal, and the United Kingdom. The industrial sector consisted primarily of manual labor and a male workforce, while the tertiary sector was primarily a female and white-collar workforce. According to the European Trade Union Confederation (2005),

> . . . in the UK, some 80 percent of temporary agency work is in the service and public sectors, while three-quarters is in construction and manufacturing industry in France. In most of the EU-15, the majority of workers are male, but in all three Nordic countries there are more women, and proportions are roughly equal in the Netherlands and the UK.

Table 9.1 Temporary Agency Work in the European Union, 1999

Country	Number of agency workers	Agency work as % of total employment
Austria	24,277	0.7
Belgium	62,661	1.6
Denmark	18,639	0.7
Finland	15,000	0.6
France	623,000	2.7
Germany	243,000	0.7
Greece	0	0.0
Ireland	9,000	0.6
Italy	31,000	0.2
Luxembourg	6,065	3.5
Netherlands	305,000	4.0
Portugal	45,000	1.0
Spain	109,000	0.8
Sweden	32,000	0.8
United Kingdom	557,000	2.1
EU total	2,080,642	1.4

SOURCE: EIRO (2000).

A second estimate of the prevalence of TAW was developed by the French employer organization for TWA, Syndicat des Entreprises de Travail Temporaire (SETT). This organization published estimates for 2004 derived from national sources for only eight EU countries. A comparison of Tables 9.1 and 9.2 suggests a relatively large increase from 1999 to 2004 in TAW in the United Kingdom, but no clear trend in the other countries.

Both tables reflect national historical differences in the treatment and regulation of TAW in the context of all forms of temporary work. Actual changes suggest that there are two reasons why limitations imposed by regulation based on the types of jobs and industrial sector are being reduced. First, there has been an increased acceptance over time of TAW in countries that for a long time were reluctant to expand TAW. This will result in a relaxation of these regulations. Second, temporary work agencies are developing their businesses to provide their services wherever temporary help is needed, and even when temporary help for long periods of time is required (European Trade Union Confederation 2005). Regulations are likely to be relaxed as employers become more dependent on these services.

Finally, what Tables 9.1 and 9.2 do not show is the importance of TAW in labor flows into and out of unemployment, and out of and into employment. The 1999 EIRO report provided this information for a few countries. For example, TAW in Spain accounts for 12.5 percent of new employment contracts. This is not surprising since temporary work arrangements of various types are often entry-level jobs for persons entering the labor force and for those with relatively low levels of skills.

DEFINING TEMPORARY AGENCY WORK AND TEMPORARY EMPLOYEES

In an effort to standardize the social protections provided to employees hired through atypical employment contracts, the EU authorities in the second half of the 1990s organized negotiations between the EU-level social partners (employers and unions) on "flexibility in working time and security for workers."[6] The European negotiations focused on three types of atypical employment: part-time work, fixed-term contracts, and TAW. It was expected that some European standard-

Table 9.2 Temporary Agency Work in Europe, 2004

Country	Number of agency workers	Agency work as % of total employment
Belgium	75,100	1.8
France	569,300	2.1
Germany	350,000	0.9
Italy	154,400	0.6
Netherlands	180,000	3.0
Portugal	48,000	0.9
Spain	120,000	0.7
Sweden	39,000	1.0
UK	1,052,000	3.5

SOURCE: Syndicat des Entreprises de Travail Temporaire (2005).

ization of the definitions and regulations in all three areas would result. EU-level negotiations were concluded successfully on part-time work in 1997 and on fixed-term contract work in 1999. They produced two official directives from the European authorities. The negotiations on TAW were the last to be organized, but in May 2001 they failed despite repeated efforts to resolve differences.

The EU-level collective negotiations on TAW failed because the social partners were unable to negotiate an acceptable compromise. Unions blamed employers for the failure. They perceived employers as trying to completely deregulate TAW. However, the employer representatives were divided among themselves along two lines: there was conflict between the interests of the client firms and temporary work agencies, and the objectives of employers varied from one country to another. The only result of the negotiations was a common "declaration" that mainly stressed the general principle of equal treatment between temporary agency workers and permanent employees.

Even this declaration was ambiguous on some points and was hardly discussed by the national members of the employers' organization. It did not clarify what aspects of permanent employment should be the reference points for equal treatment, nor whether the permanent employment was in the TWA or the client firm. Making such determinations was not an easy task in the European context. Some countries legally restrict the role of a TWA to offering temporary workers who are temporary employees of the TWA to client firms, while in other countries a TWA can in addition select, train, and hire permanent employees for their future employers. Consequently, the TWAs under these two different regulations are not the same businesses.

Further EU Actions to Standardize TAW Regulations

After the failure of the TWA negotiations, the European authorities decided to seek an agreement between EU member governments instead of employers and unions. The basis for this step was the prior declaration by the EU social partners of the principle of equality of treatment of temporary agency workers and permanent employees. In March 2002 the European Commission issued a "draft directive" on temporary work. It was studied and extensively amended by the European Parliament in November 2002. Although the general principle of

equal treatment was accepted, there was much discussion of the defini-
tions of the comparable workers and the acceptance of the possibility of
EU members being exempted or allowed to deviate from the principle
(European Industrial Relations Observatory 2002).

The formal objective of the directive proposed in November 2002
by the Commission of European Communities is to ensure better working conditions for temporary workers. This directive defines TWA and
TAW and the workers that will be covered. The Employment, Social
Policy, Health and Consumer Affairs Council examined the directive in
March and June 2003, but an agreement was not reached (European Industrial Relations Observatory 2003). According to the European Trade
Union Confederation (2005), adoption of such an "essential piece of
social legislation" is blocked by a minority of EU member states, name-
ly: Denmark, Germany, Ireland, and the United Kingdom. Since then,
nothing more has been done.

Differences in National Definitions of TAW

The major difficulty confronted in the EU discussions is that the
national laws are very dissimilar and do not provide even a minimum
basis for a common perspective on which an EU-level agreement can
be developed. On TAW issues the situation is characterized by such
significant heterogeneity between countries that regulations do not even
use the same vocabulary. Recent changes in national regulations do not
modify this general picture. There is no agreement on what is called
"temporary agency work" and how is it specified relative to other forms
of temporary work or even to standard employment contracts. Furthermore, there is no agreement on what is called a "temporary work agency" or how is it specified relative to other forms of services provided
to firms or to the other forms of three-way relationships between an
employee, an employer who has signed an employment contract with
an employee, and another employer for whom the employee is working
(e.g., service subcontracts or some workforce lending or leasing). Due
to this lack of a common approach, the EU authorities' proposals have
been written in relatively vague language to avoid conflicts with the
specific regulations of the member nations.

In some countries such as France, Germany, and the Netherlands,
TAW is fully recognized as a specific employment relationship. In oth-

ers, the definitions and regulations are vague, and there are no clearly defined categories. Consequently, the available information on atypical employment and TAW is extremely diverse and of variable quality. The public debate at both the national and European levels over appropriate regulatory and collective bargaining approaches to TAW reflects the lack of accurate, high-quality data and standardized definitions of the activities being measured.

The 1999 EIRO survey indicated that there are three approaches to the definition of TAW in Europe: 1) TAW is not clearly distinguished from other forms of flexible work and therefore can be measured poorly at best; 2) TAW is determined solely by identifying the companies given the status known as a TWA; the temporary employment businesses thus are formally recognized, but their temporary employees are not; and 3) a defined legal status is given to both the temporary employment agencies and to the employees working for them, so TWA employment can be relatively easily measured.[7] These approaches are discussed below for the countries using each approach.

No Distinction between TAW and Other Flexible Work

Temporary agency work is not clearly distinguished from other forms of flexible work in a few countries such as Finland, Ireland, and the United Kingdom. The lack of reliable quantitative data on TWA in these countries makes it difficult to determine whether this situation reflects a very small amount of this type of work in these countries or the lack of a precise definition that distinguishes TAW from other forms of employment, particularly other forms of temporary work. This data measurement problem can be illustrated by using the United Kingdom as an example. According to Morris (2002), the British Department of Trade and Industry reported 600,000 temporary agency workers in 2002 in the United Kingdom, contrasting markedly with two other reports. In spring 2002 the British Labour Force Survey reported 275,000 workers (Office for National Statistics 2002), while the Recruitment and Employment Confederation (REC) reported 1,336,699 workers (REC 2002).

There is no precise definition of TAW in any of the three countries. In Finland the contract binding a temporary employment agency to its employees is almost identical to the contract required by regulations for temporary work. Irish regulations hardly intervene in the relationship between temporary work agency and the worker since the Irish worker has been considered an employee of the client company for a long time.

In the United Kingdom no unique status is granted to TAW. It depends on the same regulations as any temporary work regardless of whether workers are employed directly by the client firm or by the employment agency, or even are independent. This treatment of TAW reflects two factors. First, it is frequently the same company that acts both as an employment agency and as a temporary employment agency as the term is used in this chapter. No statutory regulation now distinguishes one activity from the other. As for the formal employment relationship itself, the courts must determine the employer to whom the employee is contractually bound: the employment agency or the client company. Second, temporary workers increasingly can be self-employed. This means that the agency is only a structure that manages administrative procedures associated with the employment of the temporary workers.

However, in the beginning of the 1990s the situation of TAW changed in these countries. For example, in 1994 Finland abolished the existing regulations on hiring, which distinguished between permanent and temporary employees. To provide some protection for workers, the responsibilities of a temporary employment agency and its client company were clarified instead. In 1993 Ireland acknowledged that temporary contracts could be renewed repeatedly, but left it to the courts in case of conflict to determine whether employer abuses were being perpetrated. Furthermore, the principle was established that a temporary agency worker was not employed by the client company. In 1994 the United Kingdom abolished the necessity of TWAs receiving a permit to do business, and later contemplated new regulations to acknowledge that an employment relationship exists between the employee and the "employment agency." The Employment Relations Act of 1999 removed the prohibition against regulations which restricted employment agencies from paying temporary workers directly.

Defining Only Temporary Work Agencies

In some countries the presence of TAW is determined by a company status known as the "temporary work agency." The prevalence of TAW is determined solely by identifying the companies given this status. These temporary employment businesses are formally recognized, but their temporary employees are not. This pattern is quite frequent.

The TWA "status" is conferred by very different regulations in these countries, however, and usually is determined in one of two ways. The first is to issue a permit for the TWA. A company given the status of a TWA then becomes the basis for specifying the temporary nature of the employment relationship between the agency and the employees the agency sends for assignment to the client firms. The second gives a permanent contract to all employees of a TWA who are sent to an assignment. This permanent contract can be a specific one, or a standard one used for ordinary open-ended contracts. In this situation it is no longer the employment contract that separates TAW and other forms of employment but only the status of the employer. The principle of authorizing TWAs as employment agencies now seems established. However, the principle of a specific open-ended contract, or even a standard open-ended contract, being used for temporary agency employees seems to be losing ground, and is now less frequently used than before.

The different national approaches are illustrated by five countries: Spain, Germany, Norway, Austria, and the Netherlands. For example, in Spain TWAs have been legally recognized since 1994 and must be licensed by the state. The employee's contract can be either permanent or temporary.

Private TWAs in Germany are subject to the approval of the Federal Employment Department. Until 1997 TWAs were bound to their employees by a permanent contract, basically similar to any standard employment contract but the periods of work were for a strictly limited period. However, a succession of deregulatory measures in 1997, 1998, and 2003 abolished these limitations. Temporary employment contracts such as those lasting only the length of a particular assignment were introduced. For these contracts there was the possibility of reemploying temps three months after a first assignment, subject to the limitations of the common regulation of fixed-term contracts.

In Norway temporary agency work is only allowed for unskilled office or commercial work. Its regulation has established the principle of the permanent contract, but acknowledges exceptions for which employment contracts can be temporary. The number of these exceptions has risen since 1996. Today a temporary contract is more often used by TWA than a permanent one.

The content of the contract of a temporary agency employee in Austria is prescribed by regulation. It is not required to be a temporary contract, but it must stipulate the level of pay, the duration of work assignment, the amount of notice required for job termination, the nature of the work, and the place of work. Thus, while no principle requiring temporary contracts applies, the content of the contract defines the work as temporary.

From the perspective of both the status of temporary employment agencies and the content of the employee's contract, recent Dutch developments are atypical. The "Flexicurity" and "WAADI" Acts passed in January 1999 in the Netherlands abolished permits for temporary work agencies and determined that the temporary worker is progressively bound as employment continues to the employment agency by a standard contract. This means that time thresholds determine in stages the increases in employee rights and wages. After 18 months at a single client firm or 36 months at various firms, the employment contract becomes a standard open-ended contract with the TWA. Storrie (2002) judges the new Dutch legislation as "rather innovative."

Defining Both TWAs and Temporary Employees

Finally, in France, Portugal, Italy, and Belgium, a clearly defined legal status is given to the temporary employment agencies. In addition, a special status differentiates their temporary employees from other temporary workers with ordinary fixed-term contracts and their permanent employees such as the staff of the agencies.

France has been one of the leaders in the development of TAW and its regulations since it was first regulated in 1972. Consequently, information on TAW is relatively plentiful when compared to many other countries. In France, the TWA is not an ordinary firm. Until the beginning of 2005, the provision of temporary employees hired and paid by the TWA had to be the only profit-making activity of the agency. However, a new regulation in 2005 allowed a TWA to perform as ordinary employment agency in addition to its specific TWA business. The TWA also is subject to two special obligations. First, the company must file statements to document a specified level of financial resources and regularly provide the government with a full account of its activities. Second, a temporary employee of this type of company has a unique legal contract known as an "assignment contract" with prescribed content, accompanied by a set of extensive rules protecting the employee.

Some other countries have chosen similar approaches. In Portugal, TWAs must be licensed. Employment contracts are subject to specific legislation that stipulates the regulations of the three-way relationship. In Italy, TAW was forbidden until 1997. A law passed in that year authorized TAW for the first time and established the conditions for its use. The specific character of temporary work agencies was acknowledged. This legislation established a contract for temporary work that is drawn up between the TWA and the client company. In addition, special provisions were included that relate to the situation of temporary employees.

The legislation in Belgium defines the various forms of temporary work but appears to formally avoid defining a status for temporary employment agencies. However, the content required in a TAW contract is specified and known as "temporary for work on the premises of a third party." However, TAW has been affected by the general trends in Belgium toward regulating all nonstandard forms of employment. These efforts toward formal regulations include extending the required length of an employment assignment; less monitoring of employers to verify that they are observing the required length of employment, particularly by union representatives; and improving social security coverage and ongoing training for temporary agency employees.[8]

This section has discussed how regulations have been used to clarify the three-way relationship specific to TAW. Even those countries pursuing labor market deregulation to extend the use of more flexible types of employment have developed regulations to provide a clearer legal framework and better social protection for temporary workers. Thus, nontraditional forms of employment may be regulated with the ultimate goal of deregulating more traditional forms of employment. But the result is the creation of a paradoxical situation: far from deregulated flexibility, more regulation is being introduced to increase the flexibility of the labor markets.

EMPLOYER AND UNION ORGANIZATIONS AND
STRATEGIES TOWARD TAW

As discussed above, the temporary agency business in many European countries is a relatively new and poorly regulated institution. Consequently, it is not surprising that the relationships between TWA employer organizations and unions also remain relatively underdeveloped, and that collective bargaining in this sector is still evolving.[9]

In most EU countries TWAs are organized to varying degrees to create their own national employer organizations. Today in France, Luxembourg, Norway, and Portugal, there is one national employer organization. A single organization in France was created when two earlier organizations merged in 1998. In Spain and the Netherlands there are two employer groups. Employers are not organized in a separate association in only a few countries, such as in Sweden.

In contrast to employers' organizations, the organization of temporary agency workers in specialized unions is rare, as reported in the 1999 EIRO survey. The report on Italy is the only one that indicates that unions are exploring concerns related to separate unions for temporary workers. However, although union attitudes toward TAW are generally changing as the importance of labor market flexibility is acknowledged, unions remain largely hostile to TAW. It is this hostility that explains why unions favor bargaining with the client firm rather than the TWA, despite the fact that regulations identify the employer for the purposes of collective bargaining as the TWA instead of the client firm.

As a result of the relative lack of employer and employee organizations, the organization of industrial relations in the TAW businesses remains relatively weak. A number of TWAs are not covered by the agreement between sectoral organizations of the social partners. These TWAs conclude work agreements with their own work councils. Germany is one notable exception, however. An employer organization for the TWA businesses, the Unternehmensverband für Zeitarbeit e.V (UZA), was founded in 1969. The first collective bargaining agreement for TAW was signed in 1970.

Employer and Union Attitudes toward TAW

The relations between TAW employers and unions are fraught with tensions and conflicts that arise from the relatively recent growth in most countries of temporary agency work. All employers who are potential users of TAW understand the benefits of temporary employment. They now advocate flexibility in employment arrangements and appreciate the options provided by TAW for adjusting their labor force with fewer restricting regulations. In contrast, unions in all of the EU countries perceive the negative impact of TAW since it threatens the employment-related rights of the permanent employees. Temporary agency workers are paid less than the permanent workers, do not have equivalent social protection, and continue to be subject to employer "abuses." It is easier for employers to hire and fire temporary agency workers than permanent employees, to hire temporary workers to replace strikers, and to fire temporary workers for minor causes without an appeal process.

However, the strategic objectives of employers and unions are not always antagonistic. Since TAW in Europe is often considered by workers as the worst type of flexible employment arrangement, employers in some countries have declared their willingness to limit abuses related to TAW and tried to improve the image of this work. For example, Manpower France declared its willingness to limit TAW abuses, which led to negotiations with unions before the first TWA regulation in France in 1972. Also, the public relations activities of French temporary work agencies seek to convince workers that TAW can be highly skilled and better paid employment, which can introduce a worker to a real career for life. They try to convince potential client firms that they can provide to them highly skilled and better selected people at a lower cost. Spanish employers also agreed to limit abuses, although they disagree with the unions over what should be done. Swedish employers complain about the poor quality of temporary agency workers. They consider better training a more pressing need than any change in the regulations. German employers also have focused on finding ways to improve the relatively negative image of TAW.

However, some progress has been made, as unions generally are no longer overtly hostile to TAW. This reflects either a strategic fallback position in the face of a *fait accompli*, or the recognition that it is better to work toward the improvement of social protections that fit the special situation of TAWs. In some countries the unions now acknowledge the valid role of TAW. However, they retain the objective of providing a framework for this type of work, even if it is only to ensure that the uses of TAW remain within established limits. This is the case in the Netherlands, Denmark, and Italy.

Strategies for Compromise

The process of identifying common ground between employers and unions is not easy. However, appropriate strategies can create the conditions for compromise through collective bargaining between temporary employment agencies and unions, or client companies and unions.

France and Belgium are countries where some common ground has been found. French employers in the temporary agency industry called for standards to be adopted for TAW. Although historically the unions have long demanded a ban on TAW, they participated in the discussions. The 1990 cross-sector collective bargaining agreement, extended in the form of a law in the same year and still in effect today, deals with most aspects of the relationship between the temporary agency employer and its employees. A number of agreements in the client industry sectors relating to areas such as vocational training, safety and hygiene, and union rights have complemented this agreement. In Belgium, employers have declared themselves in favor of controlled growth for TAW. The unions within several client companies demanded long and renewable periods of temporary agency employment. However, they signed an agreement in 1997 supporting the principle that TAW is the best means for employment flexibility. This represents a major change in the attitude of the unions toward TAW.

In Italy, a cross-sector collective bargaining agreement quickly followed the enactment of the 1997 law authorizing TAW, even though differences of opinion between employers and unions delayed the passage of this law. The agreement seems to have been based on the notion that regulation by collective bargaining agreement is the only way to avoid inflexible labor markets, and that legislators should not be writing these regulations.

Even in the United Kingdom, the idea has begun to take root that some action must be taken due to the increasingly widespread use of the services of temporary work agencies. The concern is that the lack of regulation may create conflict between the dual functions of TWAs of selecting and hiring permanent workers for their clients, and providing their own workers for temporary use by the client. This turnabout in the United Kingdom attitude is particularly interesting since it is the most hostile country in Europe to any employment regulation other than the protections against discrimination. However, no major reform has been undertaken yet.

In addition to negotiations between temporary agency employers and unions, collective bargaining in client companies also can focus on TAW at either the firm level or the cross-industry level. In Austria, France, Italy, and the Netherlands, negotiations have become more prevalent in both the client company sectors and temporary employment industry, and in Italy and France, even at the cross-sector level. In a few countries, such as Belgium, Denmark, the United Kingdom, and Luxembourg, negotiations take place almost exclusively, and sometimes totally, at the level of the temporary employment agency industry. Organization in Belgium is exemplary. Since 1987 there has been a jointly run employers and unions committee in the temporary employment industry, which is similar to the organizations used for other industries in Belgium. In Finland and Sweden, however, there is no negotiation at the temporary agency industry level; negotiations occur only at client company level.

THE REGULATORY FRAMEWORK: LAW AND COLLECTIVE BARGAINING

Temporary agency work is a form of employment that has appeared in Europe because it initially provided employers with a way to avoid the constraining regulations governing standard employment. Legislated and negotiated regulations on TAW were developed in response to limit the maneuvers of employers to cases in which exceptions to the standard of employment can be justified. As employer ingenuity found ways to increase the margin for maneuvering despite, or in parallel with, the law or collective agreements with which they are supposed to comply, regulations have been updated in an effort to reduce the margin for maneuvering, reduce the scope of abuses, and impose standards.

Temporary agency work and its regulation have continued to evolve over the past 10 to 15 years, but are not reproducing the traditional industrial relations models previously used in Europe.

A typology of three regulatory frameworks is commonly used in Europe. The first model is the Latin countries (the South), where the state imposes a large number of regulations which are not always properly obeyed. The second is the German-Scandinavian model (the continental North), in which regulation has historically imposed obligatory minimum standards. Finally there is the British model, largely influenced by the dominant free market theories of the 1980s and 1990s. In this model there is an almost total absence of regulation for TAW.

The following analysis of the national reports from the EIRO centers illustrates the limitations of these traditional industrial relations models when applied to the case of TAW because new employment trends are reducing the differences between the three models and thereby the relevance of such a typology. Negotiation no longer augments the legally enforced standards as was the usual historical function of collective bargaining in many countries. Instead, negotiation may, under some conditions, remove or challenge the advantages granted to employees under the law. The interesting question is what the regulatory model of the future will be.

The Latin Model

According to the Latin model, the state imposes many regulations, but they are not always followed properly. However, there have been no regulations for TAW for a long time, and the need for a framework has surfaced only in the last few years. This change occurred in a period when the Latin model had already been altered to some extent through negotiated regulation achieved through collective bargaining. Although almost unknown in the past, negotiated regulation has become to varying degrees an accepted practice in recent years. Italy and Spain are examples of this model, while Greece and Portugal are exceptions. The early and protective regulation of TAW in France is unique.

Italy is an excellent example of the change operating within the Latin Model. According to the 1999 EIRO survey, the late recognition of TAW in this country in 1997 is attributable to the deep-seated differences in the positions taken by employers and unions toward TAW. Two collective bargaining agreements (one national across industries and the other national for the TWA business sector) were signed in 1998 immediately after this recognition. Compared to the provisions of the 1997 law, the negotiated agreements were more restrictive on certain points, such as the introduction of a maximum length for TAW assignments. However, the agreements were more flexible on other points, such as identifying new situations in which TAW can be used by a company and stipulating the rights of temporary employees. Thus, negotiation rapidly imposed its mark.

Spain has followed a pattern similar to that of Italy. Temporary agency work has been recognized in Spain by law since 1994 (with amendments in 1995 and 1997). Some unions refused any recognition of TAW. Others tried to limit the use of TAW to the strictly temporary needs of client companies or to give some special permanent contracts to temporary workers, and to provide better protections to workers. Employers recognized that abuses occurred. Finally, the collective bargaining agreements of 1997 and 1998 attempted to improve the regulation of TAW. These agreements were negotiated cross-sector and within the TWA sector, including one known as the state agreement, which was later changed into a law. The 1999 EIRO survey stressed that TAW remains a central theme of collective bargaining negotiations in Spain, but it is the subject of incessant dispute between employers and unions about the desired model of TAW.

Greece and Portugal are the exceptions to the Latin model. In Greece, as already noted, there is still no official acknowledgment of TAW either in legislation or negotiated agreements. The 1999 EIRO survey stressed that in Portugal TAW is regulated by a 1989 law. This legislation supersedes a collective bargaining agreement that has never been enforced. However, union participation is occurring now as part of the general public debate over the changes that should be made to the 1989 law.

France is a special case within the group of Latin countries due to its early and very protective regulation of TAW. Moreover, contrary to the reputation of the French government that regulates everything, regulations negotiated through collective bargaining have been part and parcel of the French legislative decisions for many years. Although the regulation of TAW in France is principally carried out by enacting legislation, on several occasions the law has only reviewed and modified a number of the issues previously negotiated by employers and unions. For example, the first French law on TAW in 1972 was based largely on the previous provisions adopted by Manpower France. Again, in 1990, the government used the option known as "extension" in the French industrial relations system to confer legal status on the provisions of the cross-sector collective bargaining agreement for the temporary work business.

The German-Scandinavian Model

The principles of the German-Scandinavian model include minimum standards imposed by legislation with almost all additional regulations imposed by collective bargaining. This model is not any better suited to the field of TAW than the Latin model. Although Austria is still a good example of this model as applied to TAW, it does not fit the other countries well (Denmark, Norway, Sweden, the Netherlands, and Germany) due to one of two considerations. In some countries the law prescribes some limits and/or principles that significantly restrict the opportunities for collective bargaining negotiations on TAW. In other countries the current trend toward deregulation and increased flexibility in employment are changing profoundly the fundamental characteristics of the relationship between legislation and negotiation to the detriment of the former.

Austrian law carefully frames the work of temporary employment agencies. These agencies must have permits to operate and observe the obligatory content of the contract binding the TWA and the employee. A TWA sector-level collective bargaining agreement complements the law on pay issues. Moreover, the collective agreements of many client companies deal specifically with the issue of TAW. The primary concern is the requirement that temporary work agency employees must be recruited on permanent contracts.

In contrast, TAW in Norway is an excellent illustration of how the legal framework significantly restricts the opportunities for collective bargaining negotiations on TAW, thereby deviating from the German-Scandinavian model. The 1999 EIRO survey emphasizes that a wide margin has developed in Norway between the laws which establish legal principles and bans on activities so that TAW is strictly regulated, relative to the actual practices of the client firms. Probably for this reason, TAW is as widespread in Norway as in many other EU countries, and now accounts for 2 percent of the labor force. The EIRO survey observes that collective bargaining seems to have neglected TAW since this sector is not yet covered by a collective bargaining agreement. However, TAW does not seem to be the subject of any significant dispute. With no information available on disputes, the report can only theorize that issues related to TAW are discussed in the in-house negotiations with the client companies.

The case of TAW in Denmark illustrates a change in the relationship between legislation and negotiation. Prior to 1990, the regulation of TAW was carried out by legislation. The law only allowed TAW in a few industries (retail and office work) and only licensed temporary employment agencies were allowed to handle it. In 1990 both sets of restrictions were lifted. Subsequently collective bargaining has grown rapidly in the newly opened industries.

Curiously, the regulation of TAW in Germany appears to be a bad example of the German-Scandinavian model. Regulations in this country have undergone a rather stormy passage. The first and only collective bargaining agreement ever reached on TAW dates back to the 1970s. The principle of a permanent contract binding a temporary employee to the TWA was laid out in the first piece of legislation in 1972. In 1989 the collective bargaining agreement was not renewed. In 1997 statutory constraints were greatly relaxed. At present temporary employees still are not covered by a collective bargaining agreement and remain outside the participation system which regulates all the German industrial relations.[10]

In the Netherlands the model of a complementary relationship between laws and negotiation is apparent. A law passed in January 1999 altered the legal framework by removing any specific definition of TAW, requirements to license temporary employment agencies, and the need to acknowledge the temporary nature of the employment contract. However, TAW has been the focus of a high degree of negotiation between temporary work agencies and unions, client companies and unions, and employers' associations of temporary work agencies and associations acting on behalf of client companies.

A similar scenario to that of the Netherlands occurred in 1991 in Sweden, when the sector called "workforce rent" was deregulated. Since the deregulation collective bargaining in Sweden has devoted more attention to TAW. For example, the local union must approve the hiring of any temporary staff, including temporary agency workers. The union also must participate in a discussion of pay between two assignments for temporary agency workers. However, this is not as radical as in the contemporary Netherlands. Despite deregulation the Swedish law still guarantees temporary agency workers some minimal protection. Examples include the possibility of being hired on a permanent contract by the client company, and prohibiting a client firm from asking its employees whose fixed-term contracts have just expired to return to work as temporary employment agency workers. The current debate primarily is focused on the possible introduction of a system of licensing by an independent authority for temporary employment agencies.

The British Model

The British model is still in effect in the United Kingdom, even though the current administration is said to be thinking of regulating the employment contract by binding the employee and the "employment agency." Since there are only a few regulations of employment relationships in the United Kingdom, and above all of TAW, firms do not have to use any innovative practices to avoid the prescriptions of the legislator.

RULES GOVERNING THE USE OF TAW AND THE PROTECTION OF EMPLOYEES

The discussion in the previous section focuses on the differences in the policy approaches used to control the use of TAW. They typically involve the joint use of legislation and collective bargaining agreements in various combinations determined by the national industrial relations systems of each EU country. In this section the discussion is focused on the key aspects of TAW that legislation or bargaining seek to regulate.

In addition to the rules that control the business of TWAs such as the requirement to have a permit to operate, the regulations control the use of TAW by client firms and provide some social protection to the temporary employee. There are four main types of regulations:

those that 1) control the length of TAW contract; 2) define the employment situations in which user firms can ask for workers from agencies; 3) require parity in the conditions of employment and pay between temporary agency workers and permanent workers doing the same work in a client company; and 4) grant union and representation rights to temporary agency workers in the client company and/or in the temporary employment agency, and regulate union and representation rights to ordinary employees and union representatives in the client company when temporary agency workers are present.

Table 9.3 presents a brief overview of the key regulated aspects of TAW. It can be observed that a deep gulf divides the countries that have deregulated TAW to varying degrees (in some cases, almost completely as in the United Kingdom) and those that are maintaining or even strengthening the legislative or negotiated framework.

Permitted Use of TAW, Contract Length, and Parity

Many European countries (Belgium, France, Italy, Luxembourg, Norway, Portugal, and Spain) always control TAW in the first three key aspects simultaneously. Therefore, regulations determine the maximum length of assignment for which a worker is hired, the circumstances in which temporary agency workers can be used, and the principle of parity in conditions of work and pay between TAW and permanent employees.

As discussed above, when TAW was legally introduced in Italy, it was with strict control of TWA businesses. The Italian law did not set any limitation on the length of assignments. However, two 1998 collective bargaining agreements limited both the use of TAW and the length of contracts. One contract that covered the TWA businesses determined that TAW could be used only in case of an absence of an employee, to provide skills that are not present within the client firm, or for any other reason negotiated through collective bargaining. The other contract was the April 1998 national multi-industry agreement. It identified which reasons are acceptable to use temporary agency workers: to provide coverage in periods of additional workload, skills not present on the labor market, and employees who could perform specific tasks that could not be performed by an employee of the firm. Contract length, including four renewals, was limited to 24 months. Other regulations required parity with permanent employees.

Since TAW was first regulated in 1972, in France the regulations have been relaxed or strengthened in response to the interest of the political majority and new choices of collective bargaining. For example, a 1990 change reintroduced a list of authorized uses for temporary agency workers which had been suppressed a few years earlier. The list limited the use to the replacement of an absent employee, the replacement of a departing employee when the job must be filled only temporarily, filling a position until a new permanent employee arrives, handling a temporary additional workload, and completing tasks defined as temporary "by nature." Temporary agency workers thus cannot be used to do the standard work of the firm, to fill core permanent jobs, or to replace strikers. The standard length of assignments is limited to 18 months, including renewals. The length of the contract must be indicated in a written contract between the employee and the employer. In some very specific situations, such as those that arise when the end of the work assignment cannot be determined at the time the contract is written, the contract can be left open-ended. However, in these cases, the written contract must indicate a minimum length for the assignment. Parity with permanent workers is formally required. In this context, the recent 2005 change is often considered a "revolution." Some new uses are authorized, which are not defined in terms of user firm needs, but in terms of worker profile: to contribute to employment policies, it is authorized to use temporary agency work for people with very low employability.

If controls are present generally in all the three areas simultaneously, there are countries where they may be very strict in some area or concerning some specific situation and weak in another. For example, in Belgium the maximum period of time for which temporary agency staff can be employed varies greatly. Temporary agency work contracts are limited to 15 days if the employee is covering for a permanent member of staff, or 12 months with possible extension for a further six months if there is an increase in company workload. Compared to Belgium, Italy with its maximum of a 24-month period and four renewals (see above) is the complete opposite.

For continental Europeans, it is not surprising to observe that the United Kingdom has no regulations stipulating a maximum length of

Table 9.3 Regulation of Key Aspects of Temporary Agency Work

Country	Regulation of maximum length of TAW contract	Restrictions on use of TAW (permitted uses)	Parity with permanent workers	Exercise of union/representation rights for TAW workers
Austria	None	Very few	Yes	No special provisions
Belgium	15 days–12 months (including renewal) depending on circumstances	Significant (replacement of employee, temporary increase in workload and special work)	Yes	Mainly in agency
Denmark	None	None	No (only by CB in some sectors)	No special provisions
Finland	None	None	No	No special provisions
France	Usually 18 months (including renewal), but 9 of 24 months in some circumstances	Significant (replacement of employees, temporary increase in workload and inherently temporary work), specific workforce groups (very low employability)	Yes	Mainly in agency
Germany	None	Very few	Introduced in the 2003 legislation, can be suppressed by CB	Divided but mainly in agency
Greece	None	None	No	No special provisions
Ireland	None	None	No	No special provisions

Italy	24 months (including 4 renewals) by CB	Significant (replacement, special skills, or—by CB—for workload peaks, specific tasks/skills)	Yes	Divided but mainly in agency
Luxembourg	12 months, including 2 renewals	Significant (specific, non-permanent jobs, not part of enterprise's normal activity)	Yes	Divided but mainly in agency
Netherlands	None	Very few	Yes	No special provisions
Norway	None	Significant (replacement, seasonal work and unpredictable, short-term changes in activity—exceptions by CB)	No	In agency
Portugal	6–12 months	Significant (replacement, temporary increases in workload, and short-lived seasonal tasks)	Yes	In agency (user company after 2 years)
Spain	No maximum in some cases, 6 months in others (up to 18 months by CB)	As for other temporary work (replacement, specific work, market circumstances, temporary increases in workload)	Yes	Mainly in the user company
Sweden	None	None	No	In agency
UK	None	Very few	No	No special provisions

NOTE: CB = collective bargaining
SOURCE: 1999 EIRO Survey (reproduced from EIRO [2000]).

contract, rules on parity, nor constraints restricting the activities of "employment agencies" to specific employment situations in which they can be used. Existing regulations only impose the principles of racial and sexual equality, and equal opportunities for the disabled and union members, for every type of employment contract.

It is more surprising to observe the same absence of regulations in Finland, Sweden, Denmark, and the same exception for parity. In Denmark, for example, collective bargaining agreements in industries using agency workers include rules on wage parity. In Sweden, wage parity is not one of the basic principles enshrined in law, but temporary agency workers have the right to the same safety and hygiene conditions as permanent staff.

Two countries have recently relaxed their regulations: Germany and the Netherlands. Prior to 1997, Germany required open-ended contracts between an agency and temporary agency workers, and restricted TAW to a list of formally defined uses. In 1997 fixed-term contracts were introduced. These contracts must have exactly the same length as the assignment in the client firm, and maximum length of the assignment was increased from 9 to 12 months. Furthermore, the use restrictions were eliminated.

The Netherlands abolished maximum length limits on contracts in 1999. At the same time the employment contract for TAW was transformed into an open-ended contract after an employee worked for 26 weeks for the same client company. Also, the regulation determining the content of every standard employment contract, whether fixed-term or open-ended, was changed. The dismissal procedure for the open-ended contracts was relaxed. Furthermore, the existing regulations on parity were maintained.

It is difficult to evaluate these changes in Germany and the Netherlands. It is not clear whether they represent deregulation or a change in the regulation of TAW (see Storrie 2002, p. 17).

Unions' Effects on Key Aspects of TAW

The regulation of TAW within a country depends on the political and social power relations and the features of the national labor markets. Predicting the union and representation rights for temporary agency workers within a country is difficult due to several considerations. First, weak, nonexplicit, and poorly formalized regulation of the conditions of TWA does not mean that unions are without any power against possible abuses by employers. It can be the opposite: union control balances the weakness of formal regulations. In Sweden, for example, where the constraints on the use of temporary agency workers are minimal, the request for temporary agency workers must be approved by employee representatives in the client company. Belgium, which otherwise imposes much more constraint, is the only other country where the agreement of employee representatives is required. In a small number of other countries, such as Germany, Italy, Norway, and Portugal, union agreement is not required, but employee representatives must be informed. In the other countries, whatever the regulations of the use of TAW—whether very detailed and strict, minimal, or no control—employers have no obligation to inform unions or employee representatives of the use of temporary agency workers.

Second, powerful unions and strictly controlled TAW do not necessary imply either specific unionization or representation rights equivalent to those of every ordinary employee. Union rights of temporary agency workers are not always recognized. And where they are recognized, this may be within the temporary employment agency, as in France, Luxembourg, and Norway, or within the client company, as in Sweden and Italy. In Germany, temporary agency workers cannot vote or stand for election to representative authorities, but may take part in meetings and consult employee representatives in their company. In Italy, the right to engage in union activity does not prevent temporary agency workers from being excluded from calculations to work out the number of seats granted to employee representatives within the user firm or the appropriate unit of the user firm.

Finally, there is little correlation between the existence of regulations on the maximum length of employment, the circumstances of the valid use of temporary agency staff, and the principles of parity on the one hand, and the recognition of temporary agency workers' union rights and the role played by the employees' representatives on the other. It can be hypothesized that the more powerful unions are, and/or the tighter the labor market conditions, the more regulation of temporary agency work can be expected. However, this hypothesis has not been empirically tested.

CONCLUSIONS AND DIRECTIONS FOR
FUTURE RESEARCH

This chapter has provided an overview of the development of TAW in the EU. However, it also has shown how large the differences in TAW are between the EU members and how difficult it is to make comparisons within the EU. Additional comparative research therefore will help us to better understand TAW and its contributions to improving labor market flexibility.

The history of temporary work agencies is highly variable within EU: some are relatively old businesses as in France, while others are very recent businesses as in Italy where TAW was authorized only a few years ago. In some countries TAW is highly regulated and strictly controlled by national legislation and collective bargaining, while in others, such as the United Kingdom, it is relatively unregulated. Even if the present dynamics suggest some convergence to more deregulated TAW, no really common definitions of TAW are used throughout the EU.

The widely varying status and regulation of TAW in the EU member states are closely linked to and dependent on those of standard employment relationships, which remain as different from one EU member to the other as those of the TAW relationships. Due to these significant cross-national differences, it is not surprising that any solid agreement at the EU level about TAW issues, even the principle of parity between temporary agency workers and permanent employees, remains illusive.

Today European labor markets are trapped between two contradictory dynamics. One set of increased pressures is working for a deregulated labor market at EU member states level. This is being countered by the increased necessity to provide some regulation at the EU level to avoid social dumping from unregulated countries, especially the new EU members from Eastern Europe.

Only one trend has emerged that allows us to predict the directions in which TAW will evolve in the future: new employment relationships are being tested by EU members as ways of making European labor markets more flexible and adaptable to the changing economic forces of the global economy. Temporary agency work is one of these new relationships; it presently represents something like a social laboratory in Europe. It can be expected to be an important issue at the heart of collective bargaining in Europe in the foreseeable future.

Several topics will provide useful insights to guide future developments in EU-level employment and industrial relations policies. First, in-depth national case studies will provide useful insights into the forces resulting in changes in labor market institutions. The cases should discuss the recent trends in the development of temporary agency work and the contribution of TAW to greater labor market flexibility. Second, more information is needed about the best way to regulate TAW. Conducting and comparing in-depth case studies in countries with different approaches to TAW will provide useful insights into the optimal policies for national regulation. Third, because at present only part-time and fixed-term contracts are measured by European surveys, while TAW is not, case studies will provide the knowledge needed to design statistical surveys to collect better comparative data on TWA and the other nonstandard employment arrangements that provide employers with options for better numerical flexibility. Fourth, national comparative case studies of the strategies of employers' organizations and unions will provide better information on issues related to the future of TAW. Specifically, it is necessary to understand why the national employer organizations did not succeed in harmonizing their positions at the European level and the implications for future harmonization efforts.

Finally, at present TAW remains primarily low-skilled jobs. However, two changes have been observed that may affect the future directions of the development of TAW. First, it has been observed in many countries that temporary work agencies are beginning to prospect labor markets with better qualified workers, but we do not know whether this is a new strategy in all European countries. Second, TAW is primarily present in the industrial sector in some European countries and in the service sector in other countries. It is not clear whether there is any convergence occurring between the European countries that will reduce these differentiations between European countries or whether such changes should be anticipated. Comparative case studies and comparative statistical surveys can be used to answer these questions.

Notes

1. The defining characteristic of TAW is the three-way relationship between the employee (the temporary agency worker), the company called the "temporary work agency" (the employer in most of the national legislation), and the client firm (the user of the employees of the temporary work agency). See Gonos (1997, p. 105) for further discussion of this relationship.
2. From 1990 through 2004, the seasonally adjusted unemployment rates in the EU-15 (the members prior to May 1, 2004, when new members were accepted) ranged from a low of 7.4 percent in 2001 to high of 10.5 percent in 1994. During the same period in the United States, the unemployment rate ranged from a low of 4.0 percent in 2000 to a high of 7.5 percent in 1992 (Bureau of Labor Statistics 2005a,b).
3. The Statistical Office of the European Communities (EUROSTAT) is the official institute for processing and publishing comparable data at the EU level. The statistical agencies of the EU member countries collect the data, but EUROSTAT works with them to define common data collection methods. EUROSTAT then consolidates the data and adjusts the data as needed so that they are comparable.
4. National estimates that are not based on a standardized definition of TAW cannot be used for any serious international comparison.
5. A summary of the study is available at the following Web site: http://www.eurofound.eu.int/working/tempagency_new.htm, updated December 2002. The summary presents the main findings and conclusions from Storrie (2002). The report is based on 15 national reports commissioned by the European Foundation for the Improvement of Living and Working Conditions.
6. Specifically, an industrial relations system for the EU is only beginning to emerge, and is in the very early stages of development. Many difficulties arise due to the fact that the national industrial relations systems are organized very differently, with varying rules for unions and different levels and competencies in collective bargaining.

    The Union of Industrial and Employers' Confederations of Europe (UNICE) on one side and the European Trade Union Confederation (ETUC) on the other are the main representatives of the national organizations and confederations for Europe-wide collective negotiations. Note that only confederations rather than the unions or associations themselves are represented in this organization of EU-level collective bargaining. Also, all of the national confederations of trade unions are not represented in ETUC. For example, one of the largest unions in France, the Confédération Générale du Travail (CGT), was not a member of ETUC until a few years ago. Furthermore, newly created national unions and confederations rarely are represented.
7. The one notable exception to these three categories is Greece. In this country even regular work is not formally defined, so there is almost no information

about the different forms of employment. However, TAW is known to exist in Greece.

8. In Europe, depending on the country, social security refers to benefits such as illness coverage and pension contributions as well as employment security and unemployment benefits.

9. There are three possible levels for collective bargaining on TWA: 1) the level of the actual TWA business when it exists in a specific sector depending on the rules of each country, 2) the level of client firms (each client sector or level of users of any sector), and 3) the cross-industry level including the TWA business and the client business.

10. The German participation system allows unions to be part of the decision system of the firm.

References

Arrowsmith, J. 2006. *Temporary Agency Work in an Enlarged European Union.* Dublin: European Foundation for the Improvement of Living and Working Conditions.

Bureau of Labor Statistics. 2005a. "Unemployment Rates in the European Union and Selected Member Countries, Civilian Labor Force Basis (1), Seasonally Adjusted, 1990–2003 and 1995–2005." ftp://ftp.bls.gov/pub/special .requests/ForeignLabor/flseur.txt (accessed June 13, 2006).

———. 2005b. "Unemployment Rate in Nine Countries, Civilian Labor Force Basis, Approximating U.S. Concepts, Seasonally Adjusted, 1990–2003 and 1995–2005." ftp://ftp.bls.gov/pub/special.requests/ForeignLabor/flsjec.txt (accessed July 24, 2006).

European Commission. 2000. *Employment in Europe 2000.* Luxembourg: Office for Official Publications of the European Union.

———. 2001. *Employment in Europe 2001: Recent Trends and Prospects.* Luxembourg: Office for Official Publications of the European Union.

———. 2002. *Employment in Europe 2002: Recent Trends and Prospects.* Luxembourg: Office for Official Publications of the European Union.

European Commission, Employment and Social Affairs. 2005. *Employment in Europe 2005: Recent Trends and Prospects.* Luxembourg: Office for Official Publications of the European Union.

European Industrial Relations Observatory (EIRO). 2000. "Temporary Agency Work in Europe." *EirObserver* 1(comparative supplement): i–iv.

———. 2002. "Parliament Proposes Amendments to Draft Temporary Agency Work Directive." http://www.eiro.eurofound.ie/2002/12/InBrief/ EU0212201N.html (accessed December 3, 2002).

———. 2003. "Council Fails to Agree on Temporary Agency Work Directive."

http://www.eiro.eurofound.ie/2003/06/Feature/EU0306206F.html (accessed June 24, 2003).

European Trade Union Confederation. 2005. "Temporary Agency Workers in the European Union." http://www.etuc.org/a/501 (accessed March 17, 2006).

Gonos, George. 1997. "The Contest over 'Employer' Status in the Postwar United States: The Case of Temporary Help Firms." *Law and Society Review* 31(1): 81–111.

Kok, Wim. 2004. *Facing the Challenge: The Lisbon Strategy for Growth and Employment.* Report from the High Level Group. http://europa.eu.int/comm/lisbon_strategy/index_en.html (accessed July 24, 2006).

Morris, G. 2002. "Temporary Work in English Law." In *Temporary Work and the Information Society.* Vol. 50, *Bulletin of Comparative Labour Relations*, R. Blanpain and R. Graham, eds. Deventer, The Netherlands: Kluwer.

Office for National Statistics. 2002. "Labour Force Survey, 2002." April. London: Office for National Statistics.

Recruitment and Employment Confederation (REC). 2002. "Annual Recruitment Industry Survey 2001/2002." London: REC.

Storrie, D. 2002. "Temporary Agency Work in the European Union." Luxembourg: Office for Official Publications of the European Communities (European Institute for the Improvement of Living and Working Conditions, Dublin, Ireland). http://www.eurofound.eu.int/publications/EF0202.htm (accessed July 24, 2006).

Syndicat des Entreprises de Travail Temporaire. 2005. Rapport économique et social 2004. http://sett.org/Web_Economique/Rapport082%E9conomique082et082social.aspx (accessed July 24, 2006).

Part 5

Challenges for the Twenty-First Century

10
Where Do We Go from Here?

Sandra E. Gleason
Pennsylvania State University

The nonstandard workforce has grown in the mature industrialized nations of the United States, Japan, and Europe. On the demand side of the labor market this growth has been a response to a common set of forces for change. These forces include the globalization of economies, deregulation of labor markets, rapid advances in technology that have created the information age, and other factors that require employers to adjust more agilely to continuous change. On the supply side of the labor market the growth has reflected the desire of many workers for more flexible employment options to accommodate life stage and life-style preferences. Due to these demand and supply forces, nonstandard employment is expected to continue to grow in the future.

The structural changes that mature industrialized nations are under-going and the resulting (sometimes negative) impact on the nonstandard labor force highlighted the inadequacies of the present labor market in-frastructures. For example, in the United States, policies, laws, and in-stitutions developed in the New Deal in the 1930s structure the current employment relationship. However, the research presented in this vol-ume shows that this system no longer meets the needs of many workers, employers, or the U.S. economy, because the premises on which the New Deal system was based have changed. Specifically, workers, who primarily were male, were expected to have a long-term, full-time em-ployment relationship with only one employer during their careers. The system required reciprocity: employers provided employees with job security; in return, employees were a loyal and committed workforce for the employer. This set of bilateral expectations—often referred to as a "psychological contract"—defined the operational concept of a "good job" (Stone 2004). In contrast, the workforce of today—particularly the more educated workers in their twenties and thirties—expects to have multiple employers during a career, is more diverse, desires greater flexibility, and has less concern for security (Kochan 1998). This expectation of a "boundaryless career" is part of the new psychological contract of the future (Stone 2004).

Some authors have noted that the current definition of a "good job" is actually relatively new because it was developed in the twentieth century. The growth of contingent and short-term employment contracts thus represents a return to the historical past when contingent employment was the norm for most workers. Nevertheless, despite the recency of our definition of "good jobs," this is the definition used to frame much of the research on employment, and continues to provide the benchmark against which alternative employment arrangements are compared (Kelloway, Gallagher, and Barling 2004).

The attention focused on nonstandard employment over the past several decades has changed the way we think about jobs, even though nonstandard employment has not—and will not—become the dominant model of employment in the countries discussed in this book. What has changed is the *perception* that a career-long tenure with one employer will no longer be the norm in the future. There is now an awareness that employees will bear more risks in the labor market than in the past as they move between different types of working-time employment arrangements, such as from full-time to part-time status.[1] The risks include job loss and fluctuations in pay. However, "these are changes of degree, not of kind. They . . . constitute . . . a reallocation within a stable institutional structure dominated by standard employment arrangements" (Jacoby 1999).

Kochan (1998) argues that the situation in the United States today is analogous to the period from the turn of the century to the 1930s prior to the New Deal. It took about 30 years to develop the intellectual foundations of the New Deal. Similarly, researchers have been studying for about 30 years the changes in nonstandard employment and the myriad forces determining them. However, they still are grappling with the realization that the fundamental premises on which the current employment relations system was built no longer apply to many workers, and trying to determine what this implies for the future. Consequently, we have not yet developed the intellectual foundation that will define the characteristics of a new system and a new social contract. Japan and the countries of the European Union (EU) also are facing a similar challenge (see Jouen and Caremier 2000). The labor market institutions that worked well after World War II no longer fit the needs of their national economies. Kochan concludes that for the future "Identifying the specific features of these institutions and policies remains the key intellectual challenge and responsibility of this, and, perhaps, if history is any guide, the next generation of researchers and professionals" (Kochan 1998, p. 245).

THE CHALLENGES FOR FUTURE RESEARCH

The challenges in the development of appropriate labor market policies for a new social contract are to clearly identify the problems that need to be addressed, measure empirically their dimensions, determine which problems are the most important and therefore worthy of policy attention, and then select the "best" policy options in light of identified trade-offs. High-quality research is fundamental to this process. It must be based on a balanced analysis of the issues, rather than perspectives expressed in the media, which tend to be skewed to either promanagement or prolabor viewpoints.

When thinking about the identification and measurement of labor market problems, it is important to consider the challenges created by the heterogeneity of nonstandard workers and ongoing evolution of the theoretical models used to analyze the demand and supply forces. The heterogeneity of this segment of the workforce requires researchers to use data that permit the analysis of the subgroups of contingent workers that are negatively affected by their employment arrangements. For example, a variety of U.S. government databases are available for this purpose, but must be combined and better organized to facilitate research (U.S. Department of Labor 1994). However, it is not always possible to find data that define precisely the groups of workers of interest, so the severity of the negative effects of contingent employment may be overstated or understated (Lester 1998).

Furthermore, the theoretical models on which empirical analysis can be based are continuing to evolve. For example, there is no general agreement on the correct theoretical model to use to frame the analysis of the labor market effects on those workers disadvantaged by contingent employment. Lester (1998) argues that we need an improved understanding of the "root harm" experienced by disadvantaged groups, which considers both workers' abilities and preferences. This harm fundamentally is underemployment resulting from a mismatch between the jobs held by workers and their skills, interests, and human capital. While the New Keynesian models of involuntary unemployment seem to offer the best analytical approach for the analysis of "root harm," they have not been tested empirically. Thus, their ability to provide insights into appropriate legal reforms is unknown (Lester 1998).

Similarly, as Michon notes in Chapter 9, cross-national research is complicated by the lack of data to compare groups of workers defined in the same way across nations and an absence of well-developed theoretical models. The reasons for variations and the extent of the diversity observed across nations in the use of different nonstandard employment arrangements have received little attention; this has hindered our understanding of how the established institutions and cultural contexts explain particular national adaptations and the variations in the rate of adaptation. However, since the 1990s the "new institutionalism" has been developing; this approach seeks to explain how rules embodied in various institutions shape economic, social, and political activities (Godard 2004, pp. 232–235). This approach requires the researcher to understand national institutions and values as a precursor to explaining national changes in response to global forces (Godard 2004, p. 246; Martin and Bamber 2004, p. 293).

CONCEPTUALIZING POLICY EFFECTS

The infrastructures of the United States, Japan, and the European Union were designed to meet the needs of an earlier era. The growth of the global economy has restructured many sectors of these economies. What is needed now are new ways to improve labor market flexibility through policy changes to, or redesign of, the infrastructure of tax, labor, and employment laws and institutions.

Two major policy approaches have been identified to provide coverage for a greater number of employees by extending coverage to contingent workers: 1) to revise the laws to expand the eligibility standards

determining coverage, and 2) to eliminate the gray areas of legal interpretations. Table 10.1 is used to illustrate how the two approaches
would affect selected employment laws in the United States.

Table 10.1 (which is based on the discussion in Chapters 5 and 6)
presents the employer's perspective on the coverage of workers under
five categories of employment laws for six types of employment arrangements. At one extreme are the full-time, permanent core employees in "good jobs," while at the other end of the spectrum are independent contractors. The legal standing of these two groups of workers
generally is clearly defined. However, these usually are not the workers
of concern to those advocating improvements in public policies affecting nonstandard employment. The workers of concern are those in the
middle—the part-time, temporary, and leased employees, differentiated
by the firm that hires them. In Table 10.1, "Yes" indicates coverage

Table 10.1 Employer Perspective: Coverage by Selected Employment Laws of Employment Relationships in the United States

Employment relationship	FICA & FUTA[a]	Qualified retirement plan	FLSA (minimum wage)	Workers' compensation	EEO laws
Full-time, permanent, core worker	Yes	Yes	Yes	Yes	Yes
Part-time worker hired by employer	Uncertain[b]	No[c]	Yes	Yes	Yes
Temporary worker hired by employer	Uncertain[b]	Uncertain[c]	Yes	Yes	Yes
Temporary worker provided by agency	Uncertain	Uncertain	Yes[d]	Uncertain	Uncertain
Leased worker provided by agency	Uncertain	Uncertain	Yes[d]	Uncertain	Uncertain
Independent contractor	No	No	No	No	No

[a] These federal statutes provide unemployment insurance, Social Security, and Medicare coverage.

[b] Workers will quality for coverage only if the eligibility criteria are satisfied (see Chapter 5).

[c] An employee must work at least 1,000 hours, the equivalent of one year of service in a 12-month period, to qualify.

[d] The contentious issue is not the payment of the minimum wage, but rather the requirement that an employee must be paid overtime pay at time and one-half after 40 hours
of work. However, independent contractors are exempt from this requirement.

by the employment laws of workers for each type of employment arrangement; "No" indicates noncoverage; and "Uncertain" indicates that coverage is uncertain and varies with the eligibility requirements, legal interpretations, and compliance. The heterogeneity of treatment resulting from varying legal definitions and interpretations used to determine when a worker is an "employee" has created what Befort (2003) describes as "a veritable regulation-free zone in portions of the contingent work landscape," a "Black Hole of Workplace Regulation."

The first policy approach is to revise the laws to expand the work-based eligibility requirements for employment-based benefits to expand eligibility, thereby covering more nonstandard workers. For example, prorated benefits could be provided for pension coverage for workers who work less than the current requirement of one year of service in a 12-month period. A variation is to include under the coverage of the statutes any industries or firms that are currently exempted from the legislation to expand the number of workers covered. This approach requires changing each law in Table 10.1, thereby affecting the workers by column.

The second policy approach is to eliminate the gray areas of legal interpretations that exclude some workers from employment protections, thereby expanding coverage to more employees. This approach can be partially successful without changing the content of the laws per se by using a two-pronged approach: clarifying terminology and improving compliance within the existing laws. The Dunlop Commission addressed the issues of confusing terminology resulting from multiple definitions of "employee" by recommending the adoption of one definition of "employer" and one definition of "employee" for all workplace laws "based on the economic realities of the employment relationship" (U.S. Department of Labor 1994). If this recommendation was followed, such as through the development of model laws and practices based on the consistent use of definitions, the laws would have to be revised. In terms of Table 10.1, most if not all of the uncertain outcomes would be eliminated if consistent definitions were used for all laws. Improved compliance would affect both the columns and the rows.

Improvements in compliance within existing laws can be achieved through several tactics. It will be helpful to employers to have clearer guidance about their legal responsibilities, such as more user-friendly guidelines for following the laws. Employer compliance is mandated when low-wage workers are unionized because union contracts clearly define these workers as "employees." In addition, some nonprofit organizations, such as the Center for a Changing Workforce (CFCW) and the National Employment Law Project (NLEP), work to enforce compliance by ensuring that employees are correctly classified by employers.

The CFCW focuses on "permatemps"[2] and provides "advice and consultations for individuals and organizations on employment issues, litigation, and public policy" while also analyzing policy and legislation related to permatemps and tracking litigation. An illustrative project is its investigation in response to a request from AFSCME Council 28 to determine whether the University of Washington Medical Center was misclassifying employees. The 2002 report presented to AFSCME stated that "there has been widespread misuse of hourly 'temporary' employees at UWMC" (Center for a Changing Workforce 2002; Hanbey 2003). Similarly, the NLEP Nonstandard Worker Project "seeks to ensure that all workers regardless of what their employer calls them—temp, independent contractor, part-timer—receive the full benefits of labor and employment laws" (National Employment Law Project).

A two-dimensional table similar to Table 10.1 also can be developed for Japan and the countries of Europe to help researchers understand the potential impact of various policy changes. However, in the case of Europe, the analysis is compounded by the presence of EU regulations. This will require a three-dimensional diagram to more fully illustrate the potential of cross-national EU policy effects.

Well-designed research can help predict and evaluate the effects of policy changes. This information then can be used to design the appropriate changes in policy based on the identified trade-offs and evaluation of economic efficiency, equity, security, and liberty of the policy (see Chapter 6 for a review of these concepts). This process of evaluations reminds us that we have choices in shaping how the forces for change in the global economy are managed. There are no ". . . overwhelming and uncontrollable market forces [that] have made the trend toward contingency as we know it inevitable" (Gonos 1997, p. 104). Furthermore, pursuing the policy changes guided by research will "open up employment policy and practice to a period of experimentation and opportunities for further learning" (U.S. Department of Labor 1994, p. 13).

DIRECTIONS FOR FUTURE RESEARCH

Throughout this book a number of topics for future research related to the intellectual challenge posed by Kochan (1998) have been discussed. These are reviewed from four perspectives. First, research can explain more fully how employers make strategic decisions regarding the best mix of permanent and nonstandard employees, as well as the best mixes of alternative employment arrangements. To guide policy choices, we need a better understanding of decision making under varying circumstances and the impact of these choices on management practices. Also, research can guide the expansion of the coverage of employment and benefits protections for contingent workers. In addition, more comparative research on the impact of variations in regulation will help to guide policy development as nations learn from each other. Finally, research can help us evaluate the effectiveness of strategies used by unions and nonprofit organizations to improve the conditions of work and economic welfare of contingent workers.

Employers' Strategic Decision Making and Management Practices

The limited empirical evidence has identified demand-side factors as dominant when explaining the growth of nonstandard employment (Kahn 2000). Progress has been made in our understanding of the complexity of employers' strategies to mix permanent workers and varieties of nonstandard employees. However, future research focused on employers' decision making can further clarify three issues. First, we need a better understanding of the factors influencing strategic decisions that result in the hiring of nonstandard workers. Second, we need better information about the conditions under which employers choose to implement standards that treat contingent employees more equitably. Finally, we need to know whether different management strategies are required for a workforce that blends permanent and contingent workers.

Research can help determine the most important factors driving the demand for nonstandard employment arrangements, and the management strategies that are the most effective in differing circumstances. As an illustration, the cost-minimizing strategy of hiring temporary workers to cover short-run needs such as the replacement of absent full-time workers is different from the strategy that focuses on long-run productivity enhancement through labor input flexibility. The latter strategy may require investing in permanent employees who are trained to be flexible in adapting to changing work assignments instead of using contingent workers. Also, we need to understand better how these strategies mesh with hiring nonstandard workers in response to business cycle changes and structural changes in the economy. For example, improved understanding of these aspects of employer decision making will help us analyze the forces affecting U.S. firms hiring part-time and temporary employees, as well as worker dispatching by temporary employment agencies and the use of part-time workers in Japan and the growth of temporary employment agencies in Europe.

Also, although standards for the equitable treatment of contingent workers are available, we have little understanding of why and when employers implement these models when the choice is voluntary. For example, the International Labor Organization (ILO) published recommendations for the equal treatment of part-time workers relative to full-time workers. The ILO recommends that part-time workers should be paid a comparable wage and have the same statutory coverage of Social Security programs on a pro-rated basis. Also, these workers should have the right to organize and bargain collectively, be protected by occupational safety and health laws and against employment discrimination, and be entitled to equivalent protections for maternity and sick leave, job termination, paid annual leave and public holidays, and transferring between part-time and full-time employment (for further discussion see Zeytinoğlu [1999]). Similarly, in 2002 the American Federation of Teachers (AFT) published "Standards of Good Practice in the Employment of Part-Time/Adjunct Faculty" (2002), which outlines appropriate standards of treatment. These standards include equitable pay and a seniority system, as well as standards to ensure adjuncts are treated with professional courtesies.[3] Research can help explain the conditions under which these guidelines will be implemented by employers.

We know that hiring many contingent employees changes the organizational culture. We need to develop strategies that effectively manage the tensions and conflicts that arise in a blended workforce of permanent and contingent workers. The management of the attitudes and performance of contingent employees may require different methods than for permanent employees; the methods also may depend on whether the workers are voluntarily or involuntarily in contingent jobs. Case studies of how various employers manage their blended work-forces should provide useful insights.

Extending Coverage of Employment Protections and Benefits

We know that employees with less education and fewer skills—notably women, minorities, younger workers, and those employed involuntarily in contingent work such as part-time jobs—have experienced the negative effects of nonstandard employment. These include lower wages and the receipt of few, if any, employment-related benefits from either the employer or the social welfare system. While some of the individuals in contingent employment can make education and lifestyle choices to move into full-time standard employment and improve their opportunities, many will be left with few options for change and therefore will remain relatively disadvantaged. Consequently, the challenge is to design a more flexible social welfare system to provide employment protections and benefits to contingent employees that mirror the protections provided to full-time permanent employees. Another way of stating this goal is to recognize that "[w]hile we cannot change the level of risk in today's economy, we can change the rules that govern how risk is shared among the participants to the economic game" (Jacoby 1999, p. 145).

Two research projects would help move us toward this goal. First, in the United States we need to measure the extent of noncoverage of the various social welfare programs at the national level. This research would provide the information for the design of methods and policy to cover those presently excluded from coverage, as well as the evaluation of unintended consequences. Researchers can evaluate the advantages and disadvantages of different designs for prorated benefits, portable pension plans, unemployment insurance, and other programs.

Because of the dominance of women in some of the most economically vulnerable forms of contingent work such as part-time employment, tracking and evaluating government efforts to support gender equality will help nations monitor their progress. In the United States attention must be given to finding ways to improve the safety net for these female workers. Japan also is seeking ways to address the needs of a changing female labor force in which fewer women are marrying and marriages are occurring later in life.[4] In the EU ". . . the social contract has failed to incorporate the high-risk groups and ought to be reviewed. Above all, it must take account of the gender divide, which has been largely disregarded until now . . ." (Jouen and Caremier 2000, p. 29).

Comparative Research on Regulation

Comparative research provides insights into how a balance between supporting flexibility and extending social protections to relatively vulnerable contingent workers can be structured using different models of regulation (Vosko 1998, pp. 26–27). This in turn requires understanding national preferences for "relative equality of compensation" and "relative equality in the form of labor market participation" since "not all forms of equality can be optimized simultaneously" (DiPrete et al. 2004). These trade-offs can be explored in studies of temporary employment agencies and efforts to "harmonize" regulations within the EU for part-time employment.

We have seen that one of the fastest-growing forms of contingent employment in the mature economies of the United States, Japan, and Europe is temporary employment arranged by temporary employment agencies (Kelloway, Gallagher, and Barling 2004, p. 111). Unlike the United States, in both Japan and Europe this growth has resulted from deliberate national policy choices. However, we do not have much empirical analysis documenting how temporary agency workers actually fare in the labor market.[5] Empirical evidence from four countries with different regulatory environments—Britain (Booth, Francesconi, and Frank 2002); France (Blanchard and Landier 2002); Sweden (Holmlund and Storrie 2002); and Spain (Dolado, García-Serrano, and Jimeno 2002)—suggests that overall an expansion of temporary jobs to increase labor market flexibility has measurable negative consequences for temporary workers relative to permanent employment (Booth, Dolodo, and Frank 2002). Further comparative research is needed to explore this finding in other countries, as well as to differentiate the impact of institutions and culture on male and female part-time workers (Pfau-Effinger 1998).

A major goal of the EU is to create a single labor market in which workers can move freely by coordinating and harmonizing the approaches to nonstandard employment used by its member nations. This requires creating consistent standards to determine the employment conditions of part-time workers and providing the same basic minimum social protections for temporary employees in all of the member nations (Vosko 1998).[6] The achievement of the EU goals will require the use of voluntary coordination of policies (referred to as the "open method of coordination") across nations and EU directives, i.e., "soft law" supplemented by "hard law" measures such as the Part-Time Workers' Directives (Ashiagbor 2004; Sciarra 2004). Researchers can study and monitor the impact of the implementation of this European Employment Strategy over time.

Finally, research can consider how the lessons learned by the mature economies can provide insights for developing countries such as People's Republic of China (PRC) and India to help them proactively design their legal structure and social safety nets to support labor market flexibility. The importance of these two nations in the global economy is growing rapidly, and their populations are moving rapidly from employment in agriculture to manufacturing and service sectors. However, in the PRC industrial restructuring reduced employment from 1993 to 2002, creating the same problems for laid-off workers as those experienced in the United States and Japan (Lu et al. 2002; Banister 2005b). In the PRC movement into contingent employment—often through migration to other parts of the country—can result in not only the loss of earnings and social welfare benefits such as pensions and unemployment pay, but also the loss of subsidies for transportation, housing, food allowances, and other benefits provided by employers (Banister 2005a).

Unions and Nonprofit Organizations as Change Agents

Labor unions and nonprofit organizations in the United States have directed their attention in recent years to improving the economic welfare of the working poor—low-wage contingent workers. Some unions see the opportunity to serve as an advocate for contingent workers as an extension of their traditional leadership roles in the protection of workers' welfare, while nonprofit organizations serve as advocates for economic justice for the working poor. Both use multiple strategies: conducting campaigns to publicize the economic realities faced by the working poor, maintaining Web sites on which information is provided to assist contingent workers and those working on their behalf, sponsoring research on the factors that determine the opportunities of the working poor, organizing community efforts, and pursuing legislative and political initiatives. In addition, unions are working to organize these workers. However, we know relatively little about how widespread such efforts are and what their actual impact may be. Case studies of the effectiveness of these change agents should yield insights into the impact of a variety of strategies on employment and wages.

Stone (2004) argues that this expansion of union activities into the community and political action to represent a broader segment of the workforce, including contingent workers, is a predictable response to the transformations in the nature of work. As the attachment of employees to employers is reduced, unions must change from bargaining with one employer to bargaining with groups of employers to improve workers' compensation and conditions of work. She distinguishes two new models of union activity. The first is the "new craft unionism" based on occupations and bargaining industrywide with employer groups to facilitate worker mobility between employers. The focus is the creation of minimum standards and the provision of training.

The second model of "citizen unionism" also focuses on facilitating contingent worker mobility, setting minimum standards, and providing training, but only works within a locality or region and is not necessarily limited to a particular occupational group. In addition, efforts are made to improve the local social infrastructure through improved child care and legal assistance, and the encouragement of corporate support. Also, as discussed below, citizen unionism often is based on a collaboration between nonprofit organizations, local unions, and other local community groups working together to achieve a living wage in a specific geographic location (Stone 2004, Chapter 10).

The efforts by the AFT, the leading organizer of part-time faculty (AFT 2003), to improve the welfare of part-time teachers is an example of the new craft unionism based on occupation. It provides protections for part-time faculty while enabling them to move between employers. A two-pronged approach is used: legislative and political action, and collective bargaining. This dual strategy was used by the Washington Federation of Teachers (WFT), an AFT affiliate. In 1999 the WFT successfully pursued a public campaign for pay equity and lobbied to convince the governor and the legislature in the State of Washington to include additional funds in the state budget to increase the pay for part-time faculty. Also, the criterion for participation in the retirement plan was modified, so more part-time faculty became eligible to participate.[7] Subsequently in 2000 a prorata sick leave policy was approved for part-time faculty (AFT 2001). In addition, the AFT used collective bargaining to improve the pay, benefits, and conditions of work for part-time faculty.[8]

Another example is the media-intensive multiunion campaign begun in 2004 that focused on retail workers employed by Wal-Mart. It was led by the AFL-CIO to pressure Wal-Mart to become a better corporate citizen by increasing its wages and health benefits. Because of the size of the company, no single union can handle the challenge alone. The campaign was not designed as a unionization effort, but rather as a means of publicizing the relatively low wages that Wal-Mart pays throughout the United States, as well as the impact of the introduction of its supercenters into specific locations (Greenhouse 2004; Quisumbing 2005).

Case studies of these and other union activities can help us understand the conditions that determine whether a union will try to organize low-wage contingent workers, the factors determining which strategies are selected by the unions and why, and which organizing strategies are the most effective for different groups of contingent workers. Comparative research on the strategies used by unions in other countries also may provide insights into strategies for unions in the United States, and perhaps vice versa.

Examples of citizen unionism are the California Partnership for Working Families (CPWF) and Working Today. As part of their broader commitment to economic justice, these nonprofit organizations are working for both decent standards of living for low-wage contingent workers and employer compliance in properly classifying employees (see Chapter 5). Their approach is aimed at improving social welfare through the payment of a living wage higher than the legally mandated minimum wage to all eligible workers. This objective is consistent with the employer responsibilities identified by the United Nations Subcommission on the Promotion and Protections of Human Rights (2003)[9]:

> Transnational corporations and other business enterprises shall provide workers remuneration that ensures an adequate standard

of living for them and their families. Such remunerations shall take
due account of their needs for adequate living conditions with a
view towards progressive improvement.

CPWF is a nonprofit, statewide consortium that links organizations
in four major population areas: the East Bay area of San Francisco,
Los Angeles, San Jose, and San Diego. It is committed to an emerging
model of economic development that includes as the primary goal "the
creation of economic opportunity and the reduction of poverty and social inequality" so that development works for the benefit of communities rather than just providing profits to developers and sales tax income
(California Partnerships for Working Families; Center on Policy Initiatives 2004; Karjanen and Baxamusa 2003). Ordinances and agreements
already have been passed which require the payment of a "living wage"
in the East Bay, Los Angeles, and San Jose. One of the CPWF partners,
the Center for Policy Initiatives (CPI) in San Diego, is presently spear-
heading the San Diego Living Wage Campaign.[10] More than 20 unions
support this initiative in San Diego.

Another example is Working Today, which was created in 1995 to
place on the national agenda the issues of part-time workers and others
in temporary and short-term jobs. This national network includes a variety of organizations ranging from labor unions to community groups.
One of its first projects was the Portable Benefits Fund created to provide access to affordable health insurance (Horowitz 2000; Working
Today).

Case studies of organizations such as CPWF and Working Today
can help explain the strategies selected, the factors determining which
strategies are most effective, and the actual impact on the welfare of
contingent workers.[11] While these groups have often used city-by-city
campaigns, we do not know whether this is the most effective way to
generate change. Also, although there are more than 120 living wage
laws across the United States, we do not know much about the extent
of their actual impact on working families. For example, the Berkeley
Living Wage Ordinance of 1999 requires city contractors and developers who receive project subsidies of more than $100,000 to pay the liv-
ing wage rate of $11.37 an hour (California Partnerships for Working
Families). However, this means that many low-wage workers are not
covered. We do not know whether employers have found ways to avoid
complying with the law or what the unintended consequences, either

positive or negative, for covered and noncovered workers are. We do not know what factors will explain the success or failure of approaches such as the Portable Benefits Fund.

CONCLUSION

All labor market participants, whether employers, employees, or unions, operate within the legal framework of their nations and the expectations of their societies. What they can and cannot do is regulated by government, which can play a supportive role or create barriers to change. Each nation therefore has to choose how it will address the challenges of designing its future employment relations system to explicitly include workers in nonstandard employment arrangements. The challenge for the future is to develop public policies to protect the truly contingent workers at least as well as we protect workers in standard employment arrangements.

Research will provide guidance for the selection of the components chosen by employers, unions, and governments for this future system. It also will help identify better approaches to balancing the employer and the employee interests.[12] The need is for flexibility and efficiency while treating all employees equitably in a world of rapid and continuous economic change. What is sought is "a more humane model of flexibility" (Jouen and Caremier 2000, p. 135).

Notes

1. For a detailed discussion of the factors determining the dynamics of transitional labor markets see O'Reilly, Cebrián, and Lallement (2000).
2. The CFCW was created in 1999 in Seattle, Washington. Permatemps are defined as contingent employees who have been misclassified by employers and therefore ineligible for job security, equal pay, and benefits.
3. Many adjunct faculty, along with graduate students, perceive themselves to be exploited by the low pay and poor working conditions at colleges and universities in the United States. They are seeking unionization as a means of addressing their employment concerns. Unions as diverse

as the California Part-Time Faculty Association, the National Education Association, and the AFT have been organizing these contingent faculty. See Smallwood (2002).

4. This situation is a source of concern to the Japanese national government. Since the latter half of the 1970s the birth rate has followed a steady downward trend. The country experienced in 2004 the lowest rate of population growth since 1899 when data collection began, and international migration adds to the population only marginally. At the same time the population is aging rapidly, and much faster than in Western Europe and the United States. For example, it is projected that in 2030 the percentage of the population aged 65 and over in the United States will be about 19 percent, while in Japan it will be about 30 percent. See Ujimoto (2000) and Japanese Ministry of Internal Affairs and Communications (2006).

5. It is important to remember that temporary employment firms are not necessarily inherently bad actors in the labor market. However, the way in which they conduct their business has disadvantaged the workers they hire by not providing many of the job protections available to full-time core workers. While temporary employment arrangements provide employers with an option for flexibility, they also relieve employers to varying degrees depending on the country from some of the costs associated with permanent employees.

6. The "European Framework Agreement on Part-Time Work" was signed in June 1997. The agreement states the principle of nondiscrimination that "part-time workers shall not be treated in a less favorable manner than comparable full-time workers solely because they work part-time unless different treatment is justified on objective grounds" (p. 242). It also requires the member states to identify and eliminate obstacles that will limit part-time employment opportunities. Employers are expected to facilitate the movement of employees between part-time and full-time work and vice versa. However, this is not a comprehensive agreement. There is no reference to social security issues since these matters are left to each country. The wording in the nondiscrimination statement also permits employers to treat part-time and full-time workers differently under some circumstances. See European Union (1997). For a detailed discussion of the tension within the EU as it works to increase labor market flexibility see Teague (1999).

7. A recommendation also was made by the state agency overseeing community colleges to increase the number of full-time jobs and to use fewer part-time faculty.

8. Collective bargaining also was used to restore full-time faculty positions and negotiate provisions which permit full-time nontenured faculty to move to tenure-track positions. See Chapter 4 for additional examples of the use of collective bargaining to improve pay, benefits, and conditions of work.

9. Similar standards also have been set by other groups such as Social Accountability International (SAI), a nonprofit organization based in the United States. SAI provides codes of conduct for business community organizations such as the Association of Community Organizations for Reform Now (ACORN) that also are pursuing policy changes to create living wage ordinances. However, while such goals are expressed as ethical goals, it is not easy to reach agreement on a specific standard, although minimal standards can be set. Not surprisingly, the U.S. Chamber of Commerce, along with other business groups, has actively opposed the creation of living wage standards (Lafer 2005). For a more detailed discussion of codes of social accountability which support the concept of the living wage, see Wheeler (2005).

10. The CPI provides information and serves as an advocacy group for workers in "retail and service jobs—jobs that are often just or above the minimum wage with no health care benefits." In 1994 the first living wage was adopted in Baltimore. See Center on Policy Initiatives (2006).

11. For additional examples of innovative ways to improve the welfare of nonstandard employees see Carré and Joshi (2000).

12. For an expanded discussion of the importance of balancing employer and employee interests see Budd, Gomez, and Meltz (2004).

References

American Federation of Teachers (AFT). 2001. *Marching toward Equity: Curbing the Exploitation and Overuse of Part-Time and Non-tenured Faculty.* Washington, DC: American Federation of Teachers.

———. 2002. *Standards of Good Practice in the Employment of Part-Time/ Adjunct Faculty.* Washington, DC: American Federation of Teachers.

———. 2003. "Fighting for the Profession: A History of AFT Higher Education" (March). http://www.aft.org/higher_ed/pubs-reports/reportslist_chron .htm (accessed April 2, 2006).

Ashiagbor, D. 2004. "The European Employment Strategy and the Regulation of Part-Time Work." In *Employment Policy and the Regulation of Part-Time Work in the European Union: A Comparative Analysis,* S. Sciarra, P.

Davies, and M. Freedland, eds. Cambridge: Cambridge University Press, pp. 35–62.

Banister, J. 2005a. "Manufacturing Earnings and Compensation in China." *Monthly Labor Review* 128(8): 22–40.

———. 2005b. "Manufacturing Employment in China." *Monthly Labor Review* 128(7): 11–29.

Befort, S.F. 2003. "Revisiting the Black Hole of Workplace Regulation: A Historical and Comparative Perspective of Contingent Work." *Berkeley Journal of Employment and Labor Law* 24(1): 153–178.

Belous, R.S. 1999. *The Contingent Economy: The Growth of the Temporary, Part-Time and Subcontracted Workforce.* Washington, DC: National Planning Association.

Blanchard, O., and A. Landier. 2002. "The Perverse Effects of Partial Labour Market Reform: Fixed-Term Contracts in France." *The Economic Journal* 112(480): 214–244.

Booth, A.L., J.J. Dolado, and J. Frank. 2002. "Symposium on Temporary Work—Introduction." *The Economic Journal* 112(480): 181–188.

Booth, A.L., M. Francesconi, and J. Frank. 2002. "Temporary Jobs: Stepping Stones or Dead Ends?" *The Economic Journal* 112(480): 189–213.

Budd, J.W., R. Gomez, and N.M. Meltz. 2004. "Why a Balance is Best: The Pluralist Industrial Relations Paradigm of Balancing Competing Interests." In *Theoretical Perspectives on Work and the Employment Relationship,* B.E. Kaufman, ed. Champaign, IL: Industrial Relations Research Association pp. 195–227.

California Partnership for Working Families. http://www.californiapartnership .org (accessed March 26, 2006).

Carré, F., and P. Joshi. 2000. "Looking for Leverage in a Fluid World: Innovative Responses to Temporary and Contracted Work." In *Nonstandard Work: The Nature and Challenges of Changing Employment Arrangements,* F. Carré, M.A. Ferber, L. Golden, and S.A. Herzenberg, eds. Champaign, IL: Industrial Relations Research Association, pp. 313–339.

Center for a Changing Workforce. 2002. "A Million Hours of 'Temporary Work': How the UW Hospitals Mislabel Hundreds of Employees to avoid providing Health Insurance." Seattle, Washington. http://www.cfcw.org/ uwmcReport11-02.pdf (accessed March 27, 2006).

Center on Policy Initiatives. 2004. *Hidden Costs: The Public Cost of Low-Wage Jobs in San Diego.* Research report, San Diego, March. http://www .onlinecpi.org/campaigns_living_wage.html (accessed March 27, 2006).

———. 2006. Living Wage Campaigns. http://www.onlinecpi.org/campaigns_ living_wage.html (accessed March 27, 2006).

DiPrete, T.A., D. Goux, E. Maurin, and A. Quesnel-Valle. 2004. "Work and

Pay in Flexible and Regulated Labor Markets: A Generalized Perspective on Institutional Evolution and Inequality Trends in Europe and the U.S." http://www.soc.duke.edu/~tdiprete/web/unified021404.pdf (accessed March 27, 2006).

Dolado, J.J., C. García-Serrano, and J.F. Jimeno. 2002. "Drawing Lessons from the Boom of Temporary Jobs in Spain." *The Economic Journal* 112(480): 270–295.

European Union. 1997. "European Framework Agreement on Part-Time Work." http://www.itcilo.org/campaigns_living_wage.html (accessed March 27, 2006).

Godard, J. 2004. "The New Institutionalism, Capitalist Diversity, and Industrial Relations." In *Theoretical Perspectives on Work and the Employment Relationship,* B.E. Kaufman, ed. Champaign, IL: Industrial Relations Research Association, pp. 229–264.

Gonos, G. 1997. "The Contest over 'Employer' Status in the Postwar United States: The Case of Temporary Help Firms." *Law and Society Review* 31(1): 81–110.

Greenhouse, S. 2004. "Unions Plan Big Drive for Better Pay at Nonunion Wal-Mart." *The New York Times,* Dec. 11.

Hanbey, M. 2003. "TANF Leavers and Temp Work in Washington State, 1998–2000." Master's thesis, University of Washington. http://www.cfcw.org/TANFTempsStudy.pdf (accessed March 27, 2006).

Holmlund, B., and D. Storrie. 2002. "Temporary Work in Turbulent Times: The Swedish Experience." *The Economic Journal* 112(480): 245–269.

Horowitz, S. 2000. "New Thinking on Worker Groups' Role in a Flexible Economy." In *Nonstandard Work: The Nature and Challenges of Changing Employment Arrangements,* F. Carré, M.A. Ferber, L. Golden, and S.A. Herzenberg, eds. Champaign, IL: Industrial Relations Research Association, pp. 393–398.

Jacoby, S.M. 1999. "Are Career Jobs Headed for Extinction?" *California Management Review* 42(1): 123–145.

Japanese Ministry of Internal Affairs and Communications. 2006. *Statistical Handbook of Japan.* Chapter 2, "Population." http://www.stat.go.jp/English/data/handbook/c02cont.htn//cha2_2 (accessed April 2, 2006).

Jouen, M., and B. Caremier. 2000. *The Future of Work.* Luxembourg: Office for Official Publications of the European Communities.

Kahn, S. 2000. "The Bottom-Line Impact of Nonstandard Jobs on Companies' Profitability and Productivity." In *Nonstandard Work: The Nature and Challenges of Changing Employment Arrangements,* F. Carré, M.A. Ferber, L. Golden, and S.A. Herzenberg, eds. Champaign, IL: Industrial Relations Research Association, pp. 235–265.

Karjanen, D., and M. Baxamusa. 2003. *Subsidizing Wal-Mart: A Case Study of the College Grove Redevelopment Project.* Research report by the Center for Policy Initiatives, San Diego, November. http://www.onlinecpi.org (accessed March 26, 2006).

Kelloway, E.K., D.G. Gallagher, and J. Barling. 2004. "Work, Employment, and the Individual." In *Theoretical Perspectives on Work and the Employment Relationship,* B:E. Kaufman, ed. Champaign, IL: Industrial Relations Research Association, pp. 105–131.

Kochan, T.A. 1998. "Back to Basics: Creating the Analytical Foundations for the Next Industrial Relations System." *Proceedings of the Fiftieth Annual Meeting of the Industrial Relations Research Association*: 236–246.

Lafer, G. 2005. "The Critical Failure of Workplace Ethics." In *The Ethics of Human Resources and Industrial Relations,* J.W. Budd and J.G. Scoville, eds. Champaign, IL: Labor and Employment Relations Association, pp. 273–297.

Lester, G. 1998. "Careers and Contingency." *Stanford Law Review* 51(1): 73–145.

Lu, M., S. Liu, J. Fan, and Y. Yan. 2002. "Employment Restructuring during China's Economic Transition." *Monthly Labor Review* 125(8): 25–31.

Martin, R. and G.J. Bamber. 2004. "International Comparative Employment Relations Theory: Developing the Political Economy Perspective." In *Theoretical Perspectives on Work and the Employment Relationship,* B.E. Kaufman, ed. Champaign, IL: Industrial Relations Research Association, pp. 293–320.

National Employment Law Project. http://www.nelp.org (accessed March 27, 2006).

O'Reilly, J., I. Cebrián, and M. Lallement, eds. 2000. *Working-Time Changes: Social Integration through Transitional Labour Markets.* Cheltenham, UK: Edward Elgar Publishing, Ltd.

Pfau-Effinger, B. 1998. "Culture or Structure as Explanations for Differences in Part-Time Work in Germany, Finland and the Netherlands?" In *Part-Time Prospects: An International Comparison of Part-Time Work in Europe, North America and the Pacific Rim,* J. O'Reilly and C. Fagan, eds. London: Routledge, pp. 177–198.

Quisumbing, M. 2005. "Corporate Responsibility and Labor: Choosing Where to Buy Groceries: The High Price of Wal-Mart's 'Always Low Prices: Always.'" *Journal of Law and Social Challenges* 7(1): 111–140.

Sciarra, S. 2004. "New Discourses in Labour Law: Part-Time Work and the Paradigm of Flexibility." In *Employment Policy and the Regulation of Part-Time Work in the European Union: A Comparative Analysis,* S. Sciarra, P.

Davies, and M. Freedland, eds. Cambridge: Cambridge University Press, pp. 3–34.

Smallwood, S. 2002. "Faculty Union Issues Standards for Treatment of Adjuncts." *The Chronicle of Higher Education,* 48 (August 2) A:12.

Stone, K.V.W. 2004. *From Widgets to Digits: Employment Regulations for the Changing Workplace.* Cambridge: Cambridge University Press

Teague, T. 1999. *Economic Citizenship in the European Union: Employment Relations in the New Europe.* London: Routledge.

Ujimoto, K.V. 2000. "The Aging of Japanese Society: Human Resource Management in Transition." In *Japan after the Economic Miracle: In Search of New Directions,* P. Bowles and L.T. Woods, eds. Dordrecht, The Netherlands: Kluwer Academic Publishers, pp. 169–183.

United Nations Subcommission on the Promotion and Protection of Human Rights. 2003. "Norms on the Responsibilities of Transnational Corporations and Other Business Enterprises with Regard to Human Rights." http://www1.umn.edu/humanrts/links/norms-Aug2003.html (accessed March 27, 2006).

U.S. Department of Labor. 1994. *The Dunlop Commission on the Future of Worker-Management Relations—Final Report.* Washington, DC: U.S. Department of Labor.

Wheeler, H.N. 2005. "Globalization and Business Ethics in Employment Relations." In *The Ethics of Human Resources and Industrial Relations,* J.W. Budd and J.G. Scoville, eds. Champaign, IL: Labor and Employment Relations Association, pp. 115–140.

Working Today. http://www.workingtoday.org (accessed March 27, 2006).

Vosko, L.F. 1998. "Regulating Precariousness? The Temporary Employment Relationship Under the NAFTA and the EC Treaty." *Industrial Relations* 53(1): 2–34.

Zeytinoğlu, I.U. 1999. "International Policymaking: The ILO Standards on Changing Work Relationships." In *Changing Work Relationships in Industrialized Economies,* edited by I.U. Zeytinoğlu. Philadelphia: John Benjamins Publishing Company, pp. 219–237.

The Authors

Jay B. Barney holds the Bank One Chair in Corporate Strategy at the Fisher College of Business, Ohio State University, where he teaches strategic management.

Douglas Becker was a graduate assistant at the time the chapter was written. He is currently a Human Resource Professional for the Visteon Corporation in Dearborn, Michigan.

Venkat Bendapudi is an assistant professor of management and human resources at the Fisher College of Business, Ohio State University.

Thomas A. Coens was a labor and employment law attorney until his untimely death in December 2002. He practiced law most recently of counsel with the Lansing, Michigan, firm of Knaggs, Harter, Brake, and Schneider, P.C., and taught periodically for the School of Labor and Industrial Relations of Michigan State University.

Sandra E. Gleason is the associate dean for faculty and research and a professor in the Office of the Vice President for Commonwealth Campuses of Pennsylvania State University.

David B. Greenberger is an associate professor, chair of the Department of Management and Human Resources, and academic director of information technology at the Max M. Fisher College of Business at Ohio State University.

Robert L. Heneman is a professor of management and human resources and director of graduate programs in labor and human resources in the Max M. Fisher College of Business at Ohio State University.

Kazunari Honda is an associate professor in the faculty of economics at Kokugakuin University.

M. Catherine Lundy is a professor in the School of Labor and Industrial Relations at Michigan State University.

Stephen L. Mangum is senior associate dean for academic programs and a professor of management and human resources at the Max M. Fisher College of Business, Ohio State University.

Douglas J. Miller is an assistant professor of business administration at the University of Illinois, Urbana–Champaign.

François Michon is research director of the Centre National de la Recherche Scientifique (CNRSFrance).

Cynthia Ozeki is an assistant professor of management at California State University, Dominguez Hills.

Karen Roberts is a professor in the School of Labor and Industrial Relations at Michigan State University.

Alvin L. Storrs is a professor at the Michigan State University–Detroit College of Law.

Judith Tansky is a senior lecturer in labor and human resources in the Max M. Fisher College of Business at Ohio State University.

Akira Wakisaka is a professor of economics at Gakushuin University in Tokyo.

Jeffrey B. Wenger is an assistant professor of public administration and policy in the School of Public and International Affairs at the University of Georgia.

Courtney von Hippel is on the faculty of the School of Psychology at the University of New South Wales in Sydney, Australia.

Index

The italic letters *f*, *n*, and *t* following a page number indicate that the subject information of the heading is within a figure, note, or table, respectively, on that page.

About the Institute

The W.E. Upjohn Institute for Employment Research is a nonprofit research organization devoted to finding and promoting solutions to employment-related problems at the national, state, and local levels. It is an activity of the W.E. Upjohn Unemployment Trustee Corporation, which was established in 1932 to administer a fund set aside by Dr. W.E. Upjohn, founder of The Upjohn Company, to seek ways to counteract the loss of employment income during economic downturns.

The Institute is funded largely by income from the W.E. Upjohn Unemployment Trust, supplemented by outside grants, contracts, and sales of publications. Activities of the Institute comprise the following elements: 1) a research program conducted by a resident staff of professional social scientists; 2) a competitive grant program, which expands and complements the internal research program by providing financial support to researchers outside the Institute; 3) a publications program, which provides the major vehicle for disseminating the research of staff and grantees, as well as other selected works in the field; and 4) an Employment Management Services division, which manages most of the publicly funded employment and training programs in the local area.

The broad objectives of the Institute's research, grant, and publication programs are to 1) promote scholarship and experimentation on issues of public and private employment and unemployment policy, and 2) make knowledge and scholarship relevant and useful to policymakers in their pursuit of solutions to employment and unemployment problems.

Current areas of concentration for these programs include causes, consequences, and measures to alleviate unemployment; social insurance and income maintenance programs; compensation; workforce quality; work arrangements; family labor issues; labor-management relations; and regional economic development and local labor markets.